qooxdoo
Beginner's Guide

Develop Rich Internet Applications (RIA) with qooxdoo

Rajesh Kumar Bachu

Mohamed Raffi

PUBLISHING

BIRMINGHAM - MUMBAI

qooxdoo
Beginner's Guide

First published: December 2011

Production Reference: 1161211

Published by Packt Publishing Ltd.
Livery Place
35 Livery Street
Birmingham B3 2PB, UK.

ISBN 978-1-84951-370-8

www.packtpub.com

Cover Image by Duraid Fatouhi (duraidfatouhi@yahoo.com)

Credits

Authors
Rajesh Kumar Bachu
Mohamed Raffi

Reviewers
Ehsun Behravesh
Liang Yuxian Eugene

Acquisition Editor
Dilip Venkatesh

Development Editor
Meeta Rajani

Technical Editors
Vrinda Amberkar
Kedar Bhat

Copy Editors
Brandt D'Mello
Leonard D'Silva

Project Coordinator
Michelle Quadros

Proofreaders
Mario Cecere
Aaron Nash

Indexer
Hemangini Bari

Graphics
Valentina D'Silva
Manu Joseph

Production Coordinators
Prachali Bhiwandar
Alwin Roy

Cover Work
Prachali Bhiwandar

About the Authors

Rajesh Kumar Bachu has over six years experience in the design and development of enterprise applications and mobile games. He is good at programming in Java and J2EE technologies. He has worked extensively in qooxdoo application development and has migrated an enterprise application to qooxdoo. You can find more about him at `http://in.linkedin.com/in/rajbachu`.

I am pleased to acknowledge my colleagues with whom I worked and learned qooxdoo, my co-author, Raffi, for bringing me on-board to write this book and qooxdoo team, who have actually given me the pleasure to write on qooxdoo.

My special thanks to my parents. I would like to thank all my friends who directly or indirectly helped me to complete this book.

My thanks to all those who have been involved with this book, especially to Mary Nadar, Dilip Venkatesh, Michelle Quadros, Meeta Rajani, Ehsun Behravesh, Liang Yuxian Eugene, Vrinda Amberkar, and Kedar Bhat.

Mohamed Raffi is an Enterprise Application Specialist. His area of work includes architecture, design, development, training, and mentoring. He has over thirteen years of product development experience in a variety of Java and JavaScript-based technologies and frameworks. You can find more about him at http://in.linkedin.com/in/raffimd and he writes his thoughts at http://thoughtstoblog.blogspot.com.

My sincere thanks to Packt Publishing for this opportunity. I would like to thank my co-author Rajesh for sharing the effort of writing this book. I am proud of the qooxdoo team for creating such a wonderful RIA framework. Also, I would like to thank all my colleagues for all the learning they have provided me with.

I appreciate all the support provided by my parents and my wife in writing this book. My grandpa would be so proud (I wish he would have been here to see this).

My thanks to all who were involved with this book, especially to Mary Nadar, Dilip Venkatesh, Michelle Quadros, Meeta Rajani, Ehsun Behravesh, Liang Yuxian Eugene, Vrinda Amberkar, and Kedar Bhat.

About the Reviewers

Ehsun Behravesh is a 28 year old post-graduate student at Universiti Putra, Malaysia (`http://www.upm.edu.my/`). He is majoring in Distributed and Parallel Computing. He is holds a bachelor's degree from the London Metropolitan University (`http://www.londonmet.ac.uk/`). He started programming when he was in high school and he has developed software systems for almost 10 years. He is a fan of open source software and one of his open source projects, MyPasswords (`http://sourceforge.net/projects/mypasswords7/`), won a comparison competition on LinuxFormat, January 2011 magazine. He loves computer programming, music, and animals.

I want to thank my wife who has always encouraged me to work and study. I also want to thank my parents who helped me to study abroad.

Liang Yuxian Eugene most recently completed an internship as a frontend engineer with Yahoo!, Taiwan after completing a double degree in Business Administration and Computer Science at National Cheng Chi University, Taipei, Taiwan.

He is also the author of *JavaScript Testing Beginner's Guide, Packt Publishing*.

Eugene enjoys solving difficult problems creatively in the form of building web applications using Python/Django/Tornado Web and JavaScript/jQuery. He is also passionate about social media, social network analysis, social computing, recommendation algorithms, link analysis, data visualization, data mining, information retrieval, business intelligence, and intelligent user interfaces.

Eugene seeks to solve business problems with Computer Science.

He can be reached at http://www.liangeugene.com.

Firstly, as a technical reviewer, I want to thank all the great folks at Packt Publishing for giving me the opportunity to work with such a great team of people.

Secondly, I want to thank my family and friends for their kind understanding and putting up with my incredibly busy schedule.

Lastly, I want to thank all the people I have met and have helped me out here-and-there along the way. It has been a great journey.

www.PacktPub.com

Support files, eBooks, discount offers, and more

You might want to visit www.PacktPub.com for support files and downloads related to your book.

Did you know that Packt offers eBook versions of every book published, with PDF and ePub files available? You can upgrade to the eBook version at www.PacktPub.com and as a print book customer, you are entitled to a discount on the eBook copy. Get in touch with us at service@packtpub.com for more details.

At www.PacktPub.com, you can also read a collection of free technical articles, sign up for a range of free newsletters and receive exclusive discounts and offers on Packt books and eBooks.

http://PacktLib.PacktPub.com

Do you need instant solutions to your IT questions? PacktLib is Packt's online digital book library. Here, you can access, read and search across Packt's entire library of books.

Why Subscribe?

- Fully searchable across every book published by Packt
- Copy and paste, print and bookmark content
- On demand and accessible via web browser

Free Access for Packt account holders

If you have an account with Packt at www.PacktPub.com, you can use this to access PacktLib today and view nine entirely free books. Simply use your login credentials for immediate access.

Table of Contents

Preface

Rich Internet Application (RIA) provides the capability to deliver feature-rich web applications, enables you to develop web applications with most of the desktop application's characteristics, and improves the usability of the web application. Over the last few years, many frameworks have arrived and are available to develop the Rich Internet Applications in different technologies.

qooxdoo is one of the comprehensive open source RIA frameworks. qooxdoo allows you to develop cross-browser RIAs in object-oriented JavaScript, which helps greatly to re-use application code, and hence reduces the application size. It provides a wide range of off-the-shelf UI widgets. qooxdoo comes with a rich feature set when compared to most of the other RIA frameworks. qooxdoo is completely based on JavaScript. It provides a variety of tools to build, optimize, generate documentation, and more. qooxdoo framework supports multiple browsers, multi-language deployment, custom look and feel, unit testing, automation testing, and much more.

In the past few years, all the major Internet applications or enterprise applications have been developed or migrated to RIA to support all the features that are provided in the desktop applications. This helps the organizations to keep the customers happy and also improves application deployment and maintenance.

qooxdoo is an open source framework. It has been there since 2005 and it is a quite stable framework now. If you are watching and waiting for the right time to migrate your application to qooxdoo, this is the right time, in my opinion.

What this book covers

Chapter 1, *What is qooxdoo?*, helps the developer to get an overview of the qooxdoo framework, to get to know what the framework provides, to know the architecture of the qooxdoo framework, and to get a feel of the RIA developed in qooxdoo.

Chapter 2, Say Hello to qooxdoo World!, guides the developer in setting up the development environment for the qooxdoo framework, to understand the communication with the server, and to set up one of the RPC servers that comes as a contribution project.

Chapter 3, Core Programming Concepts, explains the core programming concepts of qooxdoo. This chapter is a very important chapter as it explains the implementation syntax of basic object-oriented concepts such as class, interface, and so on. This chapter will help the developer to construct the application code in an object-oriented way.

Chapter 4, Working with Layouts and Menus, explains the layout design, toolbars, and menu bars.

Chapter 5, Working with Widgets, helps the developer to know about the various widgets available in the qooxdoo framework.

Chapter 6, Working with Forms and Data, explains form handling and data store support in the qooxdoo framework.

Chapter 7, Testing and Debugging, explains how to test and debug the qooxdoo application, as well as how to fix the identified issues.

Chapter 8, Internationalization, helps the developer to internationalize and localize the qooxdoo application to multiple languages.

Chapter 9, Working with Themes, aids the developer in understanding the theme support in qooxdoo and in designing a custom theme for the application.

Chapter 10, Performance, helps the developer to monitor and improve the performance of the qooxdoo application.

Chapter 11, Miscellaneous, covers a few miscellaneous topics that complete your understanding of qooxdoo.

Appendix, Pop Quiz Answers, contains the answers to all the pop quiz questions for all the chapters.

References: It contains the references used in this book.

What you need for this book

qooxdoo is completely based on object-oriented JavaScript. So, what you should be well versed in is just JavaScript. If you know the object-oriented concepts and have worked with any object-oriented language, such as Java, it will really help you to understand the qooxdoo programming concepts pretty quickly. Even if you haven't worked with any of the object-oriented languages, it is okay; you can learn the object-oriented concepts with qooxdoo.

Even though it is web development, you don't need to know HTML, DOM, CSS, and so on. qooxdoo generates HTML in runtime from the JavaScript code that you have written.

Who this book is for

This book is intended for the client-side developers who design and develop Internet web applications and enterprise web applications. If you want to start developing RIA in qooxdoo, this book would be of great help to jump start your development. If you are already developing qooxdoo applications, this book will help you to go through the qooxdoo framework quickly to improve your contribution to your project.

This book helps the beginners in qooxdoo to easily set up the development environment and explains the concepts in an order that can easily be grasped by beginners.

This book also provides an idea for the architects and lead developers to know about qooxdoo and evaluate the framework.

This book is also intended for the desktop application developers who want to move into RIA development and develop rich Internet applications and rich enterprise web applications.

Conventions

In this book, you will find several headings appearing frequently.

To give clear instructions of how to complete a procedure or task, we use:

Time for action – heading

1. Action 1
2. Action 2
3. Action 3

Instructions often need some extra explanation so that they make sense, so they are followed with:

What just happened?

This heading explains the working of tasks or instructions that you have just completed.

You will also find some other learning aids in the book, including:

Pop quiz

These are short multiple-choice questions intended to help you test your own understanding.

You will also find a number of styles of text that distinguish between different kinds of information. Here are some examples of these styles, and an explanation of their meaning.

Code words in text are shown as follows: "Besides regular classes, it offers `abstract`, `static`, or `singleton` classes."

A block of code is set as follows:

```
<!DOCTYPE html PUBLIC "-//W3C//DTD XHTML 1.1//EN" "http://www.w3.org/
TR/xhtml11/DTD/xhtml11.dtd">
<html xmlns="http://www.w3.org/1999/xhtml" xml:lang="en">
<head>
  <meta http-equiv="Content-Type" content="text/html; charset=utf-8"
/>
```

Any command-line input or output is written as follows:

```
E:\>python
ActivePython 2.7.1.3 (ActiveState Software Inc.) based on
Python 2.7.1 (r271:86832, Feb  7 2011, 11:30:38) [MSC v.1500 32 bit
(Intel)] on win32
Type "help", "copyright", "credits" or "license" for more information.
>>>
```

New terms and **important words** are shown in bold. Words that you see on the screen, in menus or dialog boxes for example, appear in the text like this: "Click on the **Add Feed** menu in the toolbar and add any feed that you want to put into the feed reader."

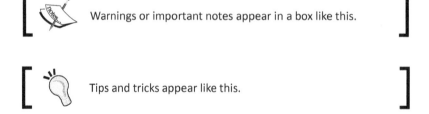

Warnings or important notes appear in a box like this.

Tips and tricks appear like this.

Reader feedback

Feedback from our readers is always welcome. Let us know what you think about this book—what you liked or may have disliked. Reader feedback is important for us to develop titles that you really get the most out of.

To send us general feedback, simply send an e-mail to `feedback@packtpub.com`, and mention the book title via the subject of your message.

If there is a topic that you have expertise in and you are interested in either writing or contributing to a book, see our author guide on `www.packtpub.com/authors`.

Customer support

Now that you are the proud owner of a Packt book, we have a number of things to help you to get the most from your purchase.

Downloading the example code

You can download the example code files for all Packt books you have purchased from your account at `http://www.PacktPub.com`. If you purchased this book elsewhere, you can visit `http://www.PacktPub.com/support` and register to have the files e-mailed directly to you.

Errata

Although we have taken every care to ensure the accuracy of our content, mistakes do happen. If you find a mistake in one of our books—maybe a mistake in the text or the code—we would be grateful if you would report this to us. By doing so, you can save other readers from frustration and help us improve subsequent versions of this book. If you find any errata, please report them by visiting `http://www.packtpub.com/support`, selecting your book, clicking on the **errata submission form** link, and entering the details of your errata. Once your errata are verified, your submission will be accepted and the errata will be uploaded on our website, or added to any list of existing errata, under the Errata section of that title. Any existing errata can be viewed by selecting your title from `http://www.packtpub.com/support`.

Piracy

Piracy of copyright material on the Internet is an ongoing problem across all media. At Packt, we take the protection of our copyright and licenses very seriously. If you come across any illegal copies of our works, in any form, on the Internet, please provide us with the location address or website name immediately so that we can pursue a remedy.

Please contact us at copyright@packtpub.com with a link to the suspected pirated material.

We appreciate your help in protecting our authors, and our ability to bring you valuable content.

Questions

You can contact us at questions@packtpub.com if you are having a problem with any aspect of the book, and we will do our best to address it.

1

What is qooxdoo?

This chapter introduces the qooxdoo framework to you, explains the architecture, explores the framework features, briefs you about the GUI widget library, and provides an overall understanding about the qooxdoo framework. It takes you through an application developed in qooxdoo and also explains the application that we are going to develop throughout this book.

In this chapter, we'll cover the following:

- ◆ A feel of an RIA developed in qooxdoo
- ◆ Architecture of the qooxdoo SDK
- ◆ qooxdoo framework features
- ◆ Event-based Rich UI Programming
- ◆ GUI Library
- ◆ The application to be developed in this book—Team Twitter
- ◆ What you should know and what you don't need to know

By the end of this chapter, you will have an understanding of the qooxdoo RIA framework and the programming languages or technologies required to develop an application in qooxdoo.

Let's begin to understand qooxdoo.

A feel of an RIA developed in qooxdoo

Before anything, let's get a feel for an application developed in qooxdoo. This will give a rough idea about the things that you can develop, depending on the features in that application. You can do more than that with qooxdoo. The following screenshot will give you an overview of the feed reader application:

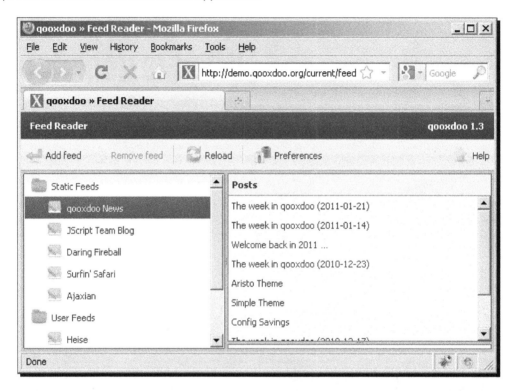

Time for action – play with the feed reader application

Go to the qooxdoo demo feed reader URL (`http://demo.qooxdoo.org/current/feedreader/`), play with the feed reader application, and feel the qooxdoo application. Perform all the operations available in the application; observe the AJAX behavior, desktop-like features, and so on. Compare the behavior of this application with any typical web application. You can perform the following operations:

Adding a feed to the feed reader

Click on the **Add Feed** menu in the toolbar and add any feed that you want to put into the feed reader. Let's add the feed to the Google Open Source Blog. Enter **Google Open Source Blog** in the **Title** field and **http://feeds.feedburner.com/GoogleOpenSourceBlog** in the **URL** field. Click on the **Add** button. This will add a feed to the **User Feeds** section:

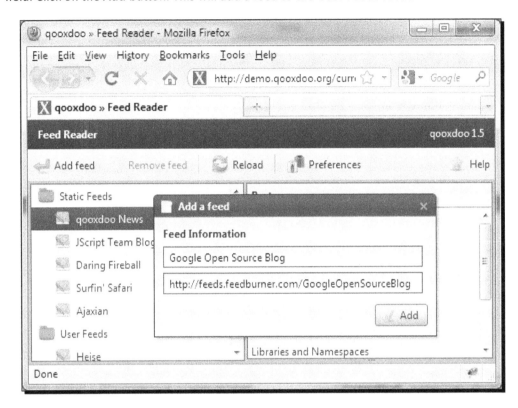

 You must have observed that the add feed action displayed a modal dialog box without disturbing the existing content, and on add action, it just added a feed under the **User Feeds** section. It did not reload the entire page displayed in the browser. That is the beauty of AJAX applications.

Checking the feeds

Clicking on the RSS feed nodes on the tree panel will load the feeds on the right-hand side panel. Once you click on a particular feed post on the top pane in the right-hand side panel, it will load the details of that particular feed post on the bottom of the right-hand side panel. Go to **User Feeds** | **Google Open Source Blog** and check the **Google Open Source Blog** feed.

If you observe closely, it just loads the required data on the respective content area without disturbing user context or without reloading the entire page (as shown in the following screenshot). This is done through AJAX. In AJAX applications, the application just sends and receives the required data and updates only the impacted portion in the GUI. This helps to retain the user context, improves performance because of less transfer of data between client and server, and improves the usability of the GUI:

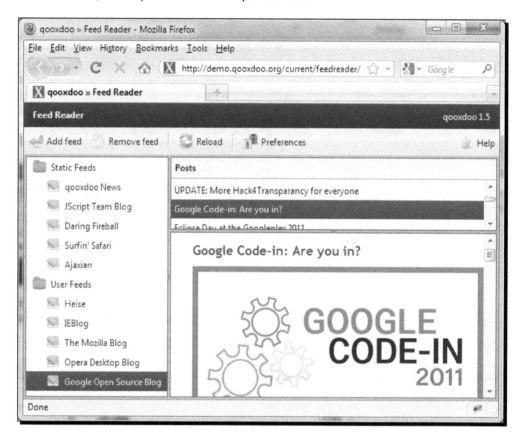

Try the following actions, too:

- **Reload**
- **Preferences**
- **Remove feed**

What just happened?

You played with a **Rich Internet Application** (**RIA**) developed in qooxdoo. Let's have a look at the key aspects provided by an RIA developed in qooxdoo.

User context

AJAX-based RIA does not reload the whole page every time; instead it just loads the required data in the respective content area. This is the main differentiating aspect in RIA. It holds the user context all the time, thus the user experience is very much appreciated by the users. RIA applications do not open multiple browser windows, as it is done in the traditional web application using `window.open()`. Instead, it uses the modal dialog and avoids the floating browser windows. RIA applications do not wipe out the whole page and reload the new page, as it is done in traditional web applications; instead, they retain the user context, send and receive only the necessary data, and update only the changed or impacted portion of the screen. qooxdoo is an RIA framework based on AJAX.

Desktop characteristics

RIA provides rich features developed through the off-the-shelf widgets provided by RIA frameworks such as qooxdoo. Because of this, RIA provides rich user experience. You have seen the toolbar, split-pane, modal dialog, and so on in the feed reader application. There are many more widgets provided by qooxdoo for various purposes that you'll come to know about in the coming chapters.

GUI library

qooxdoo provides a wide range of widgets in the GUI library, which helps you to develop your application pretty quickly with all the rich features. For example, qooxdoo provides the `Tree` widget that does not come with the plain HTML, it supports column sorting on the table and the remote data model for the table. There are many more widgets with very nice features that are readily available for you. You don't have to spend time to develop these things on your own in HTML and struggle between multiple browser implementations. Instead, just focus on your application's functionalities.

Architecture of qooxdoo SDK

Architecture of the qooxdoo SDK is pretty neatly done to hide the modules that include internal parts such as HTML rendering, multiple browser handling, and so on in different layers and provide the GUI toolkit on top of all the layers.

Let's explore the architecture of the qooxdoo framework to know more about the framework capability:

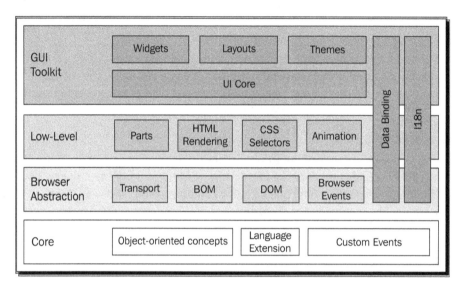

Core layer

qooxdoo is an object-oriented framework and its working is based on event programming. All the core framework modules are in this layer. You don't have to worry about this until you contribute to the qooxdoo framework.

Browser Abstraction layer

This layer abstracts the document-object model, browser-based events, and so on. This layer is also an internal layer; you don't have to worry about this until you contribute to the qooxdoo framework.

Low-Level layer

This layer contains all the modules that work over the Browser Abstraction layer to achieve actual things on the browser. It contains the modules to render the HTML, select the CSS based on the themes, to animate things, and so on. In addition to these, it has a module called Parts, which helps to divide your application into multiple parts and load only the necessary parts required at any point of time to improve the performance. You need to know only about the Parts module in this layer; the rest of the modules are internal to the qooxdoo implementation.

GUI Toolkit layer

This layer is exposed to the users. You should know all of the modules in this layer. It has a separate module for core UI classes. The widgets and layouts are developed over the core UI. qooxdoo provides a wide range of layouts and widgets for you. Once you know all the layouts provided by the qooxdoo framework, it will be easy to pick the right layout for your needs. It provides a full-blown set of widgets. You can learn the basic widgets first and the other widgets as and when you need to use them. The qooxdoo framework separates the style part into a separate module called Themes, which allows you to change the look and feel of your application without touching the application logic code. This is based on JavaScript, not CSS. The qooxdoo framework supports keyboard navigation, focus handling, tab handling, and drag-and-drop functionalities.

Data Binding

This functionality is available across multiple layers. Basically, this provides a way to attach the data source to the UI widget. The data could be fetched from a file, web server, or web service, and the store will fetch the data from any of these sources and attach that to the data model of the UI widget. The controller will make sure that the data is displayed in the view part of the widget. One of the data sources can be YQL API or REST API from twitter.

Internationalization

This functionality is also available across multiple layers. qooxdoo supports the internationalization of the application, so that you can localize your application to support locale information for virtually every country in the world. You need to prepare your application code to read from the locale files, and as you translate the texts to multiple locales, your application will work as per the locale that is chosen in the application.

qooxdoo framework features

qooxdoo is an entirely object-oriented framework based on JavaScript. This framework is properly organized on the basis of namespaces. It supports most of the modern browsers, provides utilities to generate documentation based on javadocs such as comments, and also supports themes and internationalization. In this section, you will learn about all these features.

Let's check all the features provided by the qooxdoo framework. This will improve your knowledge on qooxdoo and help you further understand the qooxdoo framework.

Language

- The qooxdoo application runs in most of the modern web browsers, including:
    - Internet Explorer 6+
    - Firefox 2+
    - Opera 9+
    - Safari 3.0+
    - Chrome 2+

- No plugins (ActiveX, Java, Flash, or Silverlight) are required. It is completely based on JavaScript.
- Non-critical modifications of the native JavaScript objects to allow for easy integration with other libraries and custom code.
- Cross-browser JavaScript 1.6 (string/array generics).

Object-orientation

- Framework is fully class-based
- Framework uses namespaces. It avoids the conflicts in global variables
- Besides regular classes, it offers `abstract`, `static`, or `singleton` classes
- Constructor and destructor support
- Multiple access specifiers—`public`, `protected`, and `private`
- Single inheritance and full polymorphism
- Java-like interfaces
- Ruby-like mixins
- So-called dynamic properties, a very convenient and powerful way to have optimized `setter` and `getter` methods generated from simple configuration

Programming

- Purely client-side JavaScript
- No need to know HTML, DOM, or CSS
- Complete support for event-based programming
- Development of qooxdoo applications fully supported on all platforms; for example, Windows, Linux, all flavors of Unix, and Mac OS X
- Quick start for easy evaluation of the framework without the need to install any software
- Skeletons are pre-configured for full-featured custom applications
- Many sample applications and examples
- Designed for high performance
- Framework has no issue of memory leak
- Aids in developing memory-leak free user applications
- Extensive logging capabilities (for example, different log appenders and Firebug support)
- Straightforward debugging (for example, object introspection and benchmarking)
- Browser history management, that is, browser back/forward button, bookmarks
- Cookies
- Generic JavaScript pretty printer/code formatter for unified code style

Internationalization

- Built-in internationalization (i18n) and localization (l10n) support
- Support for all languages and locales, at least on this planet
- Based on the comprehensive **Common Language Data Repository (CLDR)**
- Internally using the mature GNU `gettext` tools
- Well-known translation file format (`.po`)
- Support by professional, free translation tools (PO editors) on all platforms

API reference

- Extended javadoc-like source code comments
- Full API reference for both framework and custom applications
- Online (`http://api.qooxdoo.org/`) and offline API viewer applications

Testing

◆ Integrated unit testing framework (test runner)

◆ Integrated functional testing framework (simulator)

Deployment

◆ Generation of a self-contained and easily-deployable build version

◆ Complexity of the build process hidden behind user-friendly commands

◆ JavaScript compression (removal of whitespaces, and so on)

◆ Automatic dependency resolution of JavaScript classes; no need for manual `require()` statements or tweaking a custom build

◆ Automatic linking of JavaScript classes (JS linker)

◆ Copying of required static resources like images or other external files into a self-contained build

◆ String extraction (tremendous performance improvement for IE6)

◆ Shortening and obfuscating local variables and/or private members

◆ Optional browser-specific variant for each supported browser (For example, Firefox-only build)

◆ Generation of build versions depending on user-defined variants, which allows for different products from the same code base

◆ Removal of debug statements within the application code before deployment

Migration

◆ Support for easy migration of custom applications from one framework release to another

◆ Migration in the qooxdoo framework is painless as it is technically easy to carry out

◆ Fully integrated into the regular build system

◆ All non-ambiguous changes are done automatically for maximum convenience and to avoid manual find/replace errors

◆ All ambiguous or semantic changes that require some developer decision are put into a comprehensive checklist

Alternative programming models

In addition to the JavaScript programming model, you can also develop qooxdoo applications using one of the following alternative programming models or development platforms. Some are not quite stable, some are not active, and some are pretty new. This book focuses only on the JavaScript programming model, which is the built-in development model of the qooxdoo framework.

- **Java/Eclipse**: Eclipse **Rich Ajax Platform** (**RAP**); for more information, see `http://eclipse.org/rap`

- **Java**: **qooxdoo Web Toolkit** (**QWT**); for more information, see `http://qooxdoo.org/contrib/project/qwt`

- **QxWT:** JSNI wrapper for the qooxdoo JavaScript library; for more information, see `http://www.ufacekit.org/index.php?cat=02_qooxdoo&page=01_QxWT`

- **LISP (qooxlisp)**: LISP programming for web applications; for more information, see `https://github.com/kennytilton/qooxlisp/wiki/`

- **XML**: XML-based GUI description; for more information, see `http://qxtransformer.org/`

The list of alternative programming models is growing. You can check the updated list at `http://qooxdoo.org/documentation/general/development_platforms`

Event-based rich UI programming

qooxdoo provides complete support for event-based programming. If you have already programmed in QT or Java Swing, you'll find qooxdoo very similar. qooxdoo separates out the view widgets, model classes, and the controllers. Listeners observe the widget all the time and fire the right event based on the action. The action could be a click, a key entry, a selection of an item, mouse over the widget, change of the value in a table cell, and so on. An example of event-based programming is shown in the following diagram:

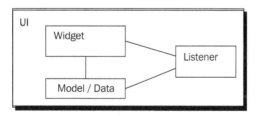

For example, you can add a listener for the Button widget to perform something on the click of a button. You can even set a command, which will be called on the execute action of the button-click event. qooxdoo provides lots of events for various widgets. For example, the List widget has many events such as changeSelection, addItem, removeItem, and so on.

GUI widget library

qooxdoo is on par with the desktop GUI toolkits such as QT, Java Swing, and so on. It provides a whole lot of off-the-shelf widgets for the GUI development. The good thing with the qooxdoo framework is the demo browser application, where you can see the behavior of each widget even without setting up the qooxdoo environment.

Similar to the feed reader application, demo browser is another application that comes with the qooxdoo framework. You can use this application to see the behavior of different widgets and select the widget that you want to use in your application. This application demonstrates various widgets, and it displays the widgets under neat categorizations such as widget, layout, UI, and so on.

In addition to the demo browser application, the qooxdoo framework provides another application called playground. As the playground application is linked with the demo browser, you can select the widget that you want to use in the demo browser, take that widget to the playground, change the code, run it, and see the behavior.

This makes it easy to select the widget in the demo browser; try it in the playground before actually trying it in your application. You can access the online version of these applications for the current qooxdoo version. You can also set these applications locally in your network if you download the qooxdoo framework. We will explore the online version of these applications in this section.

Time for action – checking the demo browser and the playground applications

Let's check the supporting tools that qooxdoo provides to explore all the widgets in the GUI Toolkit.

Demo browser

The demo browser allows you to browse through all the widgets provided by the qooxdoo framework. Double-click the tree nodes in the left panel to see the behavior on the right panel.

Go to the URL (`http://demo.qooxdoo.org/current/demobrowser/#`) and browse through all the widgets shown in the demo. The demo browser application is shown in the following screenshot:

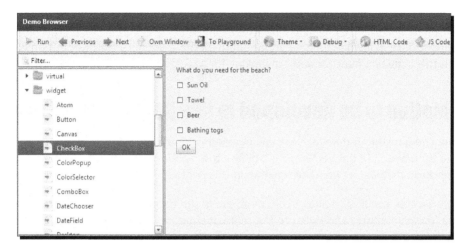

Playground

You can change the sample code and play in the playground environment provided by the qooxdoo framework. Run it immediately, and see the results. Even without setting the qooxdoo development environment, you can do some coding in the playground environment and try it. Either you can play with one of the samples in the playground environment or select one of the widgets in the demo browser, take it to the playground, and play with it.

Go to the URL `http://demo.qooxdoo.org/1.3/playground/#` and play with the widgets. The qooxdoo playground application is shown in the following screenshot:

What just happened?

You have browsed the demo and played in the playground of the qooxdoo framework. These are the pretty cool features offered by the qooxdoo framework that allow you to explore the widgets provided by the qooxdoo framework. As qooxdoo provides a lot of widgets for different purposes, it is a nice idea to browse the demo and play in the playground environment once in a while to know more about all these widgets. Another option is to carry out this activity whenever you are looking for a widget for use in your application.

Application to be developed in this book—Team Twitter

To try out the qooxdoo framework, we will develop an application across this book as we learn the framework. In this section, we'll define the high-level functional requirements of the application that we are going to develop in this book.

The Team Twitter application allows the members of the team to read the tweets written by the fellow team mates and tweet to the team. It supports tagging and filtering based on team members.

Time for action – checking the Team Twitter application

Let's define some functional requirements for the Team Twitter application.

Reading team tweets

You can read all the tweets of a team in a reverse chronological order, search the tweets for any specific keyword, or navigate through the tweets by the tags. In addition to this, you can also filter the tweets by the team members. By default, tweets from all team members are displayed:

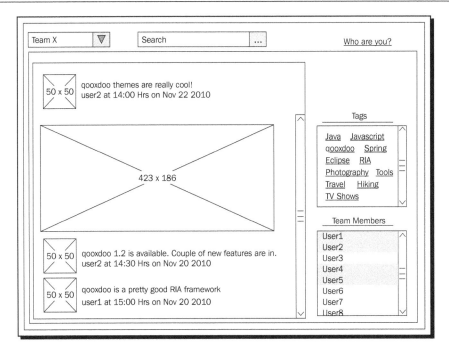

Logging in to the Team Twitter application

To tweet in a team, one should log in to the application. If he or she is not already part of the team, they can join the team.

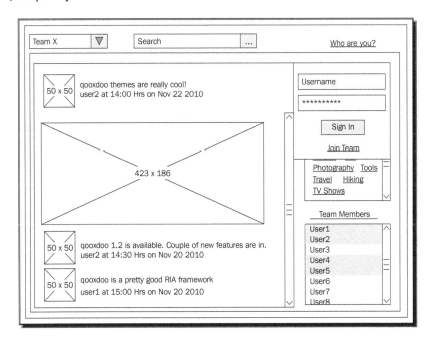

Tweeting to the team

One can tweet a text or video. One can tag the tweet to categorize it and all the tweets are displayed in reverse chronological order.

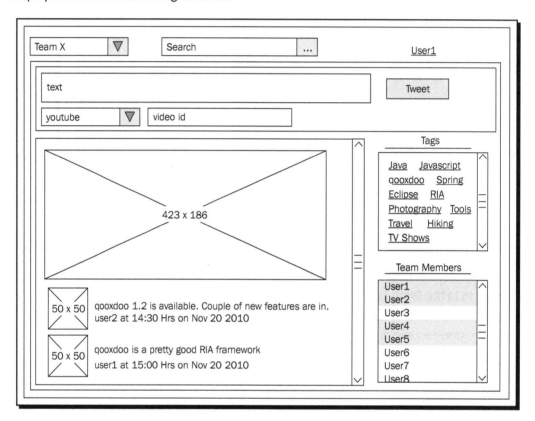

What just happened?

We have seen the high-level functional requirements of the Team Twitter application. We'll develop this application across the book as we learn more about the qooxdoo framework. In this book, all code related to the user interface development of the team twitter application will be explained in detail, but the server-side and the database part of the code will not be explained, as it is not in the scope of this book. The code for the entire application can be downloaded from the site.

What you should know and what you don't need to know

qooxdoo is completely based on object-oriented JavaScript. So, what you should know is just JavaScript. If you know the object-oriented concepts and have worked with any object-oriented language such as Java, it will really help you to understand the qooxdoo programming concepts pretty quickly. Even if you haven't worked with any object-oriented language, it is okay. You can learn the object-oriented concepts with qooxdoo.

Even though it is a web development application, you don't need to know HTML, DOM, CSS, and so on. qooxdoo generates the HTML at runtime from the JavaScript code that you have written.

Pop quiz

1. qooxdoo is a

    a. Browser-independent JavaScript framework

    b. Framework that supports object-oriented programming

    c. Event-based programming

    d. All of the above

2. qooxdoo works on most of the web browsers

    a. Yes

    b. No

3. I need to install the following on the client machine to run the qooxdoo application in a web browser

    a. ActiveX

    b. Java plugins

    c. Flash

    d. Silverlight

    e. None of the above

4. The following are possible with qooxdoo programming

    a. Code re-use through object-oriented programming

    b. Modularize the application

    c. Namespace and access control of the member variables

    d. All of the above

5. I can do the following with qooxdoo

    a. Develop an application, allow my country members to see it in their language, and show it to the world in their language

    b. Support personalization of the web application in qooxdoo

    c. Pull data from multiple data source and bind it to the widget

    d. All of the above

6. Playground allows you to

    a. Just go through the widget behavior

    b. Edit, run immediately, and see the widget behavior

Summary

We learned a lot in this chapter about the qooxdoo framework. Specifically, we:

♦ Had a feel of RIA, developed in qooxdoo

♦ Got to know the layers in the qooxdoo architecture and the layers or modules that we need to learn for GUI development

♦ Got an idea about the various features provided by the qooxdoo framework. This broadens the understanding of the qooxdoo framework

♦ Went through the widgets (if not all, as many as we could), with the help of the demo browser and the playground utilities provided by the qooxdoo framework

♦ Defined the functional requirements for the application that we are going to develop in this book

We also discussed the things we should know and the things we don't need to know. Now that we've got an overview of qooxdoo, we're ready to say "hello" to the qooxdoo world.

2
Say Hello to the qooxdoo World!

This chapter explains how to set up the environment for qooxdoo client application development, how to create a client application, and how to build and run the application. It also explains about the format of the data that is passed between client and server, the transport protocol, and the various servers supported by the qooxdoo framework.

In this chapter, you'll read about the following:

- ◆ Installing qooxdoo tools (Python/Cygwin)
- ◆ Installing qooxdoo SDK
- ◆ Creating a simple application
- ◆ Passing the data to the server using **JavaScript Object Notation** (**JSON**)
- ◆ Communicating with the server using **Remote Procedure Call** (**RPC**)
- ◆ RPC servers
- ◆ Integrating with the Java server

By the end of this chapter, the user will have the development environment for Rich Internet Applications (RIAs) based on qooxdoo. The user will also have an understanding of how the end-to-end communication takes place from client to server.

Now, let's step into the qooxdoo world to say hello.

Installing qooxdoo tools

qooxdoo provides a lot of tools to perform many activities such as creating an application, building the code, optimizing the code, generating documentation, and so on. All these tools are written in Python. So, the Python environment is required to run these tools. You don't have to know programming in Python to develop an application in qooxdoo.

Time for action – installing qooxdoo tools

For Windows OS, you can install Python from `python.org`, ActivePython from ActiveState, or the Python package with Cygwin. Python, from `python.org`, needs additional manual configuration. But the default installation of ActivePython works just fine. So, you have two options now. Either go with ActivePython if you like the Windows development environment or go with Cygwin and include the Python package if you want a Unix-like development environment. It is recommended to use ActivePython because it is simple and works well. The following sections discuss the installations for both these options.

Installing ActivePython

Go to the ActiveState website (`http://www.activestate.com/activepython/ downloads`), download the latest version of ActivePython (we used ActivePython 2.7.1 while writing this book), and install the program. The following steps will guide you through the ActivePython installation:

1. Click on the **Next** button (see the following screenshot) to start the ActivePython installation:

2. The following screenshot shows the **End-User License Agreement**. Read and agree to the license terms and click on the **Next** button:

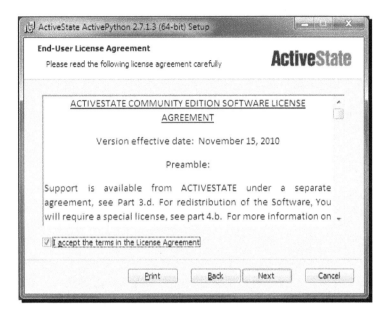

3. The following screenshot displays the list of features that are installed through this installer. Click on the **Next** button:

4. Now, the installer is ready to install the features of ActivePython. Click on the **Install** button (see the following screenshot):

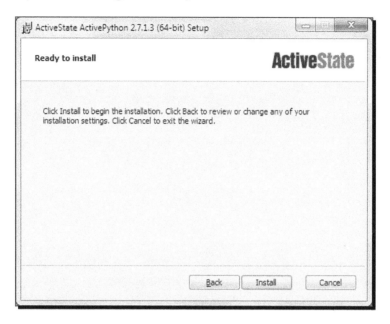

5. Once the installer has completed the ActivePython installation, you will see something similar to the following screenshot. Click on the **Finish** button:

6. To verify the ActivePython installation, open the command prompt and check the Python setup. Type `python` on the console to see whether it takes you to the Python environment. You will see the following output on your console:

```
E:\>python
ActivePython 2.7.1.3 (ActiveState Software Inc.) based on
Python 2.7.1 (r271:86832, Feb  7 2011, 11:30:38) [MSC v.1500 32
bit (Intel)] on win32
Type "help", "copyright", "credits" or "license" for more
information.
>>>
```

Installing Cygwin

Go to the Cygwin website (`http://www.cygwin.com/setup.exe`), download the Cygwin setup file, and install Cygwin.

 Cygwin is not required with the recent qooxdoo versions, as qooxdoo completely moved the dependency to Python only. You can use Cygwin with the Python package if you wish. However for the development in Windows OS, it is recommended to go with ActivePython installation as it is simple, does not require any configuration, and it works well. If you are going with ActivePython, you can skip installing Cygwin.

Run `setup.exe` to install Cygwin. The following steps will guide you through the Cygwin installation:

1. Click on the **Next** button to start installing Cygwin:

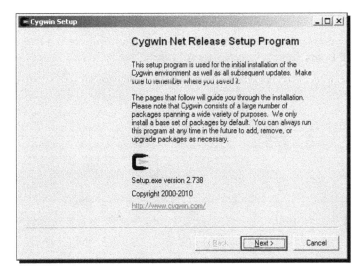

2. The following screenshot displays the options to choose a download source for the Cygwin packages. Choose the **Install from Internet** option and click on the **Next** button. Make sure that you are connected to the Internet.

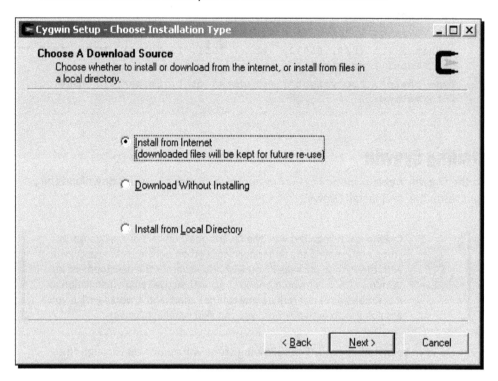

3. The following screen allows you to select the root directory for the Cygwin installation. The default value is **C:\cygwin**. If you want to install Cygwin in a different location, enter that location for the root directory. You can also specify whether you want to set up Cygwin for all users or only for the logged-in user. Select **All Users** and click on the **Next** button:

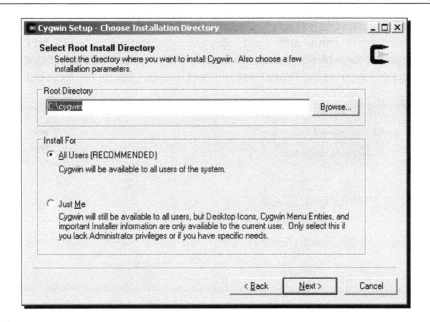

4. The next screen allows you to select the **Local Package Directory** to store the repository (see the following screenshot). Cygwin does not blow this directory away after installation. Rather, it keeps the installation files in order to remember your download choices, so that when you upgrade, you do not have to go through the tedious package selection process again. The packages can be reused later when you want to install Cygwin on another machine by selecting this directory content as a local directory in step 2 and selecting the option **Install from Local Directory** in step 2 to avoid downloading the packages from Internet. So, a non-temporary directory is recommended. Click on the **Next** button:

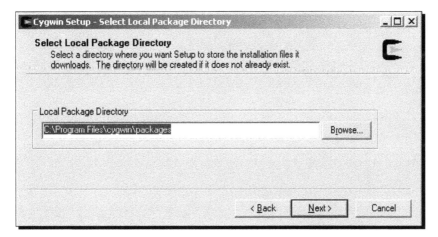

5. The following screen allows you to provide details about your Internet connection. If your internet connection is not using any proxy settings, select **Direct Connection** option. If your internet connection is using any proxy settings, select **Use HTTP/FTP Proxy** and provide the **Proxy Host** and **Port** details. Click on the **Next** button:

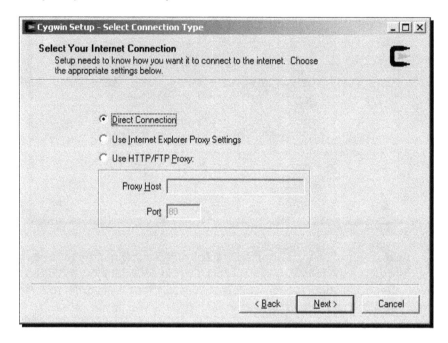

6. The following screen allows you to choose a download site. Select the download site as `http://sourceware.mirrors.tds.net` (scroll down to see it in the list). Click on the **Next** button:

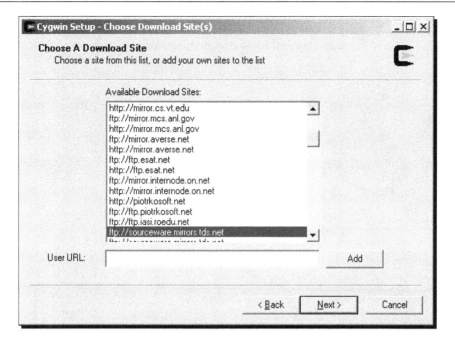

7. The following screen allows you to select the Cygwin packages. This step is important! In addition to the packages selected by default, please select the following packages required for qooxdoo. Expand the folders specified below, and click on the **Skip** link once for each of the packages specified in the following list to select the most recent version. If you click again after selection, it will be deselected. For selection, make sure the checkbox is crossed. The package column is sorted alphabetically as follows:

- **Archive**
  - **zip** (release build support)
  - **unzip** (release build support)

- **Devel**
  - **gettext** (needed for internationalization)
  - **gettext-devel** (needed for internationalization)
  - **make** (core build system)
  - **subversion** (needed for application include support)

- **Interpreters**
  - **python** (core build system)

❑ **Net**

    ❑ **curl** (needed for internationalization)

    ❑ **rsync** (support for publishing applications)

❑ **Utils**

    ❑ **diffutils** (needed for internationalization)

    ❑ **patch** (support for patching files)

    ❑ **util-linux** (general utilities)

❑ **Web**

    ❑ **wget** (needed for internationalization and application include support)

Click on the **Next** button after selecting all of the specified packages.

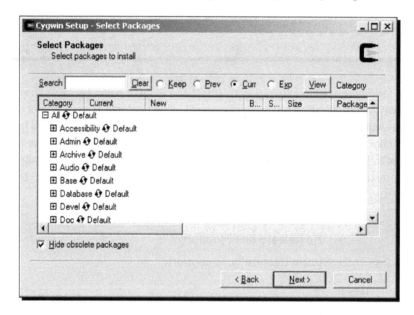

What just happened?

You have installed the tools required for the qooxdoo development environment. You can choose one of the mentioned options (ActivePython or Cygwin). Once you have set up the tools required, the next step is to install the qooxdoo SDK and start developing the application in qooxdoo.

Installing qooxdoo SDK

qooxdoo SDK provides the environment to develop, build, and test the qooxdoo applications. Once you install SDK, we are ready to develop the application.

Time for action – installing qooxdoo SDK

Go to the qooxdoo website (`http://qooxdoo.org/download`) and download the latest stable software development kit. Extract the qooxdoo SDK to `C:\qooxdoo-x.y-sdk`. We have used `qooxdoo-1.2-sdk` in the initial chapters and migrated to `qooxdoo-1.4.1-sdk` in *Chapter 11, Miscellaneous*. You can use other versions as well.

 If you want to download the `qooxdoo-1.2-sdk` version, you can download it from `http://sourceforge.net/projects/qooxdoo/files/qooxdoo-current/`. You can find all other versions, too. If you could not download the qooxdoo SDK from the default mirror site, use another mirror such as Japan Advanced Institute of Science and Technology mirror site at the following URL:

`http://sourceforge.net/projects/qooxdoo/files/qooxdoo-current/1.2/qooxdoo-1.2-sdk.zip/download?use_mirror=jaist`

The directory structure looks something like the one shown in the screenshot that follows.

Application

The `application` directory contains all the applications that are included in the qooxdoo SDK package. We have already explored some of these applications in the qooxdoo website. You can also use these applications locally in your machine instead of accessing them from the qooxdoo website. Accessing the applications locally is faster than accessing them over the Internet. During development, use the local copy in SDK. You might have to build the applications, they're not already built. You can also set up the qooxdoo SDK in one of the development server machines and make these applications available to the team.

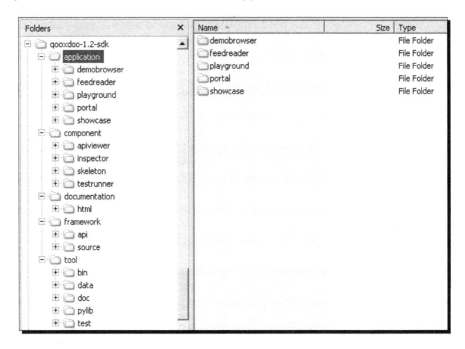

The following applications come with qooxdoo SDK and they are available under the `application` directory:

- `demobrowser`: This application allows you to browse through most of the widgets to see the behavior of the widgets and select the one required for your application.

- `feedreader`: This is a sample application that gets delivered with the qooxdoo SDK for you to get a feel of the qooxdoo application.

- `playground`: This application allows you to edit the sample code or example of the widget and play with it before actually using the widget in your application. This is one of the nice things in qooxdoo.

◆ portal: This is a simple application that demonstrates the low-level capabilities through the **Browser Object Model** (**BOM**) layer available in the qx.bom.* package. This application does not use any of the high-level widget classes. High-level widget classes use these low-level BOM layers heavily to implement the widgets.

◆ showcase: This application shows the main features of qooxdoo and provides a good overview of the qooxdoo framework.

Component

The component directory contains all the components in qooxdoo SDK. Applications in the application directory are meant for the end users, that is, the developers, and the applications in the component directory are the internal applications used by the qooxdoo framework. You can still use these components, if you understand their usage. You will use some of the components such as inspector and simulator. But some components, such as skeleton, are used internally by qooxdoo. The following directories come under the component directory:

◆ apiviewer: This component is used by the generate.py tool to generate the API reference for your application when you run the generate.py api command.

◆ inspector: This component is used by the generate.py tool to generate the inspector instance for your application when you run the generate.py inspector command. The inspector component is a powerful development tool used for live debugging. It can inspect any of the applications that are generated in inspector mode.

◆ simulator: This component provides a testing and automation environment for qooxdoo applications. It can be used to simulate the user interaction in an actual web application. You can use simulator along with inspector to automate the functional testing of your qooxdoo application.

◆ skeleton: This component contains a template to create the qooxdoo application. This component is used by the create-application.py tool to create an application.

◆ testrunner: This component provides the unit testing framework. This component is used by the generate.py tool to generate the unit test code structure for your application when you run the generate.py test or generate.py test-source command.

◆ testrunner2: This component is an experimental unit testing framework delivered in qooxdoo 1.3 which will eventually replace the testrunner component in the future. This is lighter and has an HTML-only interface. You can run the test cases even on mobile devices.

Documentation

The documentation directory contains the manual for the qooxdoo framework. The manual is in PDF as well as in HTML. You can refer to this manual to know more about qooxdoo.

Framework

The framework directory is the main directory which contains code for the qooxdoo framework. This code also follows the structure of the qooxdoo application. The directories under the framework directory are as follows:

♦ source: This directory contains the code for the qooxdoo framework. All the classes of qooxdoo are kept under the class directory. The top-level namespace or package of the qooxdoo framework is qx. All the qooxdoo framework resources such as images are under the resource directory and all the localization files are kept under the translation directory.

♦ api: This directory contains the API reference for the qooxdoo framework. You will need to refer to this most of the time. This is like javadoc for Java. Either you can use the online version from the qooxdoo website or access it locally in your machine.

Tool

This directory contains all the tools used by the framework. The directories under the tool directory are as follows:

♦ bin: This directory contains many scripts, especially generate.py and create-application.py

♦ data: This directory contains a lot of data used by different tools for various reasons such as localization, migration, and so on

♦ doc: This directory contains internal documentation about the tools

♦ pylib: This directory contains all the Python modules used by the qooxdoo framework

♦ test: This directory contains the code for unit testing of various tools

What just happened?

You have set up the qooxdoo software development kit and explored the directory structure of the qooxdoo framework to get a brief understanding of the various components and applications that come with qooxdoo.

Creating a simple qooxdoo application

We have our development environment ready; let's go and create an application in qooxdoo!

Time for action – creating a simple qooxdoo application

qooxdoo is a client-side framework and allows you to create the client application only. The qooxdoo framework also provides RPC API to communicate with the server. In this section, we will learn how to create the client application and the following sections will explain how the data is passed from client to server and how to communicate with the server.

1. Open a command window, go to `C:\qooxdoo-1.2-sdk\tool\bin`, and run the `create-application.py` command. That will show you the usage and the options of the create application script. If you have installed ActivePython, you can just type `create-application.py`, as the `.py` file type is already associated with Python application. If you have installed Python from any other source, that is, either from Cygwin or from `python.org`, you will have to associate the `.py` file type with the Python application or run Python with the `.py` file (`python create-application.py`).

 To avoid typing `python` every time, it is recommended to associate the Python application with the `.py` files. You can do so by right-clicking and opening a `.py` file. It will ask you to choose a program; just browse to the Python location. If you have any issues, run the Python application for the `.py` files. To avoid all this, it is recommended to use ActivePython.

Run the following command in the command prompt:

```
C:\qooxdoo-1.2-sdk\tool\bin>create-application.py
```

This will display a list of options of the create application script. Two of them are explained as follows:

-   `--name` or the `-n` option is for the name of application
-   `--out` or `-o` is for the output location

Other options have default values. See the other options in the console output.

2. Now, let's create the Team Twitter application. For creating this application, you can type any one of the following commands in the command prompt:

-   `create-application.py --name teamtwitter --out C:\`
-   `create-application.py -n teamtwitter -o C:\`

The preceding command creates the Team Twitter client application in the C drive.

3. Now, open the `C:\teamtwitter\source\index.html` page in the browser. It will show you the message **Application not yet ready!**. We need to build the application before running the application. In a command window, go to `C:\teamtwitter` and run the `generate.py` source command. This generates the development version of the application. Now, reload the `C:\teamtwitter\source\index.html` page in the browser. You'll see the first button; click on the button and say hello to qooxdoo world!

4. Now, let's generate the build version of the application. Go to `C:\teamtwitter` and run the `generate.py` build. This generates the deployment version of the application. Now load the page `C:\teamtwitter\build\index.html` in the browser. You'll see the **First Button** button; click on this button and say hello to qooxdoo world!

Now, let's explore the directory structure of the qooxdoo application:

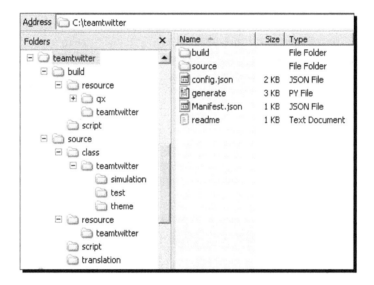

What just happened?

We have created a simple application with qooxdoo, built it, and said hello to qooxdoo world! Let's see the directories and important files that are generated on creation of the application.

Source

The `source` directory contains the development version of the application. The directories and files that come under the `source` directory are as follows:

- `class`: This directory contains all the code of the application. qooxdoo follows a complete object-oriented programming approach with a proper namespace system. You'll work under this directory most of the time to write the JavaScript classes for the application.

- `resource`: This directory contains the resource files, that is, the image files for the application. Resources also follow namespace. You can use the images that come with the qooxdoo framework. No need to copy those images from the qooxdoo framework directory to this directory. Place only the additional resource files in the application resource directory. qooxdoo framework images will be copied automatically by the generator.

- `script`: This directory contains the generated development version of the JavaScript file. It is a loader file that includes all other JavaScript files. This is generated when you run the `generate.py source`.

- `translation`: This directory contains the localization files to support internationalization of the application. If you are supporting multiple languages in your application, you need to place the `.po` files for languages other than English.

- `index.html`: This is the only HTML file (which is also simple) required for the entire qooxdoo application. This HTML file just loads the generated application JavaScript file under the script directory. The content of this file is as follows:

```
<!DOCTYPE html PUBLIC "-//W3C//DTD XHTML 1.1//EN" "http://www.
w3.org/TR/xhtml11/DTD/xhtml11.dtd">
<html xmlns="http://www.w3.org/1999/xhtml" xml:lang="en">
<head>
  <meta http-equiv="Content-Type" content="text/html;
charset=utf-8" />
  <title>teamtwitter</title>
  <script type="text/javascript" src="script/teamtwitter.js"></
script>
</head>
<body></body>
</html>
```

Build

The `build` directory contains the deployment version of the application. This whole directory's content is generated when you run the `generate.py` build. The directories and files that come under the `build` directory are listed as follows:

- ◆ `resource`: This directory contains the resource files. It contains the resources added in the application and also the resources that came with the qooxdoo framework.

- ◆ `script`: This directory contains the generated build version of the JavaScript file. It will be a single, optimized JavaScript file that contains the content from all the source JavaScript files. If your application is huge, you can split this one single JavaScript file into many by modularizing your application into parts, which gets loaded on demand.

- ◆ `index.html`: This is identical to the development version.

Manifest.json

The `Manifest.json` file contains meta information about the application. This is in the **JavaScript Object Notation (JSON)** format. It has two parts, namely, `info`, which is for the human eye and `provides`, which is used by the generator for build processing.

config.json

The `config.json` file contains the configuration used by the `generate.py` script for the build operations.

generate.py

The `generate.py` script is the proxy for the qooxdoo framework's `generator.py` script located in the `tool/bin` directory. This script generates the development and deployment version of the application.

Passing data to the server

qooxdoo uses the JSON format to transfer the data between the client browser and the web server. **JSON** is a light-weight data interchange format. JSON is very light when compared to the XML format. It is easy for humans to read and write. It is easy for machines to parse and generate. We have mentioned the JSON standard format in this section. This information is good enough to work with JSON. If you want to read more, you can visit the JSON website (`http://www.json.org/`).

JSON standard format

Structure	Syntax	Description
object	{}/{member}	object has members separated by comma.
member	pair	A member is a pair.
pair	string : value	pair is a simple key and value separated by a colon. Key is always a string and value is an object.
array	[]/[elements]	array contains elements separated by comma.
element	value	An element is a simple value.
value	string number object array true false null	A value can be a string, number, object, array, or boolean values (true, false, or null).
string	" " "<characters>"	A string literal contains space and characters. A string is very much like a C or Java string.

char	Contains any Unicode character except " or \ or any of the following control characters:
	  ◆ \"
	  ◆ \\
	  ◆ \/
	  ◆ \b
	  ◆ \f
	  ◆ \n
	  ◆ \r
	  ◆ \t
	  ◆ \u (four hexadecimal digits)
		character is any Unicode character except ", \, or control character.

number	int int frac int exp int frac exp	number can be an integer, fraction, or exponential. A number is very much like a C or Java number, except that the octal and hexadecimal formats are not used.

Structure	Syntax	Description

int	`<digit>`
	`<digit> <1 to 9 digits>`
	`<1 to 9 digits>` may include:
	    ◆ `digit`
	    ◆ `<digit> <1 to 9 digits>`
		Integer is any positive or negative digits from 1 to 9 and 0.

frac	`. <digits>`	Fraction has the digits after the "."
exp	`e <digits>`	Exponential to the power of e. Power can be any digits.
digits	`<digit> <digits>`	Digits can be multiple digits.

e	It can take any one of the following forms:
	`e`
	`e+`
	`e-`
	`e-`
	`e`
	`e+`
	`e-`
		Exponential can be positive or negative.

The `Date` object is an exception in the formatting as JavaScript does not have a literal syntax for the `Date` object.

`Date` objects are sent as the following tokens:

- The string—`new Date (Date.UTC(`
- The *year*, integer; for example, `2006`
- A comma
- The *month*, 0-relative integer; for example, `5` (that is, June)
- A comma
- The *day* of the month, integer, range: `1-31`
- A comma
- The *hour* of the day on a 24-hour clock, integer, range: `0-23`
- A comma
- The *minute* of the hour, integer, range: `0-59`

- A comma
- The *second* within the minute, integer, range: 0-59
- A comma
- The *milliseconds* within the second, integer, range: 0-999
- The string—))

A resulting date representation might therefore be:

```
new Date(Date.UTC(2006,5,20,22,18,42,223))
```

While working with date strings, you must take care with the following:

- **Whitespace**: The following points should be remembered:
  - When generating these date strings, implementations should not add whitespace before, after, or between any of the fields within the date string.
  - When parsing these date strings, implementations should allow whitespace before, after, or between any of the fields within the date string.

- **Numbers**: The following points should be remembered:
  - When generating these date strings, implementations must not add leading zeros to the numeric values in the date string. Doing so will cause them to be parsed as octal values. Numbers must be passed in decimal (base 10) notation without leading zeros.
  - When parsing these date strings, implementations must take the integer value of numeric portions of the string as base 10 values, even if leading zeros appear in the string representation of the numbers.

Within the JSON protocol and in JSON messages between peers, Date objects are always passed in UTC format.

A sample JSON content to explain the file menu contents that contain the members, pairs, values or strings, arrays, and so on In the JSON format is as follows:

```
{"menu": {
  "id": "file",
  "value": "File",
  "popup": {
    "menuitem": [
      {"value": "New", "onclick": "CreateNewDoc()"},
      {"value": "Open", "onclick": "OpenDoc()"},
      {"value": "Close", "onclick": "CloseDoc()"}
    ]
  }
}}
```

What just happened?

We got to know about the data format that is passed between client and server in qooxdoo applications.

Communicating with the server

qooxdoo uses the **Remote Procedure Call (RPC)** mechanism to call the APIs that are exposed on the server. qooxdoo RPC is based on JSON-RPC as the serialization and method call protocol. qooxdoo provides all the necessary classes in the `qx.io.remote` package. So, it is pretty simple to communicate with the server.

Setting up an RPC connection

To make remote calls, you need to create an instance of the `Rpc` class:

```
var rpc = new qx.io.remote.Rpc(
"http://localhost:8080/qooxdoo/.qxrpc",
"qooxdoo.test"
);
```

The first parameter is the URL of the server and the second is the name of the service you want to call. Class name is the fully qualified name and is case sensitive.

Making a call

When you have the `Rpc` instance, you can make synchronous and asynchronous calls based on your need:

```
// synchronous call
try {
var result = rpc.callSync("echo", "Test");
alert("Result of sync call: " + result);
} catch (exc) {
alert("Exception during sync call: " + exc);
}
```

Synchronous calls typically block the browser UI until the response comes back from the server. A user cannot perform any action until the response comes back from the server. So, try to avoid them as much as possible or use them sparingly. In synchronous calls, the method name is the first parameter followed by the parameters of the server method as mentioned in the preceding code.

The following code demonstrates asyncronous call:

```
// asynchronous call
var handler = function(result, exc) {
if (exc == null) {
alert("Result of async call: " + result);
} else {
alert("Exception during async call: " + exc);
}
};
rpc.callAsync(handler, "echo", "Test");
```

An asynchronous call does not block the browser UI until the response comes back from the server. Instead, it takes an additional first parameter that specifies a handler function that is invoked when the result of the method call is available or when an exception occurs. You can also use qooxdoo event listeners for asynchronous calls. To use qooxdoo event listeners, just use `callAsyncListeners` instead of `callAsync`.

A sample which uses an asynchronous call via event listeners is as follows:

```
var rpc = new qx.io.remote.Rpc();
var methodName = "testMethod";
rpc.addListener("completed", function(e) {
  var result = e.getData();
  // do something.........
}, this );
rpc.addListener("failed", function(e) {
  // do something on failure
  this.warn("Method call failed "+e);
}, this );
rpc.addListener("timeout", function(e) {
  // do something on timeout.
  this.warn("Method call timed out "+e);
}, this);
var result = rpc.callAsyncListeners(false, methodName);
```

Finally, to summarize, one can communicate with the server by issuing an RPC call in three different ways:

- **Synchronous** (`qx.io.remote.Rpc.callSync`): It is dangerous as it blocks the whole browser and it is not recommended to use it

- **Asynchronous** (`qx.io.remote.Rpc.callAsync`): It returns the results via a call back function

- **Asynchronous** (`qx.io.remote.Rpc.callAsyncListeners`): It returns results via event listeners

Request

RPC request contains a service which maps to the remote service. It also contains the method to be invoked in that remote service, ID of the request, and the parameters to pass as arguments to the remote service method.

```
{
"service":"qooxdoo.test",
"method":"echo",
"id":1,
"params":["Hello to Qooxdoo World!"]
}
```

Response

RPC response contains the ID to map the request call and the result of the request.

```
{
  "id":"1",
  "result":"Client said: Hello to Qooxdoo World!"
}
```

Aborting a call

If the user of the system changes his or her mind, the user can abort an asynchronous call while it's still being performed. See the following code snippet for aborting the asynchronous call:

```
// Rpc instantiation and handler function left out for brevity
var callref = rpc.callAsync(handler, "echo", "Test");
// ...
rpc.abort(callref);
// the handler will be called with an abort exception
```

Error handling

When you make a synchronous call, you can catch an exception to handle the errors. The exception object contains `rpcdetails` that describes the error in detail. The same details are also available in the second parameter in an asynchronous handler function, as well as in the events fired by `callAsyncListeners`. The following code snippet demonstrates error handling:

```
//creation of the Rpc instance left out for brevity
//error handling for sync calls
try {
var result = rpc.callSync("echo", "Test");
} catch (exc) {
showDetails(exc.rpcdetails);
}
// error handling for async calls
var handler = function(result, exc) {
if (exc != null) {
    showDetails(exc);
}
};
rpc.callAsync(handler, "echo", "Test");
//method to display error details
var showDetails = function(details) {
alert(
"origin: " + details.origin +
"; code: " + details.code +
"; message: " + details.message
);
};
```

The exception origin can be one of the following four:

◆ `qx.io.remote.Rpc.origin.server`: This occurs on the server (for example, when a non-existing method is called)

◆ `qx.io.remote.Rpc.origin.application`: This occurs inside the server application (for example, during a method call in a non-qooxdoo code)

◆ `qx.io.remote.Rpc.origin.transport`: This occurs in the communication layer (for example, when the `Rpc` instance was constructed with a URL where no backend is deployed, resulting in an HTTP 404 error)

◆ `qx.io.remote.Rpc.origin.local`: This occurs locally (for example, when the call timed out or when it was aborted)

The exception code depends on the origin. For the server and application origins, the possible code is defined by the backend implementation. For transport errors, it's the HTTP status code. For local errors, the following code is defined:

- `qx.io.remote.Rpc.localError.timeout`: A time-out occurred

- `qx.io.remote.Rpc.localError.abort`: The call was aborted

Cross-domain calls

Using the qooxdoo RPC implementation, you can also make calls across domain boundaries. On the client side, all you have to do is specify the correct destination URL in the `Rpc` constructor and set the `setcrossDomain` property to `true`. See the following code snippet:

```
var rpc = new qx.io.remote.Rpc("http://targetdomain.com/appname/.
qxrpc");
rpc.setCrossDomain(true);
```

On the server side, you need to configure the backend to accept cross-domain calls (Refer the documentation of the various backend implementations).

The origin is determined through a combination of protocol, host, and port. The `localhost` and `127.0.0.1` are treated as two different hosts. Therefore, if you access the application using `http//localhost:8080/teamtwitter`, then to access the server without enabling the cross-domain, you will have to use the following URL for the RPC calls:

`http://localhost:8080/teamtwitter/.qxrpc`

Similarly, if you access the application using `http//127.0.0.1:8080/teamtwitter`, then to access the server without enabling the cross-domain, you will have to use the following URL for the RPC calls:

`http://127.0.0.1:8080/teamtwitter/.qxrpc`

It is advisable to get the protocol, host, and port from the URL typed in the browser and construct the URL for the RPC calls that are sent to the same server.

If you really want to make cross-domain calls, you will have to set the cross-domain flag in the RPC call from the client and make sure the server running on the different host accepts the cross-domain calls.

Parameter and result conversion

All method parameters and result values are automatically converted between JavaScript and the server implementation language. During the data transfer between the client and server, the data is transferred in JSON format. So, the data gets converted from JavaScript to JSON and then to Java or any other server implementation language and vice versa. Using the Java RPC Server, you can even have overloaded methods. The correct one will be picked on basis of the provided parameters. The following table lists the JavaScript types and the corresponding JSON types and Java types at the server.

JavaScript type	JSON type	Java type
Number	number	int, long, double, Integer, Long, Double
Boolean	true, false	boolean, Boolean
String	String	String
Date	The Date object is an exception in the JSON formatting as JavaScript does not have literal syntax for date. Date objects are sent as the following tokens: new Date(Date. UTC(2006,5,20,22,18,42,223))	java.util.Date
Array	Array	java.util.Array
Object	Object	java.util.Map
Object	Object	JavaBean

All primitive data types are self explanatory. JavaScript has the Date object, which is translated to the java.util.Date object. JavaScript supports the Array object, which is translated to the java.util.Array object. Other than Number, Boolean, String, Date, and Array type are objects in JavaScript. If a JavaScript object is passed for the java.util.Map parameter in the server side, all the member variables of the object are converted to the key-value pair of the map. Similarly, when a java.util.Map is returned from the server side, all key-value pairs are translated to member variables of the JavaScript object.

JavaBeans are converted in a similar way. The properties of JavaBeans become JavaScript properties and vice versa. If a JavaScript object contains properties for which no corresponding setters exist in the JavaBeans, they are ignored. For performance reasons, recursive conversion of JavaBean and Map objects is performed without checking for cycles! If there's a reference cycle somewhere, you end up with a StackOverflowException.

The same is true when you try to send a JavaScript object to the server. If it (indirectly) references itself, you get a recursion error in the browser. Besides the fully-automatic conversions, there's also a class hinting mechanism. You can use it in case you need to send a specific sub-class to the server. However, it can't be used to instantiate classes without a default constructor yet. Future qooxdoo versions may provide more extensive class hinting support.

What just happened?

We got an understanding of how to communicate with the server from the qooxdoo client applications. We have learnt how to make synchronous and asynchronous calls, handle the error, abort the asynchronous call, and so on. We have also understood the data type mapping between the JavaScript, JSON, and the server implementation language.

RPC servers

qooxdoo is a server-agnostic framework. The qooxdoo client can communicate with any server implemented in languages such as Java, Python, Perl, PHP, and so on, provided the implementation abides by the qooxdoo JSON-RPC server guidelines. qooxdoo already provides many RPC server implementations in the contribution projects. If you don't find the server implementation in your favorite language, you can write one yourself by following the qooxdoo JSON-RPC server guidelines. The available contribution projects for the RPC Server implementation in different languages can be found at the following website. Refer to the backend projects at `http://qooxdoo.org/contrib/project`.

To know more on writing your own RPC server, you can check the following URL:

`http://manual.qooxdoo.org/1.2.x/pages/communication/rpc_server_`
`writer_guide.html`

Integrating with the Java server

qooxdoo is a client framework and it works with any server obeying qooxdoo JSON-RPC server guidelines. We'll focus on client application development in most of this book. In this section, we will set up the server environment with the qooxdoo contribution project—RPCJava. We'll use the same for the development of our book application (Team Twitter). As the scope of this book is qooxdoo client applications, in other sections, we will focus on the client application development. The complete code of the application to be developed in this book will be available for download from the publisher's website.

Time for action – integrating with the Java server

One of the qooxdoo contribution projects is RPCJava (`http://qooxdoo.org/contrib/project#rpcjava`). In early versions of qooxdoo, the server components were also bundled as the backend in the qooxdoo SDK. As it evolved, the server components have been separated into contribution projects to allow those components to grow independently from the qooxdoo client framework.

Let's set up the server development environment. To do so, just follow these steps:

1. Create the following directories:
   - `C:\teamtwitter-server`
   - `C:\teamtwitter-server\src`
   - `C:\teamtwitter-server\lib`
   - `C:\teamtwitter-server\classes`
   - `C:\teamtwitter-server\dist`
   - `C:\teamtwitter-server\webapp`

2. Download the GNU tarball of RPCJava from the SourceForge website (`http://qooxdoo-contrib.svn.sourceforge.net/viewvc/qooxdoo-contrib/trunk/qooxdoo-contrib/RpcJava/`) and extract `qooxdoo-contrib-RpcJava.tar.gz` to `C:\`.

3. Set up RPCJava in the server environment:
   - Go to `C:\RPCjava`
   - Copy the contents of `C:\RpcJava\trunk\lib` to `C:\teamtwitter-server\lib`
   - Copy the contents of `C:\RpcJava\trunk\rpc` to `C:\teamtwitter-server\src`
   - Copy the contents of `C:\RpcJava\trunk\webapp` to `C:\teamtwitter-server\webapp`
   - Copy `C:\RpcJava\trunk\build.properties.sample` to `C:\teamtwitter-server\build.properties.sample`
   - Copy `C:\RpcJava\trunk\build.xml` to `C:\teamtwitter-server\build.xml`
   - Copy `C:\teamtwitter-server\build.properties.sample` to `C:\teamtwitter-server\build.properties`

4. Download the following tools or software required for the server project and install them:

- ❏ Download the Ant tool to run the build file. Either you can download Ant from `http://ant.apache.org/` and install it or use the Ant plugin that comes with Eclipse.

- ❏ Download the latest stable **Java Development Kit (JDK)** from `http://www.oracle.com/technetwork/java/javase/downloads/index.html` and install it.

- ❏ Download the latest stable version of Tomcat from `http://tomcat.apache.org/` and install it.

5. Set the following environment variables in **My Computer | Properties | Advanced | Environment Variables**:

- ❏ Set the **ANT_HOME** environment variable, as shown in the following screenshot:

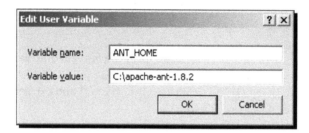

- ❏ Set the **JAVA_HOME** environment variable, as shown in the following screenshot:

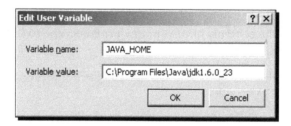

- ❏ Append the `bin` directory of Ant (`C:\apache-ant-1.8.2\bin`) in the `PATH` environment variable.

6. In C:\teamtwitter-server, edit build.properties to set your details. The following details may differ for your system:

```
applicationName = teamtwitter
deployDir = C:/softwares/tomcat5.5/webapps
qooxdooDir = C:/qooxdoo-1.2-sdk
clientApplicationDir = C:/teamtwitter
```

7. In C:\teamtwitter-server, edit the build.xml file to add the necessary targets to build the Team Twitter client source and server source. The build.xml file reads the properties from build.properties and sets the value for the various directories such as build.dir, dist.dir, application.dist.dir, and web.dir.

The target clean wipes out the old classes and creates classes and dist directories.

The target compile compiles the team twitter server code with the libraries kept under the lib directory. All the output classes are saved under the classes directory.

The following content is from the build.xml file:

```xml
<?xml version='1.0'?>
<project name="teamtwitter" default="help" basedir=".">

  <property file="build.properties" />
  <property name="build.dir" value="${basedir}" />
  <property name="dist.dir" value="${basedir}/dist" />
  <property name="application.dist.dir" value="${dist.
dir}/${applicationName}" />
  <property name="web.dir" value="${basedir}/web" />
  <target name="clean">
    <delete dir="classes" />
    <mkdir dir="classes" />
    <delete dir="${dist.dir}" />
    <mkdir dir="${dist.dir}" />
    <mkdir dir="${application.dist.dir}" />
  </target>
  <target name="compile">
    <mkdir dir="classes" />
    <javac srcdir="src" destdir="classes" debug="true"
target="1.5" source="1.5">
      <classpath>
        <fileset dir="lib">
          <include name="**.jar" />
        </fileset>
```

```
        </classpath>
      </javac>
    </target>

    <target name="client.generate-source">
      <exec executable="python" dir="${clientApplicationDir}">
        <arg value="generate.py" />
        <arg value="source" />
      </exec>
    </target>

    <target name="client.generate-build">
      <exec executable="python" dir="${clientApplicationDir}">
        <arg value="generate.py" />
        <arg value="build" />
      </exec>
    </target>

    <target name="copy.web" depends="compile, client.generate-
build">
      <!-- copy client application -->
      <copy todir="${application.dist.dir}">
        <fileset dir="${clientApplicationDir}/build">
        </fileset>
      </copy>

      <mkdir dir="${application.dist.dir}/WEB-INF" />

      <!-- copy lib -->
      <copy todir="${application.dist.dir}/WEB-INF/lib">
        <fileset dir="${build.dir}/lib">
          <exclude name="servlet-api.jar" />
        </fileset>
      </copy>

      <!-- copy classes -->
      <mkdir dir="${application.dist.dir}/WEB-INF/classes" />
      <copy todir="${application.dist.dir}/WEB-INF/classes">
        <fileset dir="${build.dir}/classes">
          <include name="**/*.class" />
          <exclude name="**/*Test.class" />
          <exclude name="**/*Tests.class" />
        </fileset>
      </copy>
```

```
    <!-- copy WE-INF -->
    <copy todir="${application.dist.dir}/WEB-INF">
      <fileset dir="${build.dir}/webapp/WEB-INF">
        <include name="**/*" />
      </fileset>
    </copy>
  </target>

  <target name="dist" depends="copy.web">
    <war destfile="${dist.dir}/${applicationName}.war"
webxml="${application.dist.dir}/WEB-INF/web.xml">
      <fileset dir="${application.dist.dir}" />
    </war>
  </target>

  <target name="deploy">
    <copy todir="${deployDir}/${applicationName}">
      <fileset dir="${application.dist.dir}">
      </fileset>
    </copy>
  </target>
  <target name="help">
  <echo message="targets available in this build file are:" />
    <echo message="clean" />
    <echo message="compile" />
    <echo message="client.generate-source" />
    <echo message="client.generate-build" />
    <echo message="copy.web" />
    <echo message="dist" />
    <echo message="deploy" />
  </target>
</project>
```

The target `client.generate-source` generates the development version of the Team Twitter client application.

The target `client.generate-build` generates the deployment version of the Team Twitter client application.

The target `copy.web` depends on targets `compile` and `client.generate-source`.

After completing the dependency targets, it copies the Team Twitter client application deployment version into the `dist` directory, creates the `WEB-INF` directory in the `dist` directory, copies all the library files except `servlet-api.jar` under the `WEB-INF/lib` directory, copies the Team Twitter server classes under the `WEB-INF/classes` directory, and copies the `web.xml` under `WEB-INF`. The `servlet-api.jar` file will be available in the Tomcat `common/lib` directory.

The target `dist` depends on the `copy.web` target. After completing the dependency target, it creates the **Web application ARchive (WAR)** file which contains both the client application and server code for the Team Twitter application.

The target `deploy` deploys the `dist` directory in the Tomcat `webapps` directory.

8. Now, let's build the Team Twitter application. Run the following build command:

```
C:\teamtwitter-server>ant dist
```

The preceding build command will build everything and generate the web application directory as well as the WAR file. Now, we have the server development environment.

9. Let's make changes in the Team Twitter client application to integrate with the server code. RPCJava comes with a `qooxdoo.test` remote service, which implements all the test methods of the qooxdoo RPC server. We can call the `echo` method from the `test` remote service to verify the client server communication.

Open the Team Twitter client application JavaScript file (`C:\teamtwitter\source\class\teamtwitter\Application.js`).

Edit the listener implementation for the button and add the following code to integrate with the RPCJava server.

```
// Add an event listener
button1.addListener("execute", function(e) {
        var rpc = new qx.io.remote.Rpc();
    rpc.setCrossDomain( false );
    rpc.setTimeout(1000);

    var host = window.location.host;
    var proto = window.location.protocol;
    var webURL = proto + "//" + host + "/teamtwitter/.qxrpc";
    rpc.setUrl(webURL);
    rpc.setServiceName("qooxdoo.test");

    rpc.callAsync(function(result, ex, id){
      if (ex == null) {
```

```
            alert(result);
        }
        else
        {
            alert("Async(" + id + ") exception: " + ex);
        }
    }, "echo", "Hello to qooxdoo World!");
});
```

10. Now, run the build again to rebuild the application:

`C:\teamtwitter-server>ant dist`

The `dist` target builds the client application code, compiles the server code, and builds the web application.

Now, run the following command to deploy the Team Twitter web application in Tomcat.

Let's deploy the application:

`C:\teamtwitter-server>ant deploy`

11. Now, start Tomcat by running the following command (`<TOMCAT_HOME>` is where you installed the Tomcat server):

`<TOMCAT_HOME>\bin\startup.bat`

12. Let's check the application from the browser. Once the Tomcat server is up and running, try to access the primitive Team Twitter application by accessing the following URL:

```
http://localhost:8080/teamtwitter/
```

Click on the **First Button** button; you'll get a response from the Team Twitter server. The server method just echoes whatever the client passed with the prefix **Client said**.

In the JSON-RPC call, the following data is sent as the request and received in the response.

The data sent in the request to the server is as follows:

```
{"service":"qooxdoo.test","method":"echo","id":1,"params":["Hello
to qooxdoo World!"]}
```

The data received in response from the server is as follows:

```
{"id":"1","result":"Client said: Hello to qooxdoo World!"}
```

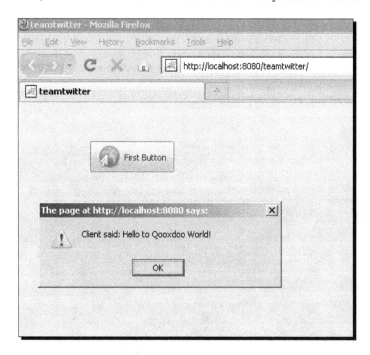

Working with Eclipse IDE

If you want to use any IDE such as Eclipse IDE, carry out the following steps (you can download the Eclipse IDE from `http://www.eclipse.org/`):

1. Create a Java project and set the project name as **teamtwitter-server**. Set the location as **C:\teamtwitter-server**, which was created earlier in step 1 in the *Time for action – integrating with the Java server* section. Click on the **Finish** button. It will automatically set everything for the project.

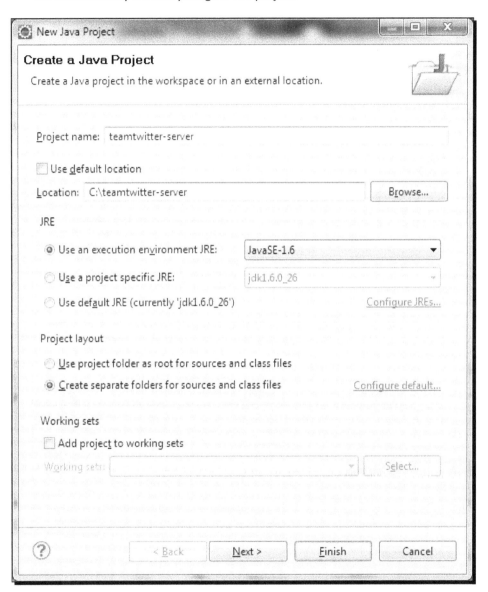

2. Now, set up the **Ant view**. If you have not enabled the Ant view, enable it by going to **Window | Show View | Ant**. In the Ant view of Eclipse, add the `build.xml` file, which is present in `C:\teamtwitter-server`. Then, you can run the Ant targets from the Eclipse IDE. The Ant tasks in the server application also build the client application based on the `build.properties` configuration, generates the final web application, and deploys it in Tomcat:

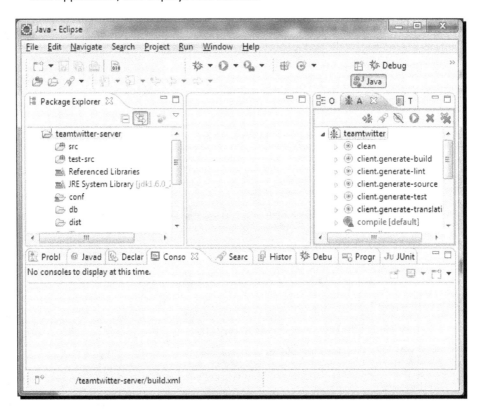

What just happened?

We have set up the RPCJava server and the server development environment. We have integrated the client application with the server, built the code, deployed the web application, and tested it.

Pop quiz

1. qooxdoo needs the following tools

    a. ActivePython and Cygwin

    b. ActivePython or Cygwin

2. Components in the qooxdoo SDK are

    a. The qooxdoo applications for the end users

    b. The qooxdoo internal applications used by the framework

3. Applications in the qooxdoo SDK are

    a. The qooxdoo applications for the end users

    b. The qooxdoo internal applications used by the framework

4. qooxdoo is a

    a. Client-side framework

    b. Server-side framework

    c. Both

5. qooxdoo prefers to send the data for communication between the client and the server in the format of

    a. XML

    b. Text

    c. JSON

6. The qooxdoo client application can communicate with the server implemented in

    a. Java only

    b. Java, Python, and Perl

    c. Any language abiding to the qooxdoo JSON-RPC server guidelines

Summary

We have set up the development environment in this chapter.

Specifically, we covered the following:

- We have set up the required tools for the qooxdoo framework
- We have set up qooxdoo SDK and explored the structure of the qooxdoo SDK
- We have created an application in qooxdoo and explored the structure of the application
- We have learnt how the data is passed between client and server
- We have learnt how communication takes place between client and server
- We have set up the Java RPC server and integrated the client code with the server

Now that we have the development environment ready, we can start learning the programming techniques in qooxdoo in the next chapter.

3
Core Programming Concepts

This chapter explains basic object-oriented features (class, object, interface, inheritance, and so on) and how these features are achieved with JavaScript in the qooxdoo framework. This chapter also explains the basic syntax of the qooxdoo programming.

JavaScript is a prototype-based scripting language that is dynamically typed and that supports object-oriented language. qooxdoo allows you to write the code in object-oriented fashion, by providing the basic syntax for each object-oriented concept. In addition to the object-oriented support, qooxdoo gives more flexibility to ease coding in JavaScript. qooxdoo framework provides many reusable components too. Let's learn the core programming concepts of qooxdoo framework, in this chapter.

In this chapter, we shall cover the following topics:

- Code comments and API documentation
- Object-oriented programming
- Interface, class, and mixin
- qooxdoo properties
- Events
- Team Twitter classes

We have already said "hello" to the qooxdoo world. Now, it is time to dive into the qooxdoo world and pick up the object-oriented programming concepts.

Code comments and API documentation

Let's learn about the comments and API documentation in qooxdoo programming before learning any other programming concepts.

The comments are non-compiled statements in the code. qooxdoo allows three different types of comments:

- **Single-line comment**: A // (double slash) is used for single-line comments, in the code. The content after the double slash, till the end of the line, is a comment. It can be used as in the following code snippet:

```
var emp = new Employee();//declared to store the employee info
```

- **Multi-line comment**: The content embedded between /* and */ is called a multi-line comment and can include multiple lines. It can be used as mentioned here:

```
/*
Line of comment
Another line of comment
*/
```

- **Doc comment**: Documentation (doc) comment is used for documenting the qooxdoo API. These are similar to javadoc or JSDoc comments. It can be used as mentioned below:

```
/**
  Documentation for the code. This will appear in API doc.
 */
```

One of the usages of the doc comment is mentioned as follows:

```
/** member functions definition */
members :{

  /** function for getting the employee data */
  getEmpInfo : function() {

    // do some thing.........
  }
}
```

The class description is taken as the first comment that starts with /**, in the file.

qooxdoo supports few HTML tags and few predefined attributes inside the doc comments, for better structure. Supported attributes are:

- `@param`: This attribute describes the parameter of a method or constructor. The `@param` attribute is followed by the name of the parameter, and type, in curly brackets, followed by a description. When the parameter is optional, the curly brackets include the default value, in addition to the type. It can be used as follows:

```
@param message {string} the message to show
@param flag {Boolean ? true}
```

- `@return`: This attribute describes the return value of a method. It can be used as follows:

```
@return {boolean} validity of the data
```

- `@throws`: This attribute describes the exception thrown by a method or constructor. It can be used as follows:

```
@throws if the search criteria is not entered completely
```

- `@see`: This attribute describes cross references to other structures (class, property, method, or constant). It can be used as follows:

```
@see com.xyz.Decorator
```

- `@link`: This is similar to the `@see` attribute but is used to link the other structures within description text. It can be used as follows:

```
<code>this.self(arguments)</code> ({@link qx.core.Object#self})
```

A sample method with the documentation is mentioned in the following code snippet:

```
/**
   @param name {string} the name of the object
   @param flag {Boolean ? true}
   @return {boolean} validity of the data
   @throws on the failure condition
   @see qx.core.Object
 */
testMethod : function( name, flag) {
   if(!flag)
   {
     throw new qx.core.ValidationError("failure", "Condition
failed");
   }
   return true;
}
```

Time for action – generating API documentation for Team Twitter

Let's generate the API documentation for our Team Twitter application.

1. Generate a nice API documentation for the Team Twitter application by running the following command in the client application directory, `C:\teamtwitter`:

```
generate.py api
```

The `api` job in the generator analyzes the code tree and generates the qooxdoo API documentation. When you run this job in your application directory, it creates a directory named `api`, under the `application` directory, and generates the API documentation for all the application classes, and the qooxdoo classes as well. In our case, it will be `C:\teamtwitter\api`.

2. Check the generated API documentation for the application. Open the file `C:\teamtwitter\api\index.html`. It will open the API viewer application for the Team Twitter application. The entire API is searchable and cross-linked.

All the qooxdoo classes fall under the `qx` package, and our application classes fall under the `teamtwitter` package:

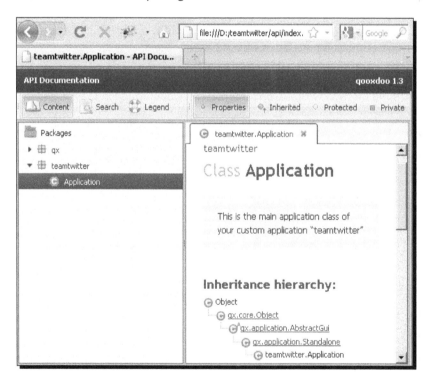

What just happened?

We generated the API documentation for the Team Twitter application and viewed the API documentation. Whenever you add new classes or modify classes, you should regenerate the API documentation to get the updated API documentation.

Object-oriented programming

Object-oriented programming is a way of organizing the code as a collection of objects that incorporate both data structure and behavior. In the real world, it is better to place the data and related methods in a class, rather than having the data structure separate from the behaviors. If you keep it separate, it will lead to data corruption, increase the complexity, and create lot of confusion, especially if the project runs on a million lines of code.

Object and class

An **object** is an instance of the class that models the related data structure and behaviors into a discrete unit. For example, `Animal` is a class that consolidates the properties of the animal, such as, name, age, weight, type, and so on, into data structures, and the behaviors, such as, eat, move, talk, and so on, defined in the class. You can instantiate the class and set the specific values for the instance. The instance with specific values stored in the data structure, and with behaviors defined in the class, is known as an object. You can create many objects from the class template and assign a different set of values for each object.

On the other hand, object-oriented programming allows you to place the related data and behavior in a class, *encapsulate* it, and expose only necessary behaviors to the outside of the class, through the use of access types (such as, `private`, `protected`, and `public`). Interfaces allow you to *abstract* the implementation of the classes. With the combination of interfaces and classes, you can achieve the runtime *polymorphism*. You can reuse the code through *inheritance* of the classes.

Encapsulation

Encapsulation means bringing the related data structure and behaviors in a class and exposing only the necessary behaviors to the members outside the class.

One can restrict the visibility of the data structure and behaviors by using the access modifiers namely, `private`, `protected`, and `public`. We can discuss more about access modifiers, while we learn about classes and members in the following sections.

Encapsulation reduces the interdependency between various parts of the code to avoid the massive ripple effects, even for a small change. The code becomes cleaner and maintainable.

Inheritance

Inheritance is the sharing of properties and behaviors among the classes, based on a hierarchical relationship. A class that inherits a class is termed a **subclass**. The subclass incorporates or inherits all the properties and behaviors from the super class, the one that is extended. It is like inheriting all wealth and characteristics from your parents.

Inheritance allows code reuse among the classes, through the class hierarchy.

Overriding

You can inherit all the properties and behaviors from the super class, but you may need to have a different behavior for a few methods implemented in the super class. You can change those behaviors by overriding the implementations. In the example mentioned earlier, implementation for the move() behavior in the Animal class may be a default implementation that might use *walk* as a mode of movement. Dogs normally run and fish actually swim, so, the move() behavior is overridden in the sub classes, as per the need.

Abstraction

Abstraction is the representation of a complex system in a simple interface. In system development, abstraction means focusing on what an object is and what it does, before deciding how it should be implemented.

Abstraction exposes a simple interface to the world and preserves the freedom to make decisions for as long as possible, by avoiding premature commitments to the details.

Polymorphism

Polymorphism means the same operation may behave differently on different classes, based on the implementation in each class. With the examples mentioned earlier, when you call move() on the dog instance, it will walk or run on the ground and when you call move() on the fish instance, it will swim in water.

The behavior is decided in runtime, based on the object on which the operation is invoked.

We have learnt the basic principles of object-oriented programming. We'll see, in the following sections, how that is achieved in qooxdoo.

Interface

Interface is a simple concept but plays a vital role. It provides abstraction on implementations and polymorphism. It is said in the basic design principles that:

- Code to an interface, rather than to an implementation
- Follow the dependency inversion principle (depend upon abstractions, not on concretions)

An interface is a contract. Interface can be implemented by any class, from any inheritance tree. One class can implement many interfaces for different purposes. Interface allows you to give a common characteristic for different classes. For example, a class that implements an interface called `Validator` will have the validation behavior implemented. Let's see how to define this contract in qooxdoo.

In qooxdoo, the items (in the contract) that can be included in an interface are discussed in the following sections.

Members

A member function of the interface can have either an empty definition or a set of preconditions to be checked. These preconditions are validated before calling the actual implementation of the class. The predefined assert functions are defined in `qx.core.Assert`. The class implementing the interface must provide the implementation for all the member functions defined in the interface.

Statics

Only constants are allowed here. The static variables are accessed through the fully qualified name (for example, `org.test.MyInterface.PI`, where `PI` is the static declared in the `org.test.MyInterface` interface).

Properties

The properties of the interface are just a name with empty map values. The class implementing the interface must have all the properties defined in the interface. Properties are discussed in more detail in the *qooxdoo properties* section in this chapter.

Events

The class implementing the interface must declare all the events defined in the interface. Events are discussed in more detail in the *Events—class level* section in this chapter.

An interface can be defined with the qx.Interface.define(<name>,<config>) method. qooxdoo allows an interface to extend one or more interfaces. Let's define an interface:

```
qx.Interface.define("org.test.MyInterface",
{
  extend : org.test.MySuperInterface,

  properties : {
    "name" : {},
    "contact" : {}
  },

  members : {
    Foo1 : function() {},
    Foo2 : function(x, y){
      this.assertArgumentsCount(arguments, 2, 2);
      this.assertString(x);
    }
  },

  events : {
    "changeValue" : "qx.event.type.Data"
  },

  statics : {
    PI : 3.14
  }
});
```

One of the basic design principles is "Code to an interface instead of coding to a class". We have learnt how to define an interface in qooxdoo and what contract items it can contain. Now, we can code an interface, first, and then implement it in the classes.

Extended Backus-Naur Form (EBNF) is the most popularly-used notation for describing context-free grammar or formal languages and is very easy to understand. You can refer to the EBNF-like syntax for interface in qooxdoo at http://manual.qooxdoo.org/1.4/pages/core/interface_quickref.html

Class

Class is the main concept and a basic unit in object-oriented programming. Effective organization of the code into proper class hierarchy improves the reusability of the code and its maintainability. You need to understand this section thoroughly to write better code.

Classes implement the methods in the interfaces. A class is a template that describes the state and behavior of the object, while the object is an instance of the class that holds the data (that is, its own state) and access to all the behaviors defined in the class. As with any other object-oriented programming language, qooxdoo allows you to define a class in JavaScript.

A class can be defined with the qx.Class.define(<name>,<map>) method. The first parameter is a fully qualified class name, and the second parameter is the map that contains all the details of the object such as constructor, destructor, members that contain instance variables, behaviors, or methods, and so on. The keys in the map are predefined in qooxdoo, and key name directly explains the object detail, namely, construct (for constructor), destruct (for destructor), members, properties, events, and so on. The allowed keys can be seen in the class syntax section.

You can extend the classes to inherit the variables and methods. Let's define a class:

```
qx.Class.define("org.test.MyClass", {
  // constructors, properties, members, and so on
});
```

As the whole definition is given in qx.Class.define(), it is called a *closed form* of class declaration. You can encapsulate the data structure and the related actions in a class, expose only the necessary actions to the members outside the class, and keep the rest of the actions (and all the data structure) as private to the class. You can create an object for the class, as follows:

```
var myObj = new org.test.Myclass();
```

The new operator is used to create an object for the class template.

Constructor and destructor

The key for the constructor in the class map is `construct`. Similarly, the key for the destructor in the class map is `destruct`. The constructor is invoked on creation of an object from the class whereas the destructor is invoked on disposal of the object. Let's add a constructor and destructor to the class map.

```
qx.Class.define("org.test.MyClass", {

// define constructor
  construct : function(){

    /* lets give info level debug statement here.
      To see that the constructor is invoked
      on creation of the class. */
    this.info("Am in Constructor of MyClass");
},

destruct : function() {
  this.info("Am in the destructor");
}
});
```

Members

Members in a qooxdoo class are the state/variable and the behaviors/methods of a class. There are two types of members, namely, class members and instance members. You can design the members as one of these types, based on the necessity.

Class members

Class members are common to all the instances of the class. They are also known as *static members*. A class member or static member can be a class variable or class method. The key for the class members in the class map is `statics`. A static member definition or declaration is similar to the other methods or variables. The best naming convention for a class or static variable is to use the uppercase notation to distinguish from instance members. Uppercase notation is only for class or static variables and not for class or static methods. Let's add a couple of class or static variables and a class or static method to the class.

```
qx.Class.define("org.test.MyClass", {

  // All class level variables and methods declared under statics
  statics : {
    //class or static variables declared here in uppercase notation
    FOO : value,
    CLASS_TYPE : "SIMPLE",
```

```
    //class or static methods declared here
      testMethod: function(){
      // do something on the class method.
       }
 }
});
```

We have seen how to declare class or static members. Let's see how to use them.

The class variable or class method can be accessed only with the fully qualified class name. As the class method is common to all the instances of the class, you need not create an instance to access the class method. You can access the class method or class variable directly from the class, with the fully qualified class name, as shown in the following code snippet:

```
org.test.MyClass.FOO = 456;
var x = org.test.MyClass.CLASS_TYPE;
org.test.MyClass.testMethod();
```

Instance members

A copy of the instance variable is created for each instance or object of the class, and the value is not common across all the instances of the class. Instance methods are invoked against the instance or the object of the class. The key for the class members in the class map is `members`. Let's add an instance variable and an instance method. To access the instance variable or instance method, you need to create an object of the class. Only a public instance variable or a public instance method can be accessed through the object reference.

```
qx.Class.define("org.test.MyClass", {

  members : {

    foo : value,

       testMethod : function(){
       // do something on the class members.
        }
 }

});

var myClass = new org.test.MyClass();
myClass.foo = 456;
myClass.testMethod();
```

We have seen the declaration of the instance members. Now, we'll learn how to encapsulate the instance members to expose only the necessary members to the outside of the class and hide the rest of the instance members in the class. This can be achieved by controlling the visibility for the instance members declared inside the class. As with all object-oriented languages, qooxdoo also supports three types of access type. As the JavaScript does not support a strong enforcing mechanism for access protection, qooxdoo uses certain coding conventions instead of the access type keywords:

- **Private**: Private members can be accessed within the defined class only. A private member name should start with a double underscore (__).
- **Protected**: Protected members can be accessed within the defined class and its derived classes. A protected member name should start with a single underscore (_).
- **Public**: Public members can be accessed even outside the class and anywhere in the code. No coding conventions to be followed for a public member name.

The following code snippet explains the declaration of instance variables with each of the access types.

```
members : {
__privateVariable : null,
    _protectedVariable : null,
    publicVariable : null
}
```

To access the static members inside instance methods, you have to use `this.self(arguments)`, thus:

```
qx.Class.define("org.test.MyClass", {

  statics : {
    FOO : 456;
  },

  members : {
    testMethod : function(){
      alert("inside test function:" + this.self(arguments).FOO );
      // do something on the instance method.
    }
  }
});
```

Static members can access other static members directly through the `this` keyword but cannot access the instance members directly.

Types

There are different types of classes, such as, static class, singleton class, and abstract class. The key for the class type in the class map is `type`, with the possible values as regular (no specific type defined), `static`, `singleton`, or `abstract`.

We have already seen a few regular classes; let's see the other types of classes.

Static class

A utility class can be defined with the `static` value for the `type` key. A static class can have static members, static variables, and static methods, only.

```
qx.Class.define("org.test.MyClass", {
  type : "static",
  statics : {
      //  variables & functions
  }
});
```

Singleton class

A singleton class can be defined with the `singleton` value for the `type` key. Only one instance of this class is allowed at any point of time. An instance of the singleton class cannot be created with the `new` operator. Instead, use the static method `getInstance()` to create and return the singleton class object. The following code snippet shows how to define a singleton class in qooxdoo:

```
qx.Class.define("org.test.MySingleton", {
  type : "singleton",
    // ......
});
```

Abstract class

An abstract class can be defined with the `abstract` value for the `type` key. The abstract class is used to provide the implementation code for the common methods in the class and leave the specific methods without any implementation. An abstract class can be extended to give the implementation for the specific methods and reuse the common methods implementation. A subclass that implements all the specific methods left without implementation, in an abstract class, can be termed as a **concrete class**. You cannot create instances of an abstract class. You can create instances of a concrete class only:

```
qx.Class.define("org.test.Animal", {
  type : "abstract",
// ......
});
```

Inheritance in qooxdoo

Similar to java, qooxdoo also supports single inheritance and does not allow multiple inheritance, that is, a class can inherit from a single super class only. As a substitute for multiple inheritance, a class can implement one or more interfaces and include one or more mixins. This inheritance is achieved with the `extend` configuration key in the class map:

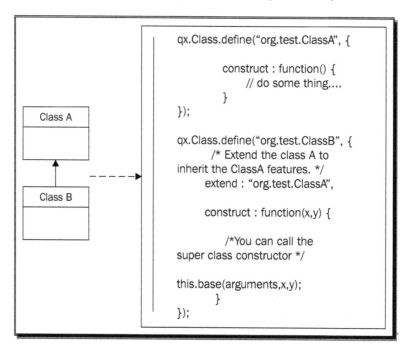

```
qx.Class.define("org.test.ClassA", {

    construct : function() {
        // do some thing....
    }
});

qx.Class.define("org.test.ClassB", {
    /* Extend the class A to
    inherit the ClassA features. */
    extend : "org.test.ClassA",

    construct : function(x,y) {

        /*You can call the
    super class constructor */

    this.base(arguments,x,y);
    }
});
```

Class A

Class B

Overriding in qooxdoo

qooxdoo allows you to override the methods in a derived class. It also allows you to call an overridden super class method implementation, from the overriding subclass method, just like calling `super()`, in Java.

qooxdoo allows two ways to call a super class method, mentioned as follows:

- `this.base(arguments, x, y …);`: This internally uses or wraps around the second method
- `Arguments.callee.base.apply(this, arguments );`: This is a JavaScript native implementation, so it's very efficient

Both of these ways are implemented in the following code snippet:

```
qx.Class.define("org.test.ClassA", {

    members : {
        baseFunction : function(x, y) {
            // do some thing......
            // Am inside base function
        }
    }
});


qx.Class.define("org.test.ClassB", {

    /* Extend the class A to inherit the ClassA features. */
    extend : "org.test.ClassA",

    members : {
        baseFunction : function(x,y) {
            // do some thing before calling base class implementation.

            /* You can call the super class constructor */
            this.base(arguments,x,y);
            //      or
            Arguments.calle.base.apply(this, x, y) ;
            // do some thing after calling base class implementation.

        }
    }
});
```

We have learnt the main concept for object-oriented programming. Now, we know how to create a class, what it can contain, how to encapsulate the members, and how to create different types of classes for different purposes.

We have also learnt how to create objects from the class and how to access the instance members and class members.

You can refer to the EBNF-like syntax for classes in qooxdoo, at the following location:

```
http://manual.qooxdoo.org/1.4/pages/core/class_quickref.html
```

Now, it's time to create a class and to implement an interface.

Let's define a class and implement the `MyInterface` interface that we defined in the earlier section.

```
qx.Interface.define("org.test.MyClass",
{
    /* Implement the interface */
  implement : org.test.MyInterface,

  members : {

    /**
     *  Some implementation for the method
     */
    foo1 : function() {
      // do something……….
    },

    foo2 : function(x, y){

      // do something……….

    },

    _applyName : function(oldValue, newValue){

    }
  },

    properties : {
      "name" : {
          check : "String",
          apply: "_applyName"
          },

      "contact" : {
            check : "String",
          validate : qx.util.Validate.email()
        }

    },

    events : {
      "changeValue" : "qx.event.type.Data"
    }
});
```

We have implemented the `MyInterface` interface in `MyClass` by abiding by the contracts defined in the interface. The implementing class gives the implementations for all the abstract/interface methods and declares all the properties and events defined in the interface.

Mixin

This concept is pulled from the Ruby programming language. qooxdoo supports single inheritance, like Java and Ruby do. The concept of modules, known as *categories* in Objective-C, is used to substitute the multiple inheritance features in Ruby. A **module** is a collection of methods. Classes can mix in a module and receive all of its methods. It is a kind of lateral merging to the inheritance hierarchy.

A mixin is a collection of members, variables, and methods; it can be merged into other classes. In qooxdoo, a mixin is very similar to a class but cannot be instantiated. Unlike interfaces, they do contain implementation code. Typically, a mixin is made up of only a few members that allow for a generic implementation of some very specific functionality. Mixins are used to share functionality, without using inheritance, and to extend/patch the functionality of existing classes. A mixin is especially used when you don't want to change the object hierarchy and just want to add few members laterally to the classes.

You can:

◆ Add a mixin to the definition of a class—all members of the mixin are added to the class definition.

◆ Add a mixin to a class after the class is defined. This enhances the functionality but is not allowed to overwrite existing members.

◆ Patch existing classes—change the implementation of existing methods. This should normally be avoided but, as some projects may need to patch qooxdoo, we should define a clean way to do so.

As with a class, a mixin can be defined with `qx.Mixin.define(<mixin name>, <mixin config map>)`. A mixin can include one or more mixins but cannot implement an interface, as it doesn't allow the inheritance and method overriding.

Defining a mixin

Let's define a mixin:

```
qx.Mixin.define("org.test.MyMixin", {
  include : org.test.MyMixin1,

  /**
   * This constructor will be called on creating an object of the
   * class for which this mixin is included.
   */
  construct : function() {

  },

  /**
   * The member functions will be added to the class.
   */
members : {

    testFunction : function(){
      alert(" Am in the mixin.");
      // do something on the class members.
    }
  }

});
```

Using a mixin in a class

Let's use a mixin in one of the classes. In the following code snippet, the org.test.
MyAnotherClass class inherits the org.test.MyClass class and uses an org.test.
MyMixin mixin:

```
qx.Class.define("org.test.MyAnotherClass", {
  extend: org.test.MyClass,
  include: org.test.MyMixin,

  members: {
    testMethod2: function() {
      // do something here…
    }
  }
}
```

We have learnt the supplementary feature, mixin, of the object-oriented concept. In recent object-oriented programming languages, this concept substitutes for the multiple inheritance concept. We have also learnt how to define and use a mixin.

You can refer to the EBNF-like syntax for mixin in qooxdoo, at the following location:

```
http://manual.qooxdoo.org/1.4/pages/core/mixin_quickref.html
```

As we have learnt about interface, class, and mixin, let's summarize the different configurations that can be defined in the configuration or map. The following table describes the key used in the configuration or map, what it is used for, where it is used, and a brief description of the configuration:

Configuration key	Type	Used in	Description
include	Mixin or Mixin[]	Class or mixin	Adds the included mixins' functionalities into the class or mixin
type	String	Class	Allows defining the type of the class. Possible string values are abstract, static, or singleton
extend	Class or Class[]	Class or interface	Allows extending a single parent class when used in a class. When used in an interface, allows single or multiple interfaces to be extended.
implement	Interface or Interface[]	Class	Allows implementing one or more interfaces.
statics	Map	Class, interface, or mixin	Static properties' map
properties	Map	Class, interface, or mixin	Properties' definitions
events	Map	Class, interface, or mixin	Events' map
members	Map	Class, interface, or mixin	Member functions and variables
construct	Function	Class or mixin	Optional function called while instantiating the class
destruct	Function	Class or mixin	Optional function called while disposing of the class instance

Time for action – writing classes for Team Twitter

Now that we have learnt the basics of object-oriented concepts of the qooxdoo framework, let's write a few classes for our Team Twitter application.

1. To start building our Team Twitter application, let's first identify the widgets that we need to develop. Let's start our coding with the following items for our Team Twitter application:

- ❑ `UserLoginForm` (creates the UI for the login form)
- ❑ `SignUpForm` (creates the UI for the signup form)
- ❑ `Tweet` widget or form

2. Let's decide how these forms should finally look. This section shows the screenshots of the forms that we need to develop. We will write the classes in step 3 to develop the **Login** form, the **Sign Up Form**, and the tweet widget or form.

3. We had a look at a few screenshots for our Team Twitter application. Now, let's write a few interfaces and classes to develop these screens.

As we are developing the initial classes only for now, we will be learning more about the reusable components and predefined widgets, in the following chapters. As we learn more, we will improve these classes by adding more details. You will not be able to see these screens until we design the layouts, add the widgets, and assemble it with the application. We will add more details to these screens in the following chapters.

Let's write one class for each form. Let's name the class for user login form `UserLoginForm`. This form extends one of the predefined container classes—`GroupBox`. We will learn more on the containers in *Chapter 4, Working with Layouts and Menus*.

Create the `UserLoginForm.js` file under `C:\teamtwitter\source\class\ teamtwitter\ui` and write the following code. This code is also available as in the `978-1-849513-70-8_03_01.txt` file under `Chapter 3` in the support files for this book:

```
qx.Class.define("teamtwitter.ui.UserLoginForm", {
  extend : qx.ui.groupbox.GroupBox,

  /**
   * Constructor
   */
  construct : function(){
    this.base(arguments);
    this._initLayout();
  },

  /**
   * MEMBERS
   */
  members : {

    /**
     * create the layout for the form.
     * @returns
     */
    _initLayout : function() {
      /* For actual layout design and adding form elements into
the form as shown in the expected screen shot */

    },

    /**
     * Should take the entered values and has to perform user
login  by validating into db.
```

```
       * @returns
       */
      loginUser : function() {

      },

      /**
       * To focus on to user name field.
       * @returns
       */
      focusOnUserName : function() {

      },


      /**
       * create the layout for the form.
       * @param Exception
       * @returns
       */
      openUserSignUpForm : function(e){

          /* planned a method for opening the form, on button click or
on firing an event. */
          }
      }
});
```

Now, let's write the class for the user signup form. Let's name the class for the signup form `UserSignUpForm`.

Create the `UserSignUpForm.js` file under `C:\teamtwitter\source\class\teamtwitter\ui` and write the following code. This code is also available as in the `978-1-849513-70-8_03_02.txt` file under `Chapter 3` in the support files for this book.

As this form should look like a window, we can extend predefined `Window` class, thus:

```
qx.Class.define("teamtwitter.ui.UserSignUpForm", {
  extend : qx.ui.window.Window,

  /**
   * Constructor
   */
  construct : function(){

  },

  /**
```

```
 * MEMBERS
 *
 */
members : {

  /**
   * create the layout for the form.
   * @returns
   */
  _initLayout : function() {

},

  /**
   * For validating user entered data
   * @param Exception
   * @returns
   */
  formValidator : function(items){

  },

  /**
   * To register user or to save user into Database, on register
button click.
   * @param Exception
   * @returns
   */
  register : function(e){

  },

  /**
   * For resetting whole form, on reset button click
   * @param Exception
   * @returns
   */
  resetForm : function(items){

  }

 }
});
```

Similarly, you can write the class for the tweet widget.

Create the `tweetWidget.js` file under `C:\teamtwitter\source\class\ teamtwitter\ui` and write the class. The code mentioned next gives you an idea and skeleton. You can fill the code blanks for the `tweetWidget` class by extending the required class and writing all the required methods:

```
qx.Class.define("_____", {
    extend : _____,
    /**
     * Constructor
     */
    _____ : function(){
    },

    members : {

        /**
         * create the layout for the form.
         * @returns
         */
        _____ : function(_____) {

        },

        _____ : function(_____) {

        },

        _____ : function(_____) {

        },

        _____ : function(_____) {
            },

        _____ : function(_____) {
        }
    }
});
```

Also, write the API documents. This gives an idea about the purpose of the method, details of the input parameters and return value, and the exception thrown in the method. Other developers can read the API document to understand the purpose of the method and its usage, and what exception has to be handled.

Similarly, identify the required classes for our Team Twitter application, as per the functional requirements mentioned in *Chapter 1*, *What is qooxdoo?*, and code them by creating new files for each, in the respective packages. Identifying the classes is itself a great skill in object-oriented programming. You will develop it as you gain experience in object-oriented programming.

Just concentrate on the individual forms, first; later, we can place each form at the right place, wherever we actually need it. Once we code the preceding classes properly, you can try to add them into the application and see how it looks (see the following screenshot). If you can do that, it is great, otherwise wait until *Chapter 4*, *Working with Layouts and Menus*, where you'll learn more on the containers and layout managers:

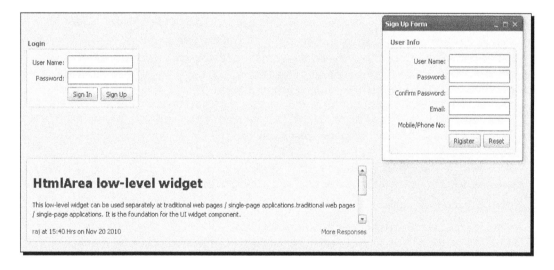

4. Now try compiling your classes to identify any syntax errors in the code. For this, use either of the following commands:

- `<teamTwitterHome>generate.py build`
- `<teamTwitter-ServerHome>ant client.generate-build`

Correct all the syntax errors, if any. Sample build and successful compilation is shown in the following screenshot:

```
[exec]    -    ................................................................
-----------------------------------------------------------------------------
[exec]    - Sorting 204 classes...
[exec] >>> Generate build version...
[exec]    - Processing translations for 2 locales...
[exec]    - Analyzing assets...
[exec]        - Compiling resource list...
[exec]    - Generating packages...
[exec]        - Compiling package #0: 10% 20% 30% 40% 50% 60% 70% 80% 90% 100%
[exec]    - Generating boot script...
[exec] >>> Done
[exec]
[exec] ===============================================================================
[exec]        EXECUTING: BUILD::BUILD-FILES
[exec] ===============================================================================
[exec] >>> Initializing cache...
[exec] >>> Copying application files...
[exec] >>> Done
BUILD SUCCESSFUL
Total time: 5 seconds
```

What just happened?

To start the development of our Team Twitter application, we had identified three screens or widgets, namely, the login form, the signup form, and the tweet widget. Then, we wrote the basic classes, following the qooxdoo programming syntax, and had successfully built the client application. These classes are just the beginning; we will enhance these classes and add more classes, as we learn more concepts in this book.

By now, you must have a good understanding of the client application environment—where to place client classes, how to build the client application, and so on.

Pop quiz-I

1. qooxdoo allows you to

    a. Write single line comments only

    b. Write single line and multiline comments

    c. Write documentation in the doc and generate the API documentation

    d. All of the above

2. In qooxdoo, interface contract includes

    a. Members

    b. Statics

    c. Properties

    d. Events

    e. All of the above

3. In qooxdoo, method declaration in the member section of an interface allows you to

    a. Just declare the method definition

    b. Declare the method definition and add assert statements and preconditions to be called before calling the implementation

4. qooxdoo supports

    a. Single inheritance only

    b. Single inheritance and multiple inheritances

    c. Single inheritance and mixins

5. A mixin is

    a. A class

    b. A collection of members, variables and methods; it can be merged into other classes laterally.

6. You would create an instance of

    a. An interface

    b. A mixin

    c. An abstract class

    d. A class that implements all the methods

7. In qooxdoo, you can do one or more of the following (you can select multiple options)

    a. Implement only one interface

    b. Implement one or more interfaces

    c. Extend only one class

    d. Extend one or more classes

    e. Include only one mixin

    f. Include one or more mixins

qooxdoo properties

A qooxdoo property management system is a very convenient mechanism, and it simplifies the code and improves the maintainability of the code. It perfectly demonstrates the framework's three virtues—elegance, power, and speed.

A qooxdoo property is a dynamic property; the framework provides a lot of in-built features for the qooxdoo properties. This is different from the variables of the object. If you want to use all the features of the qooxdoo property, go for it; otherwise, go for the member variables. Eventually, a qooxdoo property will get converted to member variables and extra supporting member functions, both provided by the qooxdoo framework. For these properties, the qooxdoo framework initializes the properties and provides few predefined methods to access the properties instead of giving direct access to the property. It reduces the overhead in writing type checks, firing change value events, validations, performance optimizations, and so on.

Let's define a couple of properties. The key for the properties in the class map is `properties`. For each property, you can configure the property features, such as, `nullable`, `init`, `check`, `inheritable`, `apply`, and so on. The following code snippet configures two properties, `foo` and `bar`, for the class `Sample`:

```
qx.Class.define("Sample", {
    .........
    properties : {
        foo : {
            init : 10,
            check : "Number"
        },
        bar : {
            nullable : true
        }
    }
    ............
});
```

Property initialization

Each property must be configured with one of the three configurations—`nullable`, `init`, or `inheritable`. This configuration of the property is used by the qooxdoo framework for initialization of the property. If it is `nullable`, qooxdoo initializes the property value as null. If it is `init`, it initializes the property with the value provided for the `init` key. If it is `inheritable`, the subclass will configure the value for that property. If you have not configured one of these configurations for each property, qooxdoo framework will not know how to initialize the property and it will raise an exception.

Predefined methods

qooxdoo framework provides the following predefined methods for properties. You can just use the predefined methods on the class reference where you declared the property:

- `setXXX(<value>)`: Sets a value to the property, for example, `this.setFoo(10)`
- `getXXX()`: Returns the value of the property, for example, `this.getFoo()`
- `initXXX(<value>)`: Initializes the value of the property, for example, `this.initFoo(10)`
- `isXXX()`: Similar to `getXXX()`, available only for the `Boolean` property, for example, `this.isAvailable()`
- `toggleXXX()`: Toggles the property value between `true` and `false`; available only for the `Boolean` property, for example, `this.toggleAvailable()`
- `resetXXX(<value>)`: Used to transfer values from parent to child widgets in the inheritance hierarchy; available only for the `inheritable` property
- `setThemedXXX(<value>)`: Used to store a separate value for the appearance of the property; available if the appearance is enabled for properties
- `resetThemedXXX(<value>)`: Used to reset the separate value for the appearance of this property; available if the appearance is enabled for properties

Property configurations

Let's look at configurations other than the `init` configuration.

Apply

Apply is an optional configuration, and the configuration key is `apply`. On modification of the property, except for the initialization, qooxdoo framework invokes the method configured for the `apply` key. The new and old values of the property are passed to this method. The configured method must be defined in the `members` section of the same class.

The best practice is to declare the apply method as protected, to avoid calling this method directly. The return value for this method is ignored. Mainly, this method is used to carry out an operation, when the value of the property is modified, except during initialization.

The following code snippet implements the `apply` configuration of the property:

```
qx.Class.define("Employee", {

  properties: {

    name : {
      apply : "_applyName"
```

```
      },
      modified : {
        init : false
      }
    },

  members : {

    /* This function is invoked on change of the property value.
        The second argument old is optional to define. */

    _applyName : function( new, old ) {
      this.setModified(true);
    }

    }

  });
```

Check

Check is an optional configuration, and the configuration key is check. This configuration is used to check the property value for many things, such as, data types, enumerated values, and to check whether regular expressions match, whether an object is an instance of a class, and whether an interface is implemented. The check configuration key is also used to check if a class is a Mixin type or a Theme type. You can also configure condition checks, or even check functions.

The following snippet of the code demonstrates the check configuration of the properties:

```
qx.Class.define("Employee", {

  properties: {

    name : {
      init : "",
      check : "String",
      apply : "_applyName"
    },
    modified : {
      check : "Boolean",
      init : false
    },
    designation : {
      init : "Assistant"
      /* Enumerated list of possible values */
```

```
          check : ["Assistant", "Programmer", "Manager"]
       }
    },

  members : {

    /* This function is invoked on change of the property value.
       The second argument old is optional to define. */

    _applyName : function( new, old ) {
      this.setModified(true);
    }

    }

});
```

You can check against one of these predefined or user-defined types:

- `Boolean`, `String`, `Number`, `Integer`, `Float`, and `Double`
- `Object`, `Array`, and `Map`
- `Error`, `RegExp`, `Function`, `Date`, `Node`, `Element`, `Document`, `Window`, and `Event`
- `Class` (incoming value must be an instance of the class)
- `Interface` (incoming value must be an instance of the class that implements the interface)
- `Mixin` and `Theme`

In addition to the check against all the types, you can check the ranges or any conditions. We can use custom checks by configuring a function for the property, as mentioned in the following code snippet. The return value of the function should be `Boolean`, returning `true` to indicate validity of the check, and `false` otherwise.

```
empid : {
  init : 0,
  check : function(value) {
    return (!isNaN(value) && value >= 0 && value <= 100);
  }
}
```

The same thing can be achieved by configuring the condition to be checked. This is more efficient, as it omits the function call.

```
empid : {
  init : 0,
  check : "!isNaN(value) && value >= 0 && value <= 100"
  }
}
```

These checks are only applied in the development (source) version of the application. qooxdoo framework removes this code in the deployment (build) version through performance optimization. Just like assertions in Java, which can be enabled or disabled in the production code, these checks will be disabled in the deployment version.

Validate

Validate is an optional configuration and the configuration key is `validate`. Property value is validated at runtime, before setting the value to the property and, if found invalid, the value will not be assigned. Instead, the function will throw a validation error. qooxdoo framework provides some default validate functions in the `qx.util.Validate` class. As the functions are static functions, you can use them directly, without creating an instance for the `Validate` class.

The following code snippet demonstrates the `validate` configuration of a property:

```
properties : {
  contactmail : {
    validate : qx.util.Validate.email()
  }
}
```

The most-used functions in the `qx.util.Validate` class are:

- `qx.util.Validate.range(<min>, <max>)`: Range validation
- `qx.util.Validate.number(<errMessage>)`: Checks if the value is a number
- `qx.util.Validate.url(<errMessage>)`: Checks if the value is a URL
- `qx.util.Validate.string(<errMsg>)`: Checks if the value is a valid string
- `qx.util.Validate.inArray(<array>, <errMsg>)`: Checks if the value is in the array
- `qx.util.Validate.regExp(<regExp>, <errMsg>)`: Checks if the value satisfies the regular expression
- `qx.util.Validate.color(<errMsg>)`: Checks if the value is a valid color

Custom validations can be done by configuring a function. You can define the function directly or provide the reference of the function that is declared in the members section of the same class. If the value of the property is not valid, the `validate` function will throw a validation error.

The following snippet of code demonstrates configuration of the user-defined `validate` function:

```
properties : {
  myProperty : {
    validate : function(value) {
      if( value > 10) {
        throw new qx.core.ValidationError( "Invalid Value. Value
should be less than 10");
      }
    }
  },

  myProperty1 : {
    validate : "_testValue"
  }
},

members : {

  _testValue : function(value) {
    // throw validation error based on the condition……..
  }
}
```

Group

Group is an optional configuration, and the configuration key is `group`. This is a convenient way to define a family or a set of properties into a group.

The following snippet of code demonstrates the configuration of `group`:

```
properties : {
  left : {
    init: 0
  },
  top : {
    init : 0
  },

  location :
    group : { "left", "top"}
  }
}
```

The `group` key is used only to group a set of properties, so that you can set all the variables at once. You still need to configure each property individually, at least for the `init` configuration.

The `group` property can be accessed as follows:

```
Obj.setLocation(40,50);  //this sets the values 40 for left & 50
for top.
```

The preceding call is equivalent to the following calls:

```
obj.setLeft(40) ;
obj.setTop(50);
```

As shown in the preceding sample, qooxdoo framework generates all the setters, getters, and resetters for the entire group.

Event—property level

Event is an optional configuration, and the configuration key is `event`. These events are mainly used to perform some operation on the change of the property value. qooxdoo framework invokes the event on the change of the property value. You can add a listener to carry out an operation on an event, whenever that event is invoked. The best practice is to name the event `change<Property Name>`. As qooxdoo provides a proper event-handling mechanism, it is well-known for event-based programming. In addition to property-level events, it also provides events at the class level, which we'll see in the *Events—class level* section, in this chapter.

The following snippet of code explains the qooxdoo events:

```
qx.Class.define("MyClass", {

  properties : {
    foo : {
      init : 0,
      /* Event "changeFoo" invoked on change of value */
      event : "changeFoo"
    }
  }

  Construct : function() {
    this.getFoo(); // returns 0
    this.setFoo(6); /* value changed. "changeFoo" event will be
fired. */
    this.getFoo(); // returns 6
    this.setFoo(6); // no change in value. So no event is fired.

  }
});
```

One can add a listener, as shown in the following code snippet. This adds a listener to the event, and that will occur on invocation of the change value event:

```
var obj = new MyClass();
obj.addListener ("changeFoo", function (e) {
  // do something……..
});
```

Property features

The major features of qooxdoo properties are discussed in the following sections.

Value checks

- Runtime checks in the development version only
- Built-in types for most common things
- Instance checks by simply defining the name of the class to check for (always use an instance of operation, as a real name is not available anymore)
- Custom checks by simply attaching a function to the declaration
- Custom checks (defined by a string) will be compiled into the resulting setters (faster than the preceding variant)
- Defines multiple possible (primitive) values, using an array

Validation

- Validation in both the development and build version
- Predefined validators for default validation
- Throws a special validation error

Convenience

- Provides `accessor` (getter) and `mutator` (setter) methods
- Toggle method for Boolean properties
- After you create an instance, qooxdoo automatically initializes properties with the `nullable` and `init` attributes defined

Notification

- Support for a custom `apply` routine
- Event-firing with a custom-named event

Advanced value handling

◆ Multivalue support—support to store different values for initialization, inheritance, style, and user, including an automatic fallback mechanism between them.

◆ Inheritance support—inheritance of properties defined by a parent widget; for example, inheritance enabled from a groupbox to all form elements. qooxdoo uses inheritance if the computed value is undefined or explicitly set to `inherit`. The `getter` method simply returns `inherit` for inheritable properties that are otherwise unset.

◆ Blocks unintentionally undefined values in all setters with an exception—to reset a value one must use the `reset` or `unstyle` methods that are in-built.

◆ Overriding a value by setting a property explicitly to `null`.

◆ Properties must be explicitly configured as `nullable` (as in .Net). The default is `false`, which means that incoming null values will result in an exception.

◆ Accessing `nullable` properties with undefined values will result in a normalization to `null`.

Performance

qooxdoo provides automatic optimization of all the setter methods to get an optimal and highly-tuned result code.

> Setter methods are generated by the framework on the first call of the setter method. So, just after the definition, you won't see the setter methods available.

Memory management

qooxdoo provides an automatic memory management mechanism. All the qooxdoo properties that contain complex data objects are disposed automatically with object disposal. The affected built-in types are already auto-configured in this way. Also, all properties that need an instance of a class, defined by using a class name in the check condition, are automatically handled.

This mechanism does not actually call `dispose()` on the object but just removes the property value, that is it dereferences the object. You still need to call `dispose()`, if necessary.

For all other properties that contain complex data, the developer must add a `dispose` key with the value `true` to the property declaration. For example, if there is no check defined, or if the check definition points to a function.

This is not needed for primitive types such as `String` and `Number`.

We have read about the overwhelming features provided by the dynamic qooxdoo properties and also about their rich feature set. Now, you know when to use the qooxdoo properties and when to use the member variables in a qooxdoo class. Let's see how to declare a property in the qooxdoo class.

You can refer to the EBNF-like syntax for properties in qooxdoo at the following location:

`http://manual.qooxdoo.org/1.4/pages/core/properties_quickref.html`

Let's summarize the different attributes allowed in the `properties` section and their significance:

Attribute or key	Value	Description
`nullable`	`true/false`	Whether null values are allowed.
`event`	String	Event name.
`init`	Value	Initialization value for the property. qooxdoo maintains these values separately, so that it can use the same values while resetting the property.
`check`	Type check	Available only in developer version. Refer to the *Check* section (under *Property configurations* section), in this chapter, for more information.
`inheritable`	`true/false`	Whether the property is inheritable from the super class.
`themeable`	`true/false`	Ability to attach theme for the property.
`group`	`[<properties>]`	Groups the properties into one group.
`validate`	Validator function	Validates the value.
`mode`	`shorthand`	Modifies the incoming data before calling the setter method of each group member. Refer to the qooxdoo manual (`http://manual.qooxdoo.org`) for more information.
`refine`	`true/false`	Redefines the `init` value of the property derived from the super class.

Events—class level

qooxdoo supports event-based programming. It also supports user-defined events. It's a kind of Observer-Observable design pattern. An observable is nothing but the event defined, and the observer is the listener registered for the observable.

This is an optional configuration in the class, and the configuration key is events; for example, value-changed event on any variable, selection-changed event on list, table row selection event, mouse-click event, drag-and-drop event, key-press event on text field, and so on. One can define one or more events in the events section in class definition.

Declaring events for a class

The following code snippet illustrates the event declaration for a class:

```
events : {
  /** Fired when the widget is clicked. */
"click": "qx.event.type.MouseEvent",
/** Fired when some thing modified in the class */
"dirty" : "qx.event.type.Data"
}
```

Adding listeners

The following code snippet illustrates how to add listeners for events:

```
// method syntax -addListener( "click", <functionCall> , <context>);
addListener("click", this.onClickFunction , this);
addListener("dirty", this.makeDirty , this);
```

Firing an event

The following code snippet illustrates how to fire events:

```
this.fireDataEvent("dirty", value, old);
```

We have learnt about class-level events. Now, we know how to declare class-level events, how to add listeners to those events, and how to fire those events.

Time for action – enhancing Team Twitter classes with properties

Let's implement what we have learnt and enhance the Team Twitter classes:

1. Identify the required properties for each class. For `tweetWidget`, we can add the following properties. This code is also available as in the `978-1-849513-70-8_03_03.txt` file under `Chapter 3` in the support files for this book:

   - userName: This should be a valid username and be of type `String` only
   - Time and date: For time and date, we can have two separate properties, and both should be of `String` type

2. Open the `C:\teamtwitter\source\class\teamtwitter\ui\tweetWidget.js` file that you created earlier in this chapter, and add the properties as mentioned in the following code snippet:

```
qx.Class.define("teamtwitter.ui.tweetWidget", {
  extend : qx.ui.groupbox.GroupBox,
  /**
   * Constructor
   */
  construct: function(){

  },

  /**
   * Properties
   */
  properties : {
     userName : {
        check : "String",
        init : " "
      },
     time : {
        check : "String",
        init : "15:40 Hrs"
      },
     date : {
        check : "String",
        init : "Nov 20 2010"
      }
   },

   members : {

     // ...............
   }
});
```

3. Now, try compiling the updated classes to identify any syntax errors in the code. For this, use either of the following commands:

- ❏ `<teamTwitterHome>generate.py build`
- ❏ `<teamTwitter-ServerHome>ant client.generate-build`

Correct all the syntax errors, if any.

In the chapters that follow, as we learn more, we can enhance the classes and add more classes.

What just happened?

We have identified certain properties of the tweet widget and enhanced the tweet widget class by adding properties as per the qooxdoo properties syntax.

After enhancing the class, we rebuilt the client application. As we modify the classes or add more classes into the client application, we will have to rebuild the client application.

Pop quiz-II

This is the second quiz in this chapter. This quiz focuses on qooxdoo properties and events.

1. When should you go for qooxdoo properties instead of member variables

   a. When I need the in-built features supported by qooxdoo

   b. When I need just the setter and getter methods

   c. I can always go for qooxdoo properties instead of member variables

2. qooxdoo property features support one or more of the following

   a. Proper initialization to property

   b. Change value events as the property value changes

   c. Property validations

   d. Value checks only in the development versions

   e. All of the above

3. qooxdoo properties support inheritance

   a. True

   b. False

4. Which configuration allows you to inherit a property

    a. `inheritable`

    b. `check`

    c. `init`

    d. `themeable`

5. Which configuration allows property initialization

    a. `inheritable`

    b. `check`

    c. `init`

    d. `nullable`

6. Which configuration allows you to validate values on runtime

    a. `nullable`

    b. `validate`

    c. `check`

7. Identify the issues in the following code snippet

```
qx.Class.define("Student", {
  properties: {
    name : {
      init : "",
      check : "String",
      apply : "_applyName"
    },
    rollNumber : {
      check : "Number",
      init : 0,
      validate : function(value){
         return value >- 100;
        }
     }
  },

members : {
   }
});
```

    a. The `_applyName()` method in `members` is missing

    b. The comma is missing at the end of Line 6 and 13

c. There are no issues

d. The `validate` configuration function must raise `validationError` on invalid value

8. Identify the issues in the following code snippet

```
qx.Class.define("Item", {
  properties: {
    paddingLeft : {
       init : 0
    },
    paddingRight : {
      init : 0
    },
    Padding : {
      Group : { paddingLeft, paddingRight, paddingTop, paddingBottom
    }
    }
    },
});
```

a. The `paddingTop` property definition is missing

b. The `paddingBottom` property definition is missing

c. The `group` configuration value is a set of strings

d. There are no issues

Summary

We have learnt about the core programming concepts of qooxdoo framework, in this chapter.

Specifically, we covered:

- ◆ Code and API doc comments
- ◆ Fundamentals of object-oriented programming
- ◆ Interface contracts in qooxdoo
- ◆ Class structure and the types of classes supported in qooxdoo
- ◆ Mixin support in qooxdoo
- ◆ Features of qooxdoo properties
- ◆ Class-level events

After learning the programming concepts, we wrote a few classes for our Team Twitter application.

This chapter is the basic foundation for qooxdoo programming. As you learn about widgets in the following chapters, you'll make use of these programming concepts for designing your user interface and also for building custom widgets.

4
Working with Layouts and Menus

This chapter focuses on the layout designs of graphical user interfaces, menu bars, and toolbars. Basically, you will learn about available layouts in qooxdoo and learn to choose the layout for the purpose of the screen. qooxdoo provides different layouts (flow, dock, grid, and so on) for different purposes, containers and menus (menu bar, toolbar, context menu, and so on).

In the last chapter, we learnt the core programming concepts, coding syntax, and object-oriented features of the qooxdoo framework. This chapter teaches you to lay out the screens for effective use of space, based on component placement, to design a layout that looks better on the addition or removal of components to the screen and resizing the screen, and so on. qooxdoo has a rich and convenient set of user interface components and also provides different layouts to place the GUI components on the screen.

In this chapter, we'll cover the following topics:

- ◆ Widgets
- ◆ Containers
- ◆ Panels
- ◆ Layout managers
- ◆ Layouts
- ◆ Menus

qooxdoo uses the generic terminology of the graphical user interface. So, it is very easy to understand the concepts involved in it.. The basic building block in qooxdoo is termed a **widget**. Each widget (GUI component) is a subclass of the Widget class. A widget also acts as a container to hold more widgets. Wherever possible, grouping of the widgets to form a reusable component or custom widget is a good idea. This allows you to maintain consistency across your application and also helps you to build the application quicker than the normal time. It also increases maintainability, as you need to fix the defect at only one place. qooxdoo provides a set of containers too, to carry widgets, and provides public methods to manage.

Let's start with the framework's class hierarchy:

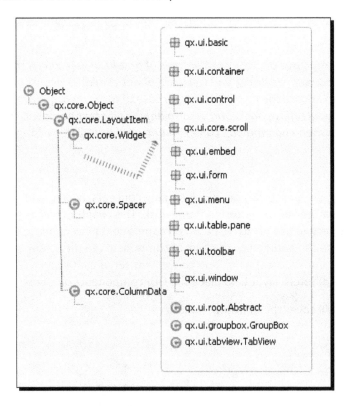

Base classes for widgets

qooxdoo framework abstracts the common functionalities required by all the widgets into a few base classes, so that it can be reused by any class through object inheritance. Let's start with these base classes.

qx.core.Object

`Object` is the base class for all other qooxdoo classes either directly or indirectly. The `qx.core.Object` class has the implementation for most of the functionalities, such as, object management, logging, event handling, object-oriented features, and so on.

A class can extend the `qx.core.Object` class to get all the functionalities defined in the this class. When you want to add any functionality to your class, just inherit the `Object` class and add the extra functionalities in the subclass.

The major functionalities of the `Object` class are explained in the sections that follow.

Object management

The `Object` class provides the following methods for object management, such as, creation, destruction, and so on:

◆ `base()`: This method calls base class method

◆ `dispose()`: This method disposes or destroys the object

◆ `isDisposed()`: This method returns a true value if the object is disposed

◆ `toString()`: This method returns the object in string format

◆ `toHashCode()`: This method returns hash code of the object

Event handling

The `Object` class provides the following methods for event creation, event firing, event listener, and so on:

◆ `addListener()`: This method adds the listener on the event target and returns the ID of the listener

◆ `addListenerOnce()`: This method adds the listener and listens only to the first occurrence of the event

◆ `dispatchEvent()`: This method dispatches the event

◆ `fireDataEvent()`: This method fires the data event

◆ `fireEvent()`: This method fires the event

◆ `removeListener()`: This method removes the listener

◆ `removeListenerById()`: This method removes the listener by its ID, given by `addListener()`

Logging

The `Object` class provides the following methods to log the message at different levels:

- `warn()`: Logs the message at warning level
- `info()`: Logs the message at information level
- `error()`: Logs the message at error level
- `debug()`: Logs the message at the debugging level
- `trace()`: Logs the message at the tracing level

Also, the `Object` class provides the methods for setters and getters for properties, and so on.

qx.core.LayoutItem

`LayoutItem` is the super most class in the hierarchy. You can place only the layout items in the layout manager. `LayoutItem` is an abstract class. The `LayoutItem` class mainly provides properties, such as, height, width, margins, shrinking, growing, and many more, for the item to be drawn on the screen. It also provides a set of public methods to alter these properties. Check the API documentation for a full set of class information.

qx.core.Widget

Next in the class hierarchy is the `Widget` class, which is the base class for all the GUI components. `Widget` is the super class for all the individual GUI components, such as, button, text field, combobox, container, and so on, as shown in the class hierarchy diagram. There are different kinds of widgets, such as, containers, menus, toolbars, form items, and so on; each kind of widgets are defined in different namespaces. We will see all the different namespaces or packages, one-by-one, in this chapter and the following chapters.

A widget consists of at least three HTML elements. The container element, which is added to the parent widget, has two child elements—the decoration and the content element. The decoration element decorates the widget. It has a lower z-index and contains markup to render the widget's background and border styles, using an implementation of the `qx.ui.decoration.IDecorator` interface The content element is positioned inside the container element, with the padding, and contains the real widget element.

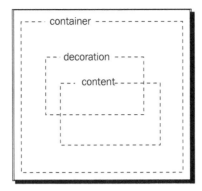

Widget properties

Common widget properties include:

- **Visibility**: This property controls the visibility of the widget. The possible values for this property are:

    - `visible`: Makes the widget visible on screen.

    - `hidden`: Hides the widget, but widget space will be occupied in the parent widget's layout. This is similar to the CSS style `visibility:hidden`.

    - `exclude`: Hides the widget and removes from the parent widget's layout, but the widget is still a child of its parent's widget. This is similar to the CSS style `display:none`.

    The methods to modify this property are `show()`, `hide()`, and `exclude()`. The methods to check the status are `isVisible()`, `isHidden()`, and `isExcluded()`.

- **Tooltip**: This property displays the tooltip when the cursor is pointing at the widget. This tooltip information consists of `toolTipText` and `toolTipIcon`.

    The different methods available to alter this property are:

    - `setToolTip()`/`getToolTip()`: Sets or returns the `qx.ui.tooltip.ToolTip` instance. The default value is `null`.

    - `setToolTipIcon()`/`getToolTipIcon()`: Sets or returns the URL for the icon. The default value is `null`.

    - `setToolTipText()`/`getToolTipText()`: Sets or returns the string text. It also supports the HTML markup. Default value is `null`.

- **Text color**: The `textColor` property sets the frontend text color of the widget. The possible values for this property are any color or `null`.

◆ **Padding**: This property is a shorthand group property for `paddingTop`, `paddingRight`, `paddingBottom` and `paddingLeft` of the widget.

The available methods are `setPadding()` and `resetPadding()`, which sets values for top, right, bottom, and left padding, consecutively. If any values are missing, the opposite side values will be taken for that side.

Also, set/get methods for each padding side are also available.

◆ **Tab index**: This property controls the traversal of widgets on the *Tab* key press. Possible values for this property are any integer or null. The traversal order is from lower value to higher value. By default, tab index for the widgets is set in the order in which they are added to the container. If you want to provide a custom traversal order, set the tab index accordingly.

The available methods are `setTabIndex()` and `getTabIndex()`. These methods, respectively set and return the integer value (0 to `32000`) or `null`.

◆ **Font**: The `Font` property defines the font for the widget. The possible value is either a font name defined in the theme, or an instance of `qx.bom.Font`, or `null`.

The available methods are:

   ❑ `setFont()`: Sets the font

   ❑ `getFont()`: Retrieves the font

   ❑ `initFont()`: Initializes the font

   ❑ `resetFont()`: Resets the font

◆ **Enabled**: This property enables or disables the widget for user input.

Possible values are `true` or `false` (Boolean value). The default value is `true`.

The widget invokes all the input events only if it is in the enabled state. In the disabled state, the widget will be grayed out and no user input is allowed. The only events invoked in the disabled state are `mouseOver` and `mouseOut`. In the disabled state, tab index and widget focus are ignored. The tab traversal focus will go to the next enabled widget.

`setEnabled()`/`getEnabled()` are the methods to set or get a Boolean value, respectively.

◆ **Selectable**: This property says whether the widget contents are selectable. When a widget contains text data and the property is true, native browser selection can be used to select the contents. Possible values are `true` or `false`. The default value is `false`.

`setSelectable()`, `getSelectable()`, `initSelectable()`, `resetSelectable()`, and `toggleSelectable()` are the methods available to modify the Selectable property.

◆ **Appearance**: This property controls style of the element and identifies the theme for the widget. Possible values are any string defined in the theme; the default value is `widget`.

`setAppearence()`, `getAppearence()`, `initAppearence()`, and `resetAppearence()` are the methods to alter the appearance.

◆ **Cursor**: This property specifies which type of cursor to display on mouse over the widget. The possible values are any valid CSS2 cursor name defined by W3C (any string) and `null`. The default value is `null`. Some of the W3C-defined cursor names are `default`, `wait`, `text`, `help`, `pointer`, `crosshair`, `move`, `n-resize`, `ne-resize`, `e-resize`, `se-resize`, `s-resize`, `sw-resize`, `w-resize`, and `nw-resize`.

`setCursor()`, `getCursor()`, `resetCursor()`, and `initCursor()` are the methods available to alter the cursor property.

qx.application

The starting point for a qooxdoo application is to write a custom application class by inheriting one of the qooxdoo application classes in the `qx.application` namespace or package. Similar to the main method in Java, the qooxdoo application also starts from the main method in the custom application class.

qooxdoo supports three different kinds of applications:

◆ `Standalone`: Uses the application root to build full-blown, standalone qooxdoo applications.

◆ `Inline`: Uses the page root to build traditional web page-based applications, which are embedded into isles in the classic HTML page.

◆ `Native`: This class is for applications that do not involve qooxdoo's GUI toolkit. Typically, they only make use of the IO (AJAX) and BOM functionality (for example, to manipulate the existing DOM).

Whenever a user creates an application with the Python script, a custom application class gets generated with a default main method. Let's see the custom application class generated for our Team Twitter application. After generation, the main function code is edited to add functionality to communicate to the RPC server and say "hello" to the qooxdoo world, as we discussed in *Chapter 2, Say Hello to the qooxdoo World!* The following code is the content of the `Application.js` class file with an RPC call to communicate with the server:

```
/**
 * This is the main application class of your custom application
"teamtwitter"
 */
qx.Class.define("teamtwitter.Application",
```

```
{
  extend : qx.application.Standalone,

  members :
  {
    /**
     * This method contains the initial application code and gets
called during startup of the application
     * @lint ignoreDeprecated(alert)
     */
    main : function()
    {
      // Call super class
      this.base(arguments);
      // Enable logging in debug variant
      if (qx.core.Variant.isSet("qx.debug", "on")) {
        // support native logging capabilities, e.g. Firebug for
Firefox qx.log.appender.Native;
        // support additional cross-browser console. Press F7 to
toggle visibility qx.log.appender.Console;
      }
      /*
        Below is your actual application code...
      */
      // Create a button
      var button1 = new qx.ui.form.Button("First Button",
"teamtwitter/test.png");
      // Document is the application root
      var doc = this.getRoot();
      // Add button to document at fixed coordinates
      doc.add(button1, {left: 100, top: 50});
      // Add an event listener
      button1.addListener("execute", function(e) {
        var rpc = new qx.io.remote.Rpc();
        rpc.setCrossDomain( false );
        rpc.setTimeout(1000);
        var host = window.location.host;
        var proto = window.location.protocol;
        var webURL = proto + "//" + host + "/teamtwitter/.qxrpc";
        rpc.setUrl(webURL);
        rpc.setServiceName("qooxdoo.test");
        rpc.callAsync(function(result, ex, id){
          if (ex == null) {
            alert(result);
          } else {
```

```
            alert("Async(" + id + ") exception: " + ex);
        }
    }, "echo", "Hello to qooxdoo World!");
    });
    }
  }
});
```

We've had an overview of the class hierarchy of the qooxdoo framework and got to know the base classes for the widgets. Now, we have an idea of the core functionalities available for the widgets, the core properties of the widgets, and the methods to manage those properties. We've received more information on the application in the qooxdoo framework.

Now, it is time to learn about the containers.

Containers

A container is a kind of widget. It holds multiple widgets and exposes public methods to manage their child widgets. One can configure a layout manager for the container to position all the child widgets in the container. qooxdoo provides different containers for different purposes.

Let's check different containers provided by the qooxdoo framework and understand the purpose of each container. Once you understand the purpose of each container, you can select the right container when you design your application.

Scroll

Whenever the content widget size (`width` and `height`) is larger than the container size (`width` and `height`), the `Scroll` container provides vertical, or horizontal, or both scroll bars automatically. You have to set the `Scroll` container's size carefully to make it work properly. The `Scroll` container is used most commonly if the application screen size is large.

The `Scroll` container has a fixed layout and it can hold a single child. So, there is no need to configure the layout for this container.

The following code snippet demonstrates how to use the `Scroll` container:

```
// create scroll container
var scroll = new qx.ui.container.Scroll().set({
  width: 300,
  height: 200
});
// adding a widget with larger widget and height of the scroll
scroll.add(new qx.ui.core.Widget().set({
```

```
    width: 600,
    minWidth: 600,
    height: 400,
    minHeight: 400
})); // add to the root widget.
this.getRoot().add(scroll);
```

The GUI look for the preceding code is as follows:

Stack

The `Stack` container puts a widget on top of an old widget. This container displays only the topmost widget. The `Stack` container is used if there are set of tasks to be carried out in a flow. An application user can work on each user interface one-by-one in order.

The following code snippet demonstrates how to use the `Stack` container:

```
// create stack container
var stack = new qx.ui.container.Stack();
// add some children
stack.add(new qx.ui.core.Widget().set({
 backgroundColor: "red"
}));
stack.add(new qx.ui.core.Widget().set({
 backgroundColor: "green"
}));
stack.add(new qx.ui.core.Widget().set({
 backgroundColor: "blue"
}));
this.getRoot().add(stack);
```

The GUI look for the preceding code is as follows:

Resizer

`Resizer` is a container that gives flexibility for resizing at runtime. This container should be used only if you want to allow the application user to dynamically resize the container.

The following code snippet demonstrates how to use the `Resizer` container:

```
var resizer = new qx.ui.container.Resizer().set({
  marginTop : 50,
  marginLeft : 50,
  width: 200,
  height: 100
});
resizer.setLayout(new qx.ui.layout.HBox());
var label = new qx.ui.basic.Label("Resize me <br>I'm resizable");
label.setRich(true);
resizer.add(label);
this.getRoot().add(resizer);
```

The GUI look for the preceding code is as follows:

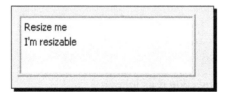

Composite

This is a generic container. If you do not want any of the specific features, such as, resize on runtime, stack, scroll, and so on, but just want a container, you can use this container. This is one of the mostly used containers.

The following code snippet demonstrates the `Composite` container usage. A horizontal layout is configured to the `Composite` container. A label and a text field are added to the container. The horizontal layout manager places them horizontally:

```
// create the composite
var composite = new qx.ui.container.Composite()
// configure a layout.
```

```
composite.setLayout(new qx.ui.layout.HBox());
// add some child widgets
composite.add(new qx.ui.basic.Label("Enter Text: "));
composite.add(new qx.ui.form.TextField());
// add to the root widget.
this.getRoot().add(composite);
```

The GUI look for the preceding code is as follows:

Window

Window is a container that has all features, such as, minimize, maximize, restore, and close. The icons for these operations will appear on the top-right corner. Different themes can be set to get the look and feel of a native window within a browser. This window is best used when an application requires **Multiple Document Interface (MDI)** or **Single Document Interface (SDI)**.

The following code snippet demonstrates a window creation and display:

```
var win = new qx.ui.window.Window("First Window");
win.setWidth(300);
win.setHeight(200);
// neglecting minimize button
win.setShowMinimize(false);
this.getRoot().add(win, {left:20, top:20});
win.open();
```

The GUI look for the preceding code is as follows:

Tabview

The Tabview container allows you to display multiple tabs, but only one tab is active at a time. The Tabview container simplifies the GUI by avoiding the expansive content spreading to multiple pages, with a scroll. Instead, the Tabview container provides the tab title buttons to navigate to other tabs. You can group the related fields into each tab and try to avoid the scroll by keeping the most-used tab as the first tab and making it active. Application users can move to other tabs, if required.

Tabview is the best example for the stack container usage. It stacks all pages one over the other and displays one page at a time. Each page will have a button at the top, in a button bar, to allow switching the page. Tabview allows positioning the button bar on top, bottom, left, or right. Tabview also allows adding pages dynamically; a scroll appears when the page buttons exceed the size.

The following code snippet demonstrates the usage of Tabview:

```
var tabView = new qx.ui.tabview.TabView();
// create a page
var page1 = new qx.ui.tabview.Page("Layout", "icon/16/apps/utilities-
terminal.png");
// add page to tabview
tabView.add(page1);
var page2 = new qx.ui.tabview.Page("Notes", "icon/16/apps/utilities-
notes.png");
page2.setLayout(new qx.ui.layout.VBox());
page2.add(new qx.ui.basic.Label("Notes..."));
tabView.add(page2);
var page3 = new qx.ui.tabview.Page("Calculator", "icon/16/apps/
utilities-calculator.png");
tabView.add(page3);
this.getRoot().add(tabView, {edge : 0});
```

The GUI look for the preceding code is as follows:

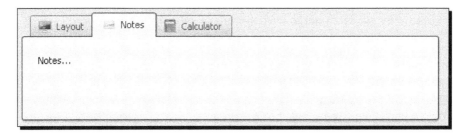

Groupbox

Groupbox groups a set of form widgets and shows an effective visualization with the use of a legend, which supports text and icons to describe the group. As with the container, you can configure any layout manager and allow adding a number of form widgets to the Groupbox. Additionally, it is possible to use checkboxes or radio buttons within the legend. This allows you to provide group functionalities such as selecting or unselecting all the options in the group. This feature is most important for complex forms with multiple choices.

The following code snippet demonstrates the usage of Groupbox:

```
// group box
var grpBox = new qx.ui.groupbox.GroupBox("I am a box");
this.getRoot().add(grpBox, {left: 20, top: 70});
// radio group box
var rGrpBox = new qx.ui.groupbox.RadioGroupBox("I am a box");
rGrpBox.setLayout(new qx.ui.layout.VBox(4));
rGrpBox.add(new qx.ui.form.RadioButton("Option1"));
rGrpBox.add(new qx.ui.form.RadioButton("Option2"));
this.getRoot().add(rGrpBox, {left: 160, top: 70});
// check group box
var cGrpBox = new qx.ui.groupbox.CheckGroupBox("I am a box");
this.getRoot().add(cGrpBox, {left: 300, top: 70});
```

The GUI look for the preceding code is as follows:

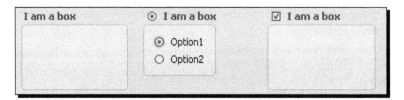

We got to know the different containers available in the qooxdoo framework. Each container provides a particular functionality. Based on the information displayed on the GUI, you should choose the right container to have better usability of the application.

Containers are the outer-most widgets in the GUI. Once you decide on the containers for your user interface, the next thing to do is to configure the layout manager for the container. Layout manager places the child widgets in the container, on the basis of the configured layout manager's policies. Now, it's time to learn how to place and arrange widgets inside the container, that is, how to lay out the container.

Layout managers

Layout managers control the position, size, and arrangement of all the widgets inside the container. The qooxdoo framework provides different layout managers for different purposes, for example, to arrange widgets horizontally or vertically, to place the widgets in rows and columns such as in a grid, to place the widgets at the corners, to place the widgets at fixed points, and so on.

When a user resizes the web page, the qooxdoo layout engine prompts the layout manager to recalculate and reposition the widgets in the container.

The different criteria or properties involved in laying out the screen are discussed in the sections that follow.

Size hint of the widget and its parent widget

Size hint is nothing but a map of boundaries, widths, and heights, and it's been calculated based on the widgets' internal widgets. qooxdoo provides two different methods to calculate and get the size hints of a widget, mentioned next:

- `getSizeHint (Boolean compute)`: This **default value for** `compute` is `true`, so it automatically computes and returns the result. Otherwise, it returns the cached values.

- `computeSizeHint ()`: This computes the size hints of the layout and returns the result. One can override this protected method in order to redesign the default algorithm.

Layout properties

The layout properties are the properties which are related to the widget's layout. These properties are pixel, flex, and percentage of width. One can set a map of all layout properties for an individual widget while adding the widget. To set this, use the `setLayoutProperties ()` method and specify the map. Map supports different key values, such as, `left`, `right`, `top`, `bottom`, `width`, `height`, **flex**, and so on; values for all these properties can be given in terms of fixed pixels (integer values), or percentages (string values). Some layout-specific properties also can be given in this map. One such property is `clearLayoutProperties ()`. This property clears the stored map of properties.

Flex is another property, which specifies the priority for the children to occupy space in the total available space. This defines the flexibility of the widget. A higher flex value gives more space for that widget. For example, if two widgets are placed in a widget such as split pane and if the first widget's flex is `1` and the second widget's flex is `2`, the total space of the split pane is considered as three parts; the first widget will occupy one part and the second widget will occupy two parts.

Auto sizing

By default, widgets are configured with some computed values for all the layout properties. So, the qooxdoo framework doesn't force the developer to set the values for any property. A developer can just create a widget and add it to the container. Most of the time, the widgets look good. If that requires any modification, the developer can modify the properties so that the layout manager takes them into consideration during the computation. For example, the widget's default value for `allowGrowX` or `allowGrowY` is `true`. So, the widget automatically gets resized based on the available room.

Growing or shrinking

The GUI should be dynamic; it should get adjusted within the available space. If the available room is less, the widgets should automatically shrink, and if more, they should grow according to the available room (see the following screenshot):

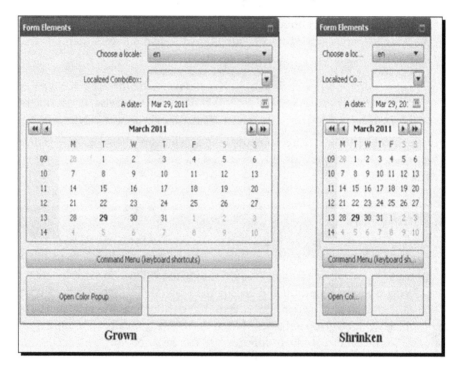

Overflow

Consider a scenario where the widget size is larger than the available room and the widget cannot shrink. In this scenario, the overflow property is used. If the overflow property is set to `true`, qooxdoo displays the whole widget by providing the required scroll bar.

qooxdoo framework provides a different set of layouts. The basic implementation is given in an abstract class (qx.ui.layout.Abstract). All the custom layouts must derive from the Abstract layout class and provide implementation for the getSizeHint(), renderLayout() and invalidateLayoutCache() methods. All the layouts provided by qooxdoo are in the qx.ui.layout package:

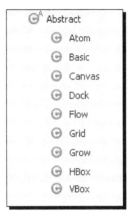

Let's check different layout managers provided by the qooxdoo framework and understand the purpose of each layout manager. Once you understand the purpose of each layout manager, you can select the right layout managers when you design your application.

Basic

This layout is very simple and is the first layout given in the qooxdoo framework. Basic layout is used to position the children in the top and left coordinates of the container.

To add any widget into a container configured with Basic layout, you should specify a map with the left and top properties. The default value for each of the properties is 0.

The following code snippet demonstrates the Basic layout. To differentiate the added widgets, let's set a different background color for each widget. For the main container, let's set white as the background color. Now, we will try adding a widget at the (100,100) position and another at the default values:

```
var container = new qx.ui.container.Composite(new qx.ui.layout.
Basic());
// adds a widget at (100,100) point.
container.add(new qx.ui.core.Widget().set({backgroundColor : "blue"}),
{left: 100, top: 100});
// adds a widget at (0,0) point.
container.add(new qx.ui.core.Widget().set({backgroundColor :
"green"}));
container.set({backgroundColor : "white"});
```

Features of the `Basic` layout are as follows:

- Basic positioning using the `left` and `top` properties
- Respects minimum and maximum dimensions without shrinking/growing
- Margins for top and left side (including negative ones)
- Respects right and bottom margins in the size hint
- Auto sizing

Canvas

This layout is also a simple layout and it provides extended features to the `Basic` layout. With this layout manager, you can position a widget relative to `top`, `left`, `right`, and `bottom` coordinates. It also allows setting the widget sizes (`width` and `height`), in terms of percentages.

The following code snippet demonstrates the `Canvas` layout:

```
var container = new qx.ui.container.Composite(new qx.ui.layout.
Canvas());
// simple positioning
container.add(new qx.ui.core.Widget().set({backgroundColor : "blue"}),
{top: 10, left: 10});
// stretch vertically with some pixel distance to the parent's top
// and bottom border
container.add(new qx.ui.core.Widget().set({backgroundColor :
"black"}), {top: 40, right: 50, bottom: 10});
// percent positioning and size
container.add(new qx.ui.core.Widget().set({backgroundColor :
"green"}), {left: "50%", top: "50%", width: "25%", height: "40%"});
container.set({backgroundColor : "white"});
```

Features of the `Canvas` layout are:

- Pixel dimensions and locations
- Percent dimensions and locations
- Stretching between left/right and top/bottom
- Minimum and maximum dimensions
- Children automatically shrink to minimum dimensions if not enough space available
- Auto sizing (ignoring percent values)
- Margins (also negative ones)
- In both `Basic` and `Canvas` layouts the spacing between the widgets cannot be specified and the overlapping of widgets is possible

Dock

The Dock layout allows you to add the widgets at the four edges of the container and the center of the container. This layout is very similar to the border layout in Java Swing. The different properties allowed in the map are edge, width, and height. The width and height properties support only the percentage values; the possible values for the edge property are north, east, west, south, and center.

The following sample code snippet demonstrates how to create and use the Dock layout:

```
var layout = new qx.ui.layout.Dock();
var w1 = new qx.ui.core.Widget();
var w2 = new qx.ui.core.Widget();
var w3 = new qx.ui.core.Widget();
var w4 = new qx.ui.core.Widget();
var w5 = new qx.ui.core.Widget();
w1.set({backgroundColor : "blue"});
w2.set({backgroundColor : "black"});
w3.set({backgroundColor : "green"});
w4.set({backgroundColor : "red"});
w5.set({backgroundColor : "orange"});
var container = new qx.ui.container.Composite(layout);
// add w1 in north edge
container.add(w1, {edge:"north"});
// add w2 in south edge
container.add(w2, {edge:"west"});
// add w3 in center
container.add(w3, {edge:"center"});
// add w4.in south edge
container.add(w4, {edge:"south"});
// add w5 in east side
container.add(w5, {edge:"east"});
container.set({backgroundColor : "white"});
   this.getRoot().add(container);
```

The Dock layout adds the widget on the edge of the container and utilizes maximum available space on that edge, while adding widgets into the container. Thus, the following widget takes the remaining space. To have a clear understanding, just change the order of adding w1, w2, w3, w4, and w5, and check the output alignment of the widgets.

There is no restriction on the number of widgets on each side; the user can add any number of widgets on each side.

Features of the Dock layout are:

- Percent width for left-/right-/center-attached child widgets
- Percent height for top-/bottom-/center-attached child widgets
- Minimum and maximum dimensions
- Prioritized growing/shrinking (flex)
- Auto sizing
- Margins and spacings
- Alignment in orthogonal axis (For example, alignX of north-attached)
- Different sort options for children

HBox

This layout allows you to add the widgets horizontally to container from left to right in a row. The properties map for this layout can have two properties, namely, width and flex, where width is percentage value and the flex is an integer value to specify the flexibility of the widget. You can specify the spacing between the widgets in this layout.

The following code snippet demonstrates how to create and configure the HBox layout with spacing of 4 between the widgets:

```
var layout = new qx.ui.layout.HBox();
layout.setSpacing(4); // apply spacing
var container = new qx.ui.container.Composite(layout);
container.add(new qx.ui.core.Widget().set({backgroundColor :
"blue"}));
container.add(new qx.ui.core.Widget().set({backgroundColor :
"black"}));
container.add(new qx.ui.core.Widget().set({backgroundColor :
"green"}));
container.set({backgroundColor : "white"});
   this.getRoot().add(container);
```

Features of the HBox layout are:

- Minimum and maximum dimensions
- Prioritized growing/shrinking (flex)
- Margins (with horizontal collapsing)
- Auto sizing (ignoring percent values)
- Percent widths (not relevant for size hint)
- Alignment (child property, qx.ui.core.LayoutItem.alignX, is ignored)
- Horizontal spacing (collapsed with margins)

- ◆ Reversed children layout (from last to first)
- ◆ Vertical children stretching (respecting size hints)

Similarly, the tweet information contains the username and time of the tweet. Those two labels were added in HBox. The username label allows clicking on it, so that the application displays the user information.

The following code snippet demonstrates the HBox layout in our Team Twitter application:

```
// create user label
var user = new qx.ui.basic.Label("<a style = 'color: rgb(126, 26,
26);'>" + this.getUserName() + "</a>");
user.setRich(true);
user.setSelectable(true);
user.setCursor("pointer");
user.addListener("click", this.userNameClicked, this);

// create time label
var dateTime = new qx.ui.basic.Label(" at " + this.getTime() + " on "+
this.getDate());
//create HBox layout manager and those two labels
var tweetInfo = new qx.ui.container.Composite();
tweetInfo.setLayout(new qx.ui.layout.HBox());
tweetInfo.add(user);
tweetInfo.add(dateTime);
```

VBox

Similar to HBox layout, the VBox layout manager allows you to add the widgets vertically to container from top to bottom in a column. You can specify the spacing between the widgets in this layout.

The following code snippet demonstrates how to create and configure the VBox layout with a spacing of 4 between the widgets:

```
var layout = new qx.ui.layout.VBox();
layout.setSpacing(4); // apply spacing

var container = new qx.ui.container.Composite(layout);
container.add(new qx.ui.core.Widget().set({backgroundColor :
"blue"}));
container.add(new qx.ui.core.Widget().set({backgroundColor :
"black"}));
container.add(new qx.ui.core.Widget().set({backgroundColor :
"green"}));
container.set({backgroundColor : "white"});
this.getRoot().add(container);
```

Features of the VBox layout are:

- Minimum and maximum dimensions
- Prioritized growing/shrinking (flex)
- Margins (with vertical collapsing)
- Auto sizing (ignoring percent values)
- Percent heights (not relevant for size hint)
- Alignment (child property, qx.ui.core.LayoutItem#alignY, is ignored)
- Vertical spacing (collapsed with margins)
- Reversed children layout (from last to first)
- Horizontal children stretching (respecting size hints)

Flow

The Flow layout positions the widgets in a flow manner or wraps the widgets within the available space. This layout manager follows the HBox layout initially, and, when the layout manager cannot accommodate the added widget horizontally adjacent to the previously added widget, the added widget will be placed in the next line; the same algorithm is followed for all the horizontal lines. This layout manager is useful when you want to add dynamic content in a container or to add multiple widgets of same type in a container.

The properties map for this layout supports only the lineBreak property, which breaks the line and places the following widgets in a new line. The Flow layout also supports the individual widgets alignment properties and the spacing between the widgets.

The following code snippet demonstrates the Flow layout:

```
this.tagCloud = new qx.ui.container.Composite();
// setting a Flow layout to the composite container
this.tagCloud.setLayout(new qx.ui.layout.Flow(5,5));
for (var i=0; i<this.tagsArray.length; i++) {
// create tag label
var tagLabel = new qx.ui.basic.Label("<a style = 'color: rgb(126, 26,
26); text-decoration:underline'>" + this.tagsArray[i] + "</a>");
tagLabel.setRich(true);
tagLabel.setSelectable(true);
tagLabel.setCursor("pointer");
tagLabel.addListener("click", this.tagClicked, this);
this.tagCloud.add(tagLabel);
}
```

Features of the `Flow` layout are:

♦ Reversing children order

♦ Manual line breaks

♦ Horizontal alignment of lines

♦ Vertical alignment of individual widgets within a line

♦ Margins with horizontal margin collapsing

♦ Horizontal and vertical spacing

♦ Height–for-width calculations

♦ Auto sizing

Grid

The `Grid` layout places the widgets in terms of two-dimensional rows and columns. It also supports the spanning of multiple rows or columns. This is one of the most useful layouts to prepare any form with labels and the input text fields, and so on.

The property map for this layout supports the row, column with row index, and column index consecutively; `rowSpan` and `colSpan` specify the number of rows or columns to span.

The following code snippet demonstrates the usage of the `Grid` layout:

```
// setting a grid layout to the composite container
this.setLayout(new qx.ui.layout.Grid(5,5));
// adding the created fields
this.add(userImg, {row : 0, column:0, rowSpan : 2});
this.add(this.twtData, {row : 0, column:1, colSpan : 2});
this.getLayout().setColumnWidth(1, 300);
this.add(hbox, {row : 1, column:1});
this.add(more, {row : 1, column:2});
```

Features of the `Grid` layout are:

♦ Flex values for rows and columns

♦ Minimal and maximal column and row sizes

♦ Manual setting of column and row sizes

♦ Horizontal and vertical alignment

♦ Horizontal and vertical spacing

♦ Column and row spans

♦ Auto sizing

qooxdoo framework provides a wide range of layout managers from a simple to a complex layout manager. We have learnt the different layout managers, layout manager features, and usage of each layout manager.

Time for action – designing layout managers for Team Twitter

Now that we have learnt the different containers and layout managers provided by the qooxdoo framework, let's design the layouts for our Team Twitter application.

1. Set the layout manager to the `UserLoginForm` class. Identify the correct layout manager and set the layout manager for the user login form. The user login form should take the input of username and password, validate the credentials, and allow the user to login. It should also allow the user to go to the registration form. To place those created widgets into the form, we can go for a `Grid` layout, where we can show the fields in terms of rows and columns. So, the best suitable layout for this form is the `Grid` layout. It will look good if we display a border with a title for the login form, therefore the best container for this widget is the `GroupBox` container. We had already created the `<TeamTwitterHomeDir>\source\class\ teamtwitter\ui\UserLoginForm.js` class. Let's set the layout manager, as shown in the following code snippet:

```
_initLayout : function() {
  this.setLegend(this.tr("Login Form"));
   // setting a grid layout to the composite container
  this.setLayout(new qx.ui.layout.Grid(5,5));
}
```

After your attempt, compare your code with the code in the `978-1-849513-70-8_04_01.txt` file under `Chapter 4` folder in the support files for this book.

2. Let's develop the widget for searching tweets. It should allow you to select the team, enter the search text, and search tweets. We also should have links for logging in and out. As this widget does not need any special features, such as, scroll, group box, and so on, the best container for this widget is the `Composite` container.

As all the fields discussed above should appear horizontally, the best layout manager for this widget is `HBox` layout manager. Let's create the class and use the `Composite` container and set the `HBox` layout manager.

Create the `TweetSearchWidget.js` file under `C:\teamtwitter\source\`
`class\teamtwitter\ui` and set the layout manager, as shown in the following
code snippet:

```
_initLayout : function() {
  // setting a grid layout to the composite container
  this.setLayout(new qx.ui.layout.HBox());
}
```

After your attempt, compare your code with the code in the `978-1-849513-70-`
`8_04_02.txt` file under `Chapter 4` folder in the support files for this book.

3. Let's set the layout manager to the `tweetWidget` class. In our Team Twitter
   application, for each tweet, we need to display the tweet text, user picture,
   tweet information, and so on. The best layout manager for this widget is the
   `Grid` layout manager.

   As we display multiple tweets in the tweet display area, it will be good to have a
   border, and optionally display the group title. The container which provides this
   functionality is called `GroupBox`. You can extend the `qx.ui.groupbox.GroupBox`
   class to use that container.

   Let's add the `Grid` layout for the `tweetWidget` that we created in the
   previous chapter. The following code just sets the `Grid` layout manager for
   the `tweetWidget`, located at `<TeamTwitterHomeDir>\source\class\`
   `teamtwitter\ui\TweetWidget.js`:

```
_initLayout : function() {
  // setting a grid layout to the composite container
  this.setLayout(new qx.ui.layout.Grid(5,5));
}
```

   After your attempt, compare your code with the code in the `978-1-849513-70-`
   `8_04_03.txt` file under `Chapter 4` folder in the support files for this book.

4. Let's develop the widget to display tags. In our Team Twitter application, the tags are
   dynamic content, and there are multiple tweets on the same tag. The best layout
   manager for the tags widget is the `Flow` layout manager. As the content is dynamic,
   we never know how many tags we need to display. So, it is better to use the `Scroll`
   container for the `Tags` panel and extend it from the `Composite` container. Let's
   develop the tags widget.

As the widget should allow the selection and deselection of the tags, it is a good idea to allow the selection and deselection of all tags at once. This functionality is provided by the enhanced version of GroupBox, CheckGroupBox. Let's use the CheckGroupBox container for the outer panel. Create the TagsWidget.js class under C:\teamtwitter\source\class\teamtwitter\ui and set the layout manager, as shown in the following code snippet:

```
_initLayout : function() {
  this.mainPanel = new qx.ui.groupbox.CheckGroupBox("Tags");
  this.mainPanel.addListener("changeValue", this.tagsClicked);
  // setting a Flow layout to the composite container
  this.mainPanel.setLayout(new qx.ui.layout.Flow(5,5));
  var scroll = new qx.ui.container.Scroll();
  scroll.set({
    allowShrinkY: false
  });
  scroll.add(this.mainPanel);
  this.add(scroll, {edge : "center"});
}
```

After your attempt, compare your code with the code in the 978-1-849513-70-8_04_04.txt file under Chapter 4 folder in the support files for this book.

5. Let's develop the widget to display the team members. This widget should display the list of users in the team. It should allow you to select multiple users.

As we display users in lists, vertically, the best layout manager is the VBox layout manager. It is a good idea to give a title and border; this functionality is provided by the GroupBox container. As the widget should allow the selection and deselection of the users, it is a good idea to allow the selection and deselection of all users at once. This functionality is provided by the enhanced version of GroupBox, CheckGroupBox. Let's use the CheckGroupBox container for this widget. Create the UsersListWidget.js file under C:\teamtwitter\source\class\teamtwitter\ui and set the layout manager, as shown in the following code:

```
qx.Class.define("teamtwitter.ui.UsersListWidget", {
  extend : qx.ui.groupbox.CheckGroupBox,

  construct : function(){
    this.base(arguments);
    this.setLayout(new qx.ui.layout.VBox());
    this._initLayout();
    this.addListener("changeValue", this.usersClicked);
  },
```

```
members : {
  _initLayout : function() {
    this.setLegend(this.tr("Team Members"));
  },
  usersClicked : function(e) {
    // <TODO> select or unselect all the users
  },
  setTeamMembers : function(teamId) {
    // <TODO> get the members of the team and display
  }
}
});
```

After your attempt, compare your code with the code in the `978-1-849513-70-8_04_05.txt` file under `Chapter 4` folder in the support files for this book.

6. Let's develop the widget that first allows you to enter the tweet text, video ID, and tag, and then to submit the tweet. As this widget does not need any special features, such as, scroll, group box, and so on, the best container for this widget is the `Composite` container. As we need to display many widgets in rows and columns, the best layout manager for this widget is `Grid` layout manager. Let's create the class, use the `Composite` container, and set the `Grid` layout manager.

Create the `TweetInput.js` file under `C:\teamtwitter\source\class\teamtwitter\ui` and set the layout manager, as mentioned in the following code snippet:

```
_initLayout : function() {
  // setting a grid layout to the composite container
  var g = new qx.ui.layout.Grid(4,5);
  g.set({
    spacingX : 10
  });
  this.setLayout(g);
}
```

After your attempt, compare your code with the code in the `978-1-849513-70-8_04_06.txt` file under `Chapter 4` folder in the support files for this book.

7. Let's design `TweetDisplayWidget` to display the tweets. We have developed the tweet widget already. `TweetDisplayWidget` just displays multiple tweet widgets vertically. The best layout manager for this widget is `VBox` layout manager. It is a good idea to display a title and border for this widget. Therefore, we can use the `GroupBox` container for this widget.

Create the `TweetsDisplayWidget.js` file under `C:\teamtwitter\source\` `class\teamtwitter\ui` and set the layout shown in the following code snippet:

```
_initLayout : function() {
  this.setLegend(this.tr("Tweets"));
  // setting a grid layout to the composite container
  this.setLayout(new qx.ui.layout.VBox());
}
```

After your attempt, compare your code with the code in the `978-1-849513-70-8_04_07.txt` file under `Chapter 4` folder in the support files for this book.

8. We have written a few widgets and set the container and layout manager. Let's assemble these widgets to form `MainWidget`.

Create the `MainWidget.js` file under `C:\teamtwitter\source\class\` `teamtwitter\ui` and try to code for the same screen as the one shown in the screenshot that follows.

To improve the usability and make use of AJAX in our application, we would like to display the login form overlapped on the home screen of the Team Twitter application, which helps to retain the context of the application. This is possible in the `Canvas` layout manager which allows you to position a widget relative to top, left, right, and bottom coordinates, or in percentages, and allows you to display overlapped content at any location. The `Basic` layout manager also supports overlapping of widgets, but the `Canvas` layout manager is an extended version of the `Basic` layout manager. So, we picked the `Canvas` layout manager over the `Basic` layout manager for the main widget. It is a good idea to display a title and set border for this widget. Therefore, we can use the `GroupBox` container for this widget.

In the `Canvas` layout, add the `TweetSearchWidget` first, so that it is displayed on the top. Provide two percent space on the left hand side. Create an instance of the `GroupBox` container for the `Content` panel and set the `Dock` layout manager for the content panel, which supports adding the widgets on the four edges and the center of the container. Add the content panel next in the main canvas layout, leaving some space on the top for the `TweetSearchWidget`. If you do not leave space, the content panel will be rendered over the `TweetSearchWidget`, which was added earlier.

In the `Content` panel, add the `TweetDisplayWidget` at the center of the `Dock` layout. As we'll display many tweets in this widget, add this widget into a scroll container and then add the scroll on the center of the `Dock` layout.

Create a `Composite` container and set the `VBox` layout manager. Add `TagsWidget` first, and then add `UsersListWidget`. Add this container on the east of the `Dock` layout. (You can refer the `978-1-849513-70-8_04_08.txt` file in the support files for writing code for the `MainWidget`):

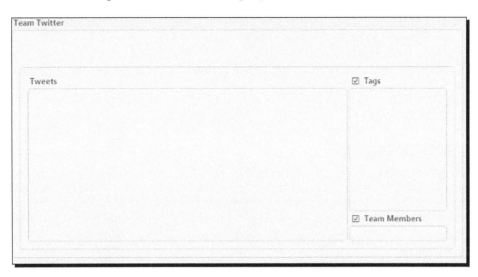

9. Let's update our application class to remove the hello world button and add the main widget of the Team Twitter application. Edit the `Application.js` file under `C:\teamtwitter\source\class\teamtwitter\` and update the code to add `MainWidget` into the application, as mentioned in the following code snippet:

```
// Document is the application root
var doc = this.getRoot();
doc.add(new teamtwitter.ui.MainWidget(), {
  left : 0,
  top : 0
});
```

After your attempt, compare your code with the code in the `978-1-849513-70-8_04_09.txt` file under `Chapter 4` folder in the support files for this book.

10. Now, try compiling your classes to identify any syntax errors in the code and fix them all. For this, use either of the following commands:
   - `C:/teamtwitter>generate.py build`
   - `C:/teamtwitter-server>ant client.generate-build`

11. Generate the complete web application distribution by running the following command:

```
C:/teamtwitter-server>ant dist
```

12. Deploy the updated web application by running the following command:

```
C:/teamtwitter-server>ant deploy
```

13. Open the Team Twitter web application in the browser and check the appearance by entering the following URL:

```
http://localhost:8080/teamtwitter/index.html
```

What just happened?

We have learnt how to select the right container and right layout manager based on the requirement.

From step 1 to step 7, we wrote a few classes for our Team Twitter application. For all those classes, we selected the right container, based on the requirement. We also selected the right layout manager for each class based on the requirement. In step 8, we assembled all the classes into a main widget. In step 9, we updated `Application.js` to display the main widget. In step 10, we built the client application. In step 11, we built the whole web application, including the server application. In step 12, we deployed the web application. In step 13, we checked the updated Team Twitter application from the web browser.

Now, let's learn the menus and toolbars to complete this chapter.

Menu, MenuBar, and ToolBar

A menu allows users to perform an action from the list of actions available in an application. It saves the space by displaying the list in pop-up or pull-down kind of widgets. A menu usually appears in a menu bar, toolbar, or as a context menu. qooxdoo provides two more components to display a menu directly in a form. Those components are `MenuButton` and `SplitButton`. When a user chooses or clicks on a menu item, the appropriate event fires and the menu item disappears. Pull-down menus or pop-up menus save space as they display menu items and sub menus over the widgets.

All menu-related classes are shown in the following screenshot:

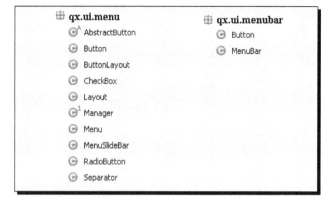

Let's explore the classes used for creating Menu, Menubar, and Toolbar.

Menu

A menu can be constructed with one or more different menu items, such as, Button, CheckBox, RadioButton, and Separator. All these items are given under the qx.ui. menu namespace and are listed as follows:

◆ Button is used to perform an action; mostly, it will bring a new screen or a dialog

◆ Checkbox is used to just select multiple options; it will not bring any screen or dialog

◆ RadioButton is used to just select a single option; it will not bring any screen or dialog

◆ Separator is used to make a separation between menu items

Menu creation

For creating a Menu object, follow these steps:

1. Create the qx.ui.menu.Menu object:

```
var menu = new qx.ui.menu.Menu();
```

2. Create the following menu items:

   ❑ `Button`: This can be added as follows:

   ```
   var btn = new qx.ui.menu.Button (<name>, <icon>, <command>,
   <submenuRef>);
   ```

   `<icon>`, `<command>` and `<submenuRef>` are optional.

   ❑ `CheckBox`: This can be added as follows:

   ```
   var chBox = new qx.ui.menu.CheckBox (<name>, <submenuRef>);
   ```

   `<submenuRef>` is optional.

   ❑ `RadioButton`: Like with `CheckBox`, you can add `RadioButton` also.
   `qx.ui.form.RadioGroup` is helpful in grouping the radio buttons.
   `RadioGroup` restricts the user from selecting more than one option
   from the group.

3. Follow the same procedure to create a submenu, as follows:

   ```
   var subMenu = new qx.ui.menu.Menu();
   var sub1Button = new qx.ui.menu.Button("Sub Option1");
   var sub2Button = new qx.ui.menu.Button("Sub Option2");
   subMenu.add(sub1Button);
   subMenu.add(sub2Button);
   ```

4. Add all the individual menu items and the submenus to the main `qx.ui.menu.`
   `Menu` object, thus:

   ```
   menu.add(btn);
   menu.add(chBox);
   menu.add(rdBtn);
   menu.add(submenu);
   ```

   One can add a separator between the menus by using the `addSeparator()` method.

5. Display the menu. Menu can be displayed on screen in different ways:

   ❑ Displaying directly: A menu can be displayed on the screen at any place just
   by setting the position using either `placeToMouse()` or `placeToPoint()`,
   and by using `show()` to show the menu at the selected point.

   ```
   menu.placeToPoint({"left" : 20, "top" : 30});
   menu.show();
   ```

   ❑ By adding the menu to `qx.ui.form.MenuButton`: This adds the menu to
   a button and the menu is displayed whenever the user clicks on the button.

   ```
   var button = new qx.ui.form.MenuButton("Menu Button", "icon/
   testicon.png", menu);
   // add to container
   this.add(button);
   ```

- ❑ Like with `MenuButton`, one can add the menu to a `SplitButton` too.

  ```
  var button = new qx.ui.form.SplitButton("Split Button",
  "icon/22/apps/preferences-users.png", menu);
  // add to container
  this.add(button);
  ```

- ❑ Displaying as a context menu: A widget has some methods available to set the menu as the context menu, where the menu pops up on right-click over the widget added. The methods available are `setContextMenu()` and `resetContextMenu()`.

- ❑ Adding menu to a `MenuBar` button: A menu can be added to a `MenuBar` button, which has to be added to a menu bar. We will learn about the menu bar in the *MenuBar* section.

- ❑ Adding a menu to a toolbar: We will learn about the toolbar in the *Toolbar* section.

Features of the `Menu` object are:

- ◆ On-demand scrolling, if the menu doesn't fit on the screen
- ◆ Menu items with text and/or icon.
- ◆ Each menu item can have a command for keyboard support.
- ◆ Menu items can have submenus.
- ◆ The menu can contain different item types:
  - ❑ Normal buttons (`menu.Button`)
  - ❑ Checkboxes (`menu.CheckBox`)
  - ❑ Radio buttons (`menu.RadioButton`)
  - ❑ Separators (`menu.Separator`) and
  - ❑ Submenus (`menu.Menu`)

MenuBar

`MenuBar` is a widget and is a container for the menu bar buttons. A menu bar contains one or more pull-down menus named with the buttons, where the menu displays whenever a user clicks on the button. Usually, a menu bar appears on top of a window. It's better to make the menu bar growable and place it on the north side of the `Dock` layout. It automatically adjusts whenever the user minimizes, maximizes or resizes the window.

A typical menu bar look, with the submenus popped up, is shown in the following screenshot:

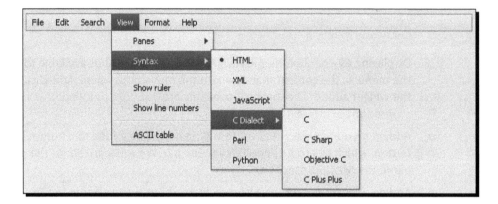

ToolBar

`ToolBar` is a widget and gives quick access to most commonly-used commands or actions in the application. Like with the `Menu` widget, all the buttons, checkboxes, radio buttons, and separators can be added. You can group some of the actions and can make them into a part of the toolbar.

The class associations for `ToolBar` are shown in the following diagram:

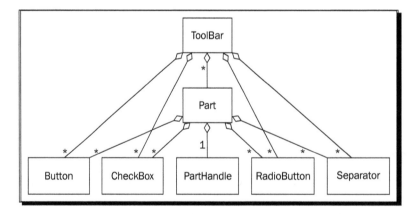

As shown in the following screenshot, a toolbar button can be shown in three ways: **Icon only**, **Label only**, or **Icon and Label**:

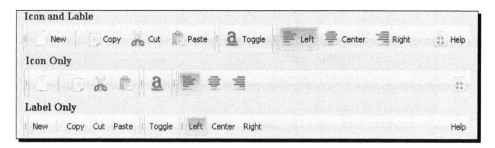

The following code snippet demonstrates the usage of the toolbar button:

```
// create the toolbar
toolbar = new qx.ui.toolbar.ToolBar();
this.getRoot().add(toolbar, { edge: 0 } );
// create and add Part 1 to the toolbar
var part1 = new qx.ui.toolbar.Part();
var newButton = new qx.ui.toolbar.Button("New", "icon/22/
actions/document-new.png");
var copyButton = new qx.ui.toolbar.Button("Copy", "icon/22/
actions/edit-copy.png");
var cutButton = new qx.ui.toolbar.Button("Cut", "icon/22/
actions/edit-cut.png");
var pasteButton = new qx.ui.toolbar.Button("Paste", "icon/22/
actions/edit-paste.png");
part1.add(newButton);
part1.add(new qx.ui.toolbar.Separator());
part1.add(copyButton);
part1.add(cutButton);
part1.add(pasteButton);
toolbar.add(part1);
// create and add Part 2 to the toolbar
var part2 = new qx.ui.toolbar.Part();
var checkBtn = new qx.ui.toolbar.CheckBox("Toggle", "icon/22/
actions/format-text-underline.png");
part2.add(checkBtn);
toolbar.add(part2);
// create and add Part 3 to the toolbar
var part3 = new qx.ui.toolbar.Part();
```

```
        var radioButton1 = new qx.ui.toolbar.RadioButton("Left",
"icon/22/actions/format-justify-left.png");
        var radioButton2 = new qx.ui.toolbar.RadioButton("Center",
"icon/22/actions/format-justify-center.png");
        var radioButton3 = new qx.ui.toolbar.RadioButton("Right",
"icon/22/actions/format-justify-right.png");
        part3.add(radioButton1);
        part3.add(radioButton2);
        part3.add(radioButton3);
        toolbar.add(part3);
        // Manager for part 3 (Radio example)
        var radioGroup = new qx.ui.form.RadioGroup(radioButton1,
radioButton2, radioButton3);
        radioGroup.setAllowEmptySelection(true);
        // create Help Button and add it to the toolbar
        toolbar.addSpacer();
        var helpButton = new qx.ui.toolbar.Button("Help", "icon/22/
actions/help-contents.png");
        toolbar.add(helpButton);
```

All `ToolBar` related classes are shown in the following screenshot:

We have learnt about the various widgets used in the menu bar and toolbar and also learnt how to construct menu bar and toolbar. Menu bars group all the main actions or operations available in the application and toolbars display the most-used actions or operations; sometimes, they display all actions or operations. Toolbars, in most applications, use only icons with tooltips, to save space, but you can use labels, if required.

Pop quiz

1. The starting point of a qooxdoo application is

   a. the main method in the custom application class

   b. a static method inside the custom application class

   c. a custom `Widget` class

2. Inline applications allow embedding into classic HTML pages

   a. True

   b. False

3. The base class for all the qooxdoo widgets is

   a. `qx.ui.core.Widget`

   b. `qx.ui.lang.Object`

   c. `qx.ui.core.Object`

   d. `qx.ui.core.LayoutItem`

4. The base class for all the qooxdoo classes is

   a. `qx.ui.core.Widget`

   b. `qx.ui.lang.Object`

   c. `qx.ui.core.Object`

   d. `qx.ui.core.LayoutItem`

5. Which container scales every widget to the available space and puts one over another?

   a. `Stack`

   b. `Composite`

   c. `TabView`

   d. `SplitPane`

6. `SplitPane` divides available space into two panes and allows resizing

   a. True

   b. False

7. Possible values for visibility are

    a. visible

    b. hidden

    c. exclude

    d. All of the above

8. Which layout allows adding widgets in rows and columns?

    a. Flow

    b. HBox

    c. VBox

    d. Grid

9. Which layout allows adding widgets at the edges of the container?

    a. Dock

    b. HBox

    c. VBox

    d. Grid

10. Which layout allows adding widgets at exact pixel values?

    a. Canvas

    b. Basic

    c. Grid

    d. Both a and b

    e. All of the above

11. Which layouts allow overlapping of the widgets?

    a. Canvas

    b. Basic

    c. Grid

    d. Both a and b

    e. All of the above

Summary

In the first three chapters, we learnt about the qooxdoo framework, feature support, syntax, and so on. In this chapter, we started learning about the graphical user interface programming.

We especially covered the following:

- We learnt about the base classes for the widgets.
- We got an idea of different containers available in the qooxdoo framework.
- We learnt about the layout manager and got a thorough understanding of different layout managers; this enables us to select the right layout manager for each container in the graphical user interface.
- We also learnt how to construct the menu bar and toolbar for the application. qooxdoo also supports the context menus that appear on the right-click action.

We have applied the knowledge gained from this chapter to lay out the screens for our Team Twitter application. Now, we know how to select the right container, how to configure the right layout manager for the container, and how to construct the menu bar and the toolbar.

Now, let's learn about the various widgets available in the qooxdoo framework, so that we can build the screens for our Team Twitter application. The next chapter explains the various widgets available in the qooxdoo framework.

5
Working with Widgets

Widgets or layout items are the basic building blocks of a graphical user interface. qooxdoo provides most of the commonly used widgets off the shelf in the framework and it also allows a user to create user-defined widgets with various themes and styles. This chapter demonstrates the usage of predefined widgets and also explaining the procedure to create user defined widgets.

In the last chapter, we learnt about graphical user interface layout designing with the qooxdoo-provided containers and layout managers. Also, we learnt the creation and usage of `Menu`, `MenuBar`, and `Toolbar`. This chapter explains the GUI components and widgets to design the individual elements in the screen. One can use a framework effectively only when one knows more about the existing widgets in the framework. To make use of the qooxdoo framework effectively, in this chapter, we mainly concentrate on the various widgets such as, labels, text fields, buttons, tables, trees, and so on, available in the qooxdoo framework.

In this chapter, we will cover the following topics:

- Basic widgets
- Form widgets
- Special widgets
- Custom widgets
- Inline widgets
- The `table` widget
- The `tree` widget
- The `treevirtual` widget

qooxdoo has a long list of off-the-shelf UI widgets. In this chapter, we will explore the various widgets available to build the graphical user interface. One can extend any of the existing widgets and can enhance the existing features too. We will learn how inheritance helps in creating brand new custom widgets. You can group all these widgets to create forms. qooxdoo framework allows you to access these form widgets generically.

Basic widgets

The basic widgets defined in the qooxdoo framework are `Label`, `Atom`, and `Image`. These widgets help in displaying the basic components such as the label or a rich HTML content label, images, icons, or icon and label together, and so on. These are defined under the `qx.ui.basic` package.

The `basic` package and the classes under it are as shown in the following screenshot:

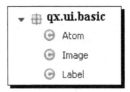

Label

The `Label` widget is used to display the text as normal text or rich text. A user cannot edit the text as it is a read-only widget. Label can be displayed in the following two modes:

- **Text mode**: This mode allows displaying normal text in different fonts, font sizes, and different styles such as bold, italic, underlined, and so on. By default, label displays normal text.

  The following code snippet demonstrates the usage of `Label` in normal mode:

  ```
  var label5 = new qx.ui.basic.Label("Big Long Label with user
  defined font").set({
          font : new qx.bom.Font(28, ["Verdana", "sans-serif"])
  });
  ```

  The GUI look for the preceding code is as follows:

  Big Long Label with user defined font

◆ **Rich mode**: This mode allows the display of HTML code with different tags including normal text. To allow these HTML tags in the label, one should set the rich property on the label to true.

The following code snippet shows the usage of the `Label` widget in rich mode:

```
var label4 = new qx.ui.basic.Label().set({
    value: "A long label text with auto-wrapping. This also may
contain <b style='color:red'>rich HTML</b> markup.",
    rich: true
});
```

The GUI look for the preceding code is as follows:

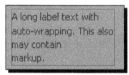

The features of the `Label` widget are listed as follows. It:

◆ Allows normal text and HTML code

◆ Allows configuring various fonts, font sizes and styles, text colors, text alignments, and so on

◆ Supports mnemonics for the actions

◆ Supports auto-wrapped text. This is supported only in rich mode

◆ Shows ellipsis (...), if the text doesn't fit in the available width

Atom

The `Atom` widget combines a label with an icon. It is one of the basic and base components for different components such as `qx.ui.form.Button`, `qx.ui.form.ListItem`, `qx.ui.form.ToggleButton`, and `qx.ui.form.HoverButton`. The `iconPosition` property allows the label to be aligned in a different direction.

Icon is an image of a format such as PNG, BMP, JPG, GIF, and so on. All the image resources have to be available in the `source\resource` folder and the required resources, whichever we are using, should be mentioned under the assets' list for the main class, where we can mention either a single image reference or the `resource` folder at once. This is shown as follows:

```
/*
*********************************************************************
#asset(teamtwitter/*)
#asset(teamtwitterxx/image.png)
*********************************************************************
*/
```

The following code snippet illustrates how to create and display atoms:

```
this.add(new qx.ui.basic.Atom("Icon Left", "icon/32/actions/go-
previous.png").set({
    backgroundColor : "#E6FAED",
    iconPosition : "left",
    allowGrowY: false
}));

this.add(new qx.ui.basic.Atom("Icon Top", "icon/32/actions/go-up.
png").set({
    backgroundColor : "#E6FAED",
    iconPosition : "top",
    allowGrowY: false
}));

this.add(new qx.ui.basic.Atom("Icon Right", "icon/32/actions/go-next.
png").set({
    backgroundColor : "#E6FAED",
    iconPosition : "right",
    allowGrowY: false
}));

this.add(new qx.ui.basic.Atom("Icon Bottom", "icon/32/actions/go-down.
png").set({
    backgroundColor : "#E6FAED",
    iconPosition : "bottom",
    allowGrowY: false
}));
```

The GUI look for the preceding code is as follows:

Features of the `Atom` widget are as follows:

◆ It toggles display among **Icon Only**, **Label Only**, and **Icon and Label** types

◆ Aligning the label on four directions (`left`, `right`, `top`, and `bottom`)

◆ Configurable space between icon and label

◆ Allows all the different features of label to be used

◆ Supports event handling on changing icon, label, gap, and show properties

Image

The `Image` widget displays an image with the specified source. A source can point to any local image in the qooxdoo application or image on the Internet, which is accessible through the URL of the image. This image class is a base class for `qx.ui.core.DragDropCursor` and `qx.ui.tree.FolderOpenButton`.

The following code snippet demonstrates the usage of the `Image` widget:

```
var big = new qx.ui.basic.Image("icon/32/actions/go-home.png");
big.setScale(true);
big.setWidth(64);
big.setHeight(64);
this.add(big);

var external = new  qx.ui.basic.Image("http://resources.qooxdoo.org/
images/logo.gif");
this.add(external);

var big1 = new qx.ui.basic.Image("icon/32/actions/go-home.png");
big.setScale(true);
big.setWidth(64);
big.setHeight(64);
big.setEnabled(false);
this.add(big1);

var external1 = new  qx.ui.basic.Image("http://resources.qooxdoo.org/
images/logo.gif");
external1.setEnabled(false);
this.add(external1);
```

The GUI look for the preceding code is as follows:

Features of the `Image` widget are as follows. It:

◆ Supports clipping, scaling, growing, and shrinking

◆ Is configurable and allows growing and shrinking on the x and y axes

◆ Supports event handling on change source, image loaded, and load failed events

◆ Supports different image formats such as PNG (with alpha transparency), GIF, and so on

◆ Enables or disables (shows in gray or blur) the image on display

◆ Allows auto-sizing

To begin with, we have learnt the basic widgets. Just before moving on to the `Form` widgets, let's have your Java server setup completed and then we will move on to the form widgets in the following section.

Time for action – enhancing the server application

It's time to enhance the server application, so that it supports the functionalities of the Team Twitter application. As the server application goes beyond this book's scope, we won't explain the server application at code level. But, we will explain how to set up the necessary libraries, provide the server code archive for the Team Twitter application, explain where to extract the server code archive, how to compile the server application, how to install the MySQL server, and how to create the database schema for the Team Twitter application. After this section, the server application provides all the necessary support for the Team Twitter client application. You can start making the RPC calls from the client to the server.

1. Let's download the required frameworks, database server, and libraries. We used Hibernate framework and Spring framework to develop the server application.

Download Spring framework (`spring-framework-2.5.6-with-dependencies.zip`) from `http://static.springsource.org/downloads/nightly/release-download.php?project=SPR`.

Download the Hibernate framework, `hibernate-distribution-3.6.5.Final-dist.zip`, from `http://sourceforge.net/projects/hibernate/files/hibernate3/3.6.5.Final/`.

Download the MySQL community server from `http://dev.mysql.com/downloads/mysql/`. Choose the correct version based on your OS type and 32-bit/64-bit OS. Download the MSI Installer.

Download the MySQL Connector/J library, `mysql-connector-java-5.1.17.zip`, from `http://dev.mysql.com/downloads/connector/j/`.

Download the Hibernate tools (`hibernate-tools-3.2.4.jar`) either from JBoss tools, which provide much functionality including the Hibernate tools. These days, they provide the JBoss tools in the form of the Eclipse plugin. Either you can download JBoss tools as the Eclipse plugin and install it, or search in Google and you might get a link where someone would have just shared this particular JAR file.

2. You will find a ZIP file named as `teamtwitter-server.zip` in the support files for this book. Extract that file in a temporary location.

Copy the directories—`conf`, `sql`, `src` to `C:/teamtwitter-server` directory.

3. Now, let's set up the database server, create the Team Twitter database, and create the Team Twitter database schema.

Install the downloaded MySQL server. Create the Team Twitter database using the SQL script, `create-db.sql`, available in the `C:\teamtwitter-server\sql` directory. The following command creates the database with the name as `tt` and grants permission to the user `ttlogin` with the password as `ttlogin`. In the following command, use the root password that you set while installing MySQL server. In the command prompt, go to `C:\teamtwitter-server\sql` and enter the following command:

```
mysql --user=root --password=<root password> < create-db.sql
```

Now, let's create the Team Twitter schema using the SQL scripts, `ddl.sql` and `initial-data.sql`, available in the `C:\teamtwitter-server\sql` directory:

```
C:\teamtwitter-server\sql>mysql --user=ttlogin --password=ttlogin
tt < ddl.sql
```

```
C:\teamtwitter-server\sql>mysql --user=ttlogin --password=ttlogin
tt < initial-data.sql
```

Check whether the database is created successfully:

```
C:\teamtwitter-server\sql>mysql --user=ttlogin --password=ttlogin
tt
```

Once you enter the preceding command, you'll get the following output:

```
Welcome to the MySQL monitor.  Commands end with ; or \g.

Your MySQL connection id is 3

Server version: 5.1.57-community MySQL Community Server (GPL)


Copyright (c) 2000, 2010, Oracle and/or its affiliates. All rights
reserved.This software comes with ABSOLUTELY NO WARRANTY. This is
free software,and you are welcome to modify and redistribute it
under the GPL v2 license Type 'help;' or '\h' for help. Type '\c'
to clear the current input statement.

mysql>
```

Enter the `show tables;` command. This will list the tables created for the Team Twitter application.

```
mysql> show tables;

+---------------+
| Tables_in_tt |
+---------------+
| team          |
| team_ttuser   |
| ttag          |
| ttuser        |
| ttweet        |
| ttweet_ttag   |
+---------------+
6 rows in set (0.01 sec)


mysql>
```

Enter `exit` to come out of the `mysql` prompt.

Now, the database for the Team Twitter application is ready.

4. Extract all the downloaded ZIP files in `C:/`. After the extraction, you should have the following directories:

   ❑ `C:/hibernate-distribution-3.6.5.Final-dist`

   ❑ `C:/spring-framework-2.5.6`

   ❑ `C:/mysql-connector-java-5.1.17`

5. Let's copy the necessary JAR files to the Team Twitter server application.

Copy the following libraries from `C:/hibernate-distribution-3.6.5.Final-dist/hibernate3.jar` **to** `C:/teamtwitter-server/lib`.

Copy the following libraries from `C:/hibernate-distribution-3.6.5.Final-dist/lib/required` **to** `C:/teamtwitter-server/lib`.

- ❑ `antlr-2.7.6.jar`
- ❑ `commons-collections-3.1.jar`
- ❑ `dom4j-1.6.1.jar`
- ❑ `javassist-3.12.0.GA.jar`
- ❑ `jta-1.1.jar`
- ❑ `slf4j-api-1.6.1.jar`

As we have copied `commons-collections-3.1.jar` from Hibernate, delete the library, `C:/teamtwitter-server/lib/commons-collections-2.1.jar`, that we copied from the RPCJava.

Copy the following libraries from the `C:/hibernate-distribution-3.6.5.Final-dist/lib/bytecode/cglib/cglib-2.2.jar` directory to the `C:/teamtwitter-server/lib` directory.

Copy the library from the `C:/hibernate-distribution-3.6.5.Final-dist/lib/jpa/hibernate-jpa-2.0-api-1.0.0.Final.jar` directory to the `C:/teamtwitter-server/lib` directory.

Copy the following libraries from the `C:/hibernate-distribution-3.6.5.Final-dist/lib/optional/c3p0/c3p0-0.9.1.jar` directory to the `C:/teamtwitter-server/lib` directory.

Copy the library from the `C:/spring-framework-2.5.6/dist/spring.jar` directory to the `C:/teamtwitter-server/lib` directory.

Copy the library from the `C:/spring-framework-2.5.6/lib/jakarta-commons/commons logging.jar` directory to `C:/teamtwitter-server/lib` directory.

Copy the library from the `C:/spring-framework-2.5.6/lib/freemarker/freemarker.jar` directory to the `C:/teamtwitter-server/lib` directory.

Copy the library from the `C:/spring-framework-2.5.6/lib/junit/junit-3.8.2.jar` directory to the `C:/teamtwitter-server/lib` directory.

Copy the library from the `C:/spring-framework-2.5.6/dist/modules/spring-test.jar` directory to the `C:/teamtwitter-server/lib` directory.

Copy the `mysql-connector-java-5.1.17-bin.jar` file from `C:/mysql-connector-java-5.1.17` to the `C:/teamtwitter-server/lib` directory.

Copy the downloaded `hibernate-tools-3.2.4.jar` file to the `C:/teamtwitter-server/lib` directory.

6. Let's modify the `build.xml` file from `C:/teamtwitter-server` to copy all the configuration files into `WEB-INF/classes`. To do this, add the following Ant script into your `copy.web` target:

```
<copy todir="${application.dist.dir}/WEB-INF/classes">
  <fileset dir="${build.dir}/conf">
    <include name="**/*" />
  </fileset>
</copy>
```

The `build.xml` file is also available as a support file named `978-1-849513-70-8_05_01.txt` file under `Chapter 5` folder in the support files for this book.

Generate the web application using the following command:

`C:\teamtwitter-server>ant dist`

Deploy the updated Team Twitter web application.

`C:\teamtwitter-server>ant deploy`

Now, your server application is ready to support all the Team Twitter functionalities and you can make the provided RPC calls from the client application.

What just happened?

We have enhanced the Team Twitter server application to provide the necessary server functionalities for the Team Twitter application. To achieve that, we have downloaded the required frameworks, database server, and libraries. We also installed the database server, copied the necessary JAR files to the `teamtwitter-server` application, compiled and generated a web application, and deployed the Team Twitter application.

Form widgets

Form is used to collect the data from the user, for example, any of the registration forms, login forms, signup forms on any website. A form is built with various form widgets such as text field, text area, button, list, and so on. As most of the form widgets are available in qooxdoo, creating complex screens is easy in qooxdoo. A form is useful to display the output information in an effective way. All these form widgets are defined under the `qx.ui.form` package.

This package consists of several components that look similar to the default HTML components such as input, button, select-option list, checkbox, and so on, whereas the qooxdoo-defined form widgets have a rich look with the possibility of configuring the themes to have a different appearance. Also, these qooxdoo widgets have the same look across the browser. The package helps to group all the widgets into a form and allows access to them in a generic way.

Let's have a look at the different components defined under this package. The following screenshot shows most of the form widgets. We will go through each and every widget individually:

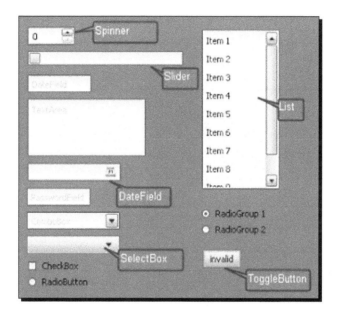

You need to use the most suitable widgets to collect the input from the user. You need to consider space restrictions, usability, and so on. If you want to collect simple text, you can use the TextField widget. If you want to collect more text, you can use the TextArea widget. If you want to collect a date, you can use the DateField widget. If you want to collect a single option from a set of choices, you can use the RadioButton widget with the RadioGroup widget. If you want to collect multiple options, you can use the CheckBox widget. If you want to collect multiple values from a list, you can use the List widget. If you want to collect a single value from a list, you can use the SelectBox widget. If you want to select a value from a range, you can use the Spinner or Slider widget.

This package defines the maximum number of interfaces for the best use of all widgets and allows access to them generically. All the `form` classes implement interfaces as per the requirements. Let's start evaluating more on this package with the defined classes, interfaces, and their usage and functionality.

Interface hierarchy

To generalize and to access all the components inside a form in a generic manner, qooxdoo provides a set of interfaces. Each interface defines the required methods and events required for the supported functionalities. All the classes in the `qx.ui.form` package implement one or more of these interfaces to implement and support the required functionalities that it provides.

Some of the interfaces defined are based on the primary data types processed by the implementing widget:

- **Number**: `qx.ui.form.INumberForm`
- **Boolean**: `qx.ui.form.IBooeanForm`
- **String**: `qx.ui.form.IStringForm`
- **Color**: `qx.ui.form.IColorForm`
- **Date**: `qx.ui.form.IDateForm`
- **Executable**: `qx.ui.form.IExecutable`
- **Form**: `qx.ui.form.IForm`
- **Range**: `qx.ui.form.IRangeForm`
- **RadioItem**: `qx.ui.form.IRadioItem`
- **Model**: `qx.ui.form.IModel`
- **Model selection**: `qx.ui.form.IModelSelection`

These interfaces and the implementing classes are shown as follows:

```
 ⓘ IBooleanForm                          ⓘ IForm                                 ⓘ IRadioItem
    ⓖ qx.ui.menu.CheckBox,                  ⓖ qx.ui.form.RadioGroup,                ⓖ qx.ui.groupbox.RadioGroupBox,
    ⓖ qx.ui.groupbox.RadioGroupBox,         ⓖᴬqx.ui.form.AbstractField,             ⓖ qx.ui.form.RadioButton,
    ⓖ qx.ui.form.RadioButton,               ⓖ qx.ui.form.Slider,                    ⓖ qx.ui.menu.RadioButton,
    ⓖ qx.ui.menu.RadioButton,               ⓖ qx.ui.form.RadioButtonGroup,          ⓖ qx.ui.tabview.TabButton,
    ⓖ qx.ui.form.ToggleButton,              ⓖ qx.ui.groupbox.GroupBox,              ⓖ qx.ui.toolbar.RadioButton
    ⓖ qx.ui.groupbox.CheckGroupBox          ⓖ qx.ui.form.Spinner,
                                            ⓖ qx.ui.control.DateChooser,         ⓘ IStringForm
 ⓘ IColorForm                               ⓖ qx.ui.form.RadioButton,               ⓖ qx.ui.basic.Label,
    ⓖ qx.ui.control.ColorSelector,          ⓖᴬqx.ui.form.AbstractSelectBox,         ⓖᴬqx.ui.form.AbstractField,
    ⓖ qx.ui.control.ColorPopup              ⓖ qx.ui.form.List,                      ⓖ qx.ui.form.ComboBox
                                            ⓖ qx.ui.form.CheckBox,
 ⓘ IDateForm                                ⓖ qx.ui.tree.Tree                    ⓘ INumberForm     ⓘ IRange
    ⓖ qx.ui.control.DateChooser,                                                    ⓖ qx.ui.form.Slider,
    ⓖ qx.ui.form.DateField               ⓘ IModel                                  ⓖ qx.ui.form.Spinner
                                            ⓖ qx.ui.form.ListItem,
 ⓘ IExecutable                              ⓖ qx.ui.groupbox.RadioGroupBox,      ⓘ IModelSelection
    ⓖ qx.ui.form.Button,                    ⓖ qx.ui.form.RadioButton,               ⓖ qx.ui.form.RadioGroup,
    ⓖᴬqx.ui.menu.AbstractButton,            ⓖᴬqx.ui.tree.AbstractTreeItem,          ⓖ qx.ui.form.RadioButtonGroup,
    ⓖ qx.ui.form.HoverButton,               ⓖ qx.ui.menu.RadioButton,               ⓖ qx.ui.form.List,
    ⓖ qx.ui.control.DateChooser,            ⓖ qx.ui.form.CheckBox,                  ⓖ qx.ui.form.SelectBox,
    ⓖ qx.ui.groupbox.RadioGroupBox,         ⓖ qx.ui.toolbar.RadioButton,            ⓖ qx.ui.tree.Tree
    ⓖ qx.ui.form.SplitButton,               ⓖ qx.ui.groupbox.CheckGroupBox
    ⓖ qx.ui.form.ToggleButton,
    ⓖ qx.ui.groupbox.CheckGroupBox
```

IBooleanForm, INumberForm, IDateForm, IColorForm, and IStringForm

All these interfaces provide essential methods and a `changeValue` event for all the widgets dealing with simple data types. Each of these interfaces provides the same set of methods and events with the respective data type supported by that interface. It allows operations such as setting, getting, and resetting generically on all the widgets such as `ColorSelector`, `CheckBox`, `RadioButton`, `RadioGroup`, `Label`, `Spinner`, and so on. In the following class diagram, XXX represents the data type supported by the interface:

```
┌─────────────────────────────────┐
│       < <Interface> >           │
│          IXXXForm               │
├─────────────────────────────────┤
│  changeValue : Data             │
├─────────────────────────────────┤
│  setValue(value : XXX) : void   │
│  getValue() : XXX               │
│  resetValue() : void            │
└─────────────────────────────────┘
```

IForm

The `qx.ui.form.IForm` interface defines a set of methods and events for every visible form widget. This interface allows us to set different properties in the methods such as `setEnabled`, `setRequired`, `setValid`, `setInvalidMessage`, and so on. The defined methods are shown in the following class diagram:

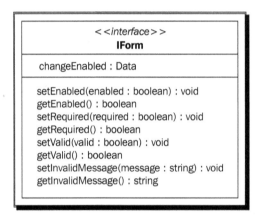

IExecutable

The `qx.ui.form.IExecutable` interface defines essential members for all executable widgets such as `Button`, `HoverButton`, and so on. All the widgets that have an action to execute will implement this interface. This interface provides methods for setting and getting commands to the widget and also provides methods to execute the action. The defined methods are shown in the following class diagram:

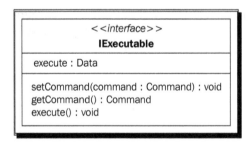

IRange

The `qx.ui.form.IRange` interface defines the essential methods for setting the minimum value, maximum value, and step value for all the widgets dealing with ranges.

```
<<interface>>
IRange

setMinimum(min : number) : void
getMinimum() : number
setMaximum(max : number) : void
getMaximum() : number
setSingleStep(step : number) : void
getSingleStep() : number
setPageStep(step : number) : void
getPageStep() : number
```

IModel

The `qx.ui.form.IModel` interface defines the essential methods for setting the data for the widget. The model is the property to store additional data that is represented by the widget. The model can store references to objects, numbers, strings, and so on. For example, `qx.ui.form.ListItem` implements the `IModel` interface. The class diagram for the `IModel` interface is as follows:

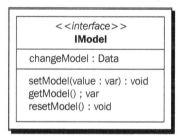

IModelSelection

The `qx.ui.form.IModelSelection` interface defines the methods for setting and retrieving the models of selected items in the widget. For example, `qx.ui.form.List` sets and returns the models of all the selected `qx.ui.form.ListItem` items in `List`. The class diagram for the `IModelSelection` interface is as follows:

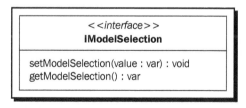

We will learn the usage of these interfaces in the following section.

Class hierarchy

The `form` widget class implements the required interfaces and helps to build complex forms with various user inputs.

The following screenshot shows a list of available classes in the `qx.ui.form` package:

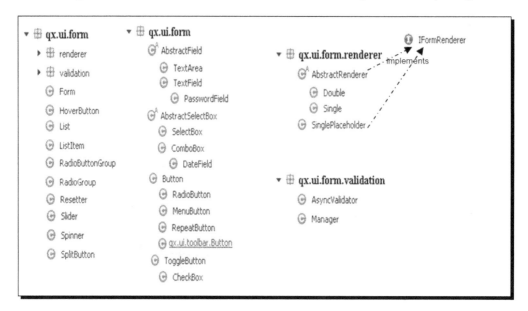

Now, we will go through the `form` widget classes.

qx.ui.form.TextField

This `TextField` is one of the most-used `form` elements. This widget allows the user to enter text in a single line. This widget is used to collect simple properties such as name. This widget supports all keys on the keyboard including *Backspace*, *Ctrl* characters, and so on. It also supports the right-click of a mouse. It fires two events: the `input` event, which is fired on every keystroke, and the `changeValue` event, which is fired on text modification.

Features of the `TextField` widget are as follows:

- Supports basic text alignment to left, center, or right.
- Allows protecting user inputs through the enabled or the `readOnly` property.
- Disabling the widget grays it out and makes it unresponsive for all types of interactions. While the text field is read-only and the modification of the value is prevented, it has no special visual indication when enabled.
- Mouse and keyboard support.

- ◆ Supports configuration of fonts.
- ◆ Allows restriction of text length entered in the widget.
- ◆ Allows handling key strokes by writing listeners to the `input` event. A user can stop the propagation of the event on a particular key press using the `stopPropagation()` method of `KeyEvent`.

qx.ui.form.TextArea

`TextArea` widget is a multiline text input form element. This widget is mainly used to collect larger text such as the description field.

Features of the `TextArea` widget are:

- ◆ It supports all the features of the `TextField` element. Additionally, it supports auto-wrapping of text.
- ◆ It allows multiple line input.

qx.ui.form.PasswordField

The `PasswordField` widget is similar to the `TextField` widget, but it hides the entered characters and displays asterisks or dots. This widget is mostly used to collect the password from the user. It is one of the most useful fields in the login form for any application.

Features of the `PasswordField` widget are:

- ◆ It supports all the features of the `TextField` element
- ◆ It hides the entered text
- ◆ It allows all special characters

qx.ui.form.CheckBox

The `CheckBox` widget represents a Boolean property, with a tick mark inside a box. This widget is used to collect an option from the user. The user can check yes or no for that option.

Features of the `CheckBox` widget are:

- ◆ It supports mouse and keyboard input
- ◆ It supports the label features too

qx.ui.form.RadioButton

A radio button allows us to choose one of the multiple options. `qx.ui.form.RadioGroup` is the class that groups the radio buttons that are added to it. `RadioGroup` restricts the user to select only one of the radio buttons.

The following code snippet demonstrates the use of `RadioButtons` and `RadioGroup`:

```
// create radio buttons for male and female
var female = new qx.ui.form.RadioButton("female");
var male = new qx.ui.form.RadioButton("male");

// create a radiogroup
var mgr = new qx.ui.form.RadioGroup();
// Group the radiobuttons by adding them to the RadioGroup
mgr.add(female, male);

// add the RadioButtons into container.
this.getRoot().add(male, {left : 10, top : 10});
this.getRoot().add(female, {left : 10, top : 30});
```

Features of the `RadioButton` widget are:

◆ It supports Boolean data type

◆ It allows the selection of one among multiple options in a group

◆ Mouse and keyboard support

◆ It fires an event on change of a value

qx.ui.form.RadioButtonGroup

`RadioButtonGroup` is similar to `RadioGroup`. In addition to that, it provides a container for the radio buttons. This widget takes care of laying out the radio buttons and adding them into a group. It is enough to add the whole `RadioButtonGroup` into the layout. Similar to the `RadioGroup` widget, the `RadioButtonGroup` widget also implements most of the form interfaces such as `qx.ui.form.IForm`, `qx.ui.form.ISingleSelection` and `qx.ui.form.IModelSelection`.

The following code snippet explains the easier way to create the preceding example:

```
// create radio buttons for male and female
var female = new qx.ui.form.RadioButton("female");
var male = new qx.ui.form.RadioButton("male");

// create a radioButtonGroup with a layout set.
var mgr = new qx.ui.form.RadioButtonGroup(new qx.ui.layout.VBox);
// Group the radiobuttons by adding them to the RadioGroup
mgr.add(female);
mgr.add( male);

// add the RadioButtons into container.
this.getRoot().add(mgr, {left : 10, top : 10});
```

The features of the `RadioButtonGroup` widget are:

- It supports Boolean data type
- It allows the selection of one among multiple options in a group
- Mouse and keyboard support
- It fires an event on change of value

qx.ui.form.SelectBox

The `SelectBox` widget allows the user to select one of the items from a set of items. The `SelectBox` widget acts like a `ComboBox`, except that the user cannot enter any data as an input. Instead, the user is only allowed to select one of the items displayed in the `SelectBox`.

The features of the `SelectBox` widget are:

- Mouse and keyboard support
- Items can be plain text, with an icon associated with the text, or only an icon
- Ellipsis and auto-scroll are supported

qx.ui.form.ComboBox

The `ComboBox` widget is a combination of a select box and a `TextField` widget. A user can either type any value in the `TextField` or select one of the multiple values in the drop-down list.

The features of the `ComboBox` widget are:

- It supports the features of a `TextField` and `SelectBox`
- Items can be plain text, with an icon associated with the text, or only an icon
- Ellipsis (...) will be shown on the item, if the item cannot be accommodated within the width

qx.ui.form.Spinner

The `Spinner` widget is a control that allows you to adjust a numerical value, typically within an allowed range. For example, month of a year (ranges from 1 to 12).

The features of the `Spinner` widget are as follows:

- Mouse and keyboard support
- Supports number format
- Configurable steps

qx.ui.form.List

The List widget is used for selecting one or more items from a given list. This widget is very similar to the select and option tags in the HTML. qooxdoo List widget provides more advantages than the HTML both in looks and functionality. The List widget's width and height can be restricted, and if the entered height is more than the restricted height, then the scroll bar is displayed by default.

List implements the form interfaces and gives flexibility in using the list inside a form to handle it generically. The implemented interfaces are qx.ui.form.IMultiSelection, qx.ui.form.IModelSelection, and qx.ui.form.IForm.

The different possible selection modes are:

- single: Only one or none can be selected
- multi: One, more, or none can be selected
- addictive: The same selection mode like multi, but each item that the user clicks on is added or removed from the selection
- one: Same as the single mode; but one selection is must

The default selection mode is single. The methods allowed to manage this selection mode are setSelectionMode() and getSelectionMode(). Each item in this list is a qx.ui.form.ListItem instance. List can contain any number of the ListItems.

Features of the List widget are as follows:

- Mouse and keyboard support
- Supports special keys like *Shift*, *Ctrl*, and so on
- Support for drag-and-drop
- Context menu support on right-click
- Supports different modes of selection, such as single, multi, addictive, and one
- Items with plain text and/or icon
- Resize and scroll support

qx.ui.form.ListItem

The ListItem widget is an item for the List widget. A user can also add the ListItem widgets to list-like widgets such as SelectBox and ComboBox. A ListItem can store data representative for the real item as text and/or icon. ListItem implements the IModel interface and gives implementation for getModel(), setModel(), and resetModel().

Features of the `ListItem` are as follows:

- ◆ Mouse and keyboard support
- ◆ Displays text and/or icon
- ◆ Supports all the features of `Atom`, as the `ListItem` is inherited from `Atom`

qx.ui.form.DateField

The `DateField` widget allows you to type the date in the specified format and displays a small, calendar icon. When you click on the calendar icon, it pops up the `DateChooser` component. The date chooser allows a user to select a particular date from the GUI interface.

The following code snippet demonstrates the usage of `DateField`. The default format for the `DateField` is `<Month> dd, yyyy`:

```
var date = new qx.ui.form.DateField();
this.getRoot().add(date);
```

The GUI's look for the preceding code is as follows:

Features of the `DateField` widget are as follows:

- ◆ Allows adding the field in any of the forms
- ◆ Supports mouse and keyboard input
- ◆ Supports user-defined date format

qx.ui.form.Button

The Button widget fires a trigger on an action. A user can trigger it either by a mouse click, or by pressing the *Enter* key or the *space* key on the keyboard. The Button widget is used to perform an action, for example, submitting the form to save an object or retrieving some values, and so on. In qooxdoo, a user can create a button by creating an instance of the qx.ui.form.Button class. When the user presses the button, the Button widget fires the execute event. It also runs the command attached to the button. But this command is optional. So, the user has the choice to perform an activity either in the execute event listener or in the command.

The following code snippet creates a button and attaches an execute event:

```
var button = new qx.ui.form.Button("Hello World");
button.addListener("execute", function(e) {
    alert("Button was clicked");
}, this);
this.getRoot().add(button, {left : 100,top  : 50});
```

The features of the Button widget are as follows:

◆ Supports displaying the image and text

◆ Mouse click or *Enter* key and *space* key in the keyboard initiates the button events

◆ Allows flexibility of the Atom and Label widgets

qx.ui.form.ToggleButton

The ToggleButton is a widget of the button type with exactly two states, namely, pressed and not pressed. If the user presses the button by clicking on it or by pressing the *Enter* or *space* key, the button toggles between the pressed and not pressed states. There is no execute event; the only event available is the changeValue event. A command can also be associated to execute while a button changes its state.

Features of the ToggleButton widget are as follows:

◆ Supports both keyboard and mouse interaction

◆ Supports all the features of the Atom widget, as it is inherited from the Atom widget.

qx.ui.form.MenuButton

On the click of a MenuButton button, the connected menu is opened or dropped down. A menu should be added to the button.

The following code snippet implements the `MenuButton` widget and its usage with the `menu` created in the previous chapter:

```
var menu = new qx.ui.menu.Menu;
var cButton = new qx.ui.menu.RadioButton("C");
var csharpButton = new qx.ui.menu.RadioButton("C Sharp");
var objcButton = new qx.ui.menu.RadioButton("Objective C");
var cplusButton = new qx.ui.menu.RadioButton("C Plus Plus");
menu.add(cButton);
menu.add(csharpButton);
menu.add(objcButton);
menu.add(cplusButton);
var button = new qx.ui.form.MenuButton("Menu Button", "icon/testicon.
png", menu);
// Add button to document at fixed coordinates
this.getRoot().add(button, {top : 20, left : 20});
```

The GUI's look for the preceding code is as follows:

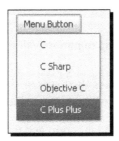

Features of the `MenuButton` widget are as follows:

- Supports all the features of a button
- Dynamically pulls down the added menu
- Supports all the menu features too like scrolling, alignment, and so on

qx.ui.form.SplitButton

The `SplitButton` acts like a normal button and shows a menu on one of the sides to open something like a history list. We have already seen the `SplitButton` and used it in the menu creation part of our previous chapter.

Features of the SplitButton widget are as follows:

◆ Keyboard and mouse support

◆ Contains text and/or icon

◆ Ellipsis and menu support

qx.ui.form.HoverButton

The HoverButton is a kind of widget that fires the execute event repeatedly while the mouse is over it. HoverButton actually starts a timer once the user places the mouse pointer over the widget and fires the execute event in regular intervals. This has many properties to configure the event firing. The properties are:

◆ firstInterval: Interval used for the first run of the timer. Usually, a greater value than the interval property value, which results in a little delayed reaction the first time. The default value is 200 milliseconds.

◆ Interval: Interval used after the first run of the timer. Usually a smaller value than the firstInterval property value, which is used to get a faster reaction. Default value is 80 milliseconds.

◆ minTimer: This configures the minimum value for the timer interval. The default value is 20 milliseconds.

◆ timeDecrease: This decreases the timer on each interval (for the next interval) until the minTimer value is reached. The default value is 2.

The following code snippet explains the creation and usage of the HoverButton with all the default values:

```
var button = new qx.ui.form.HoverButton("Hello World");
button.addListener("execute", function(e) {
  this.debug("Mouse pointer is over the widget");
}, this);
this.getRoot().add(button);
```

The GUI's look for the preceding code is as follows. The log at the bottom shows the sequence of the execute event listener activity:

```
Hello World (modified)

Hello World

Log
156498 playground.Application[495]: Starting application 'Hello World (modified)' ...
156502 playground.Application[495]: Successfully started.
158069 playground.Application[495]: Mouse pointer is over the widget
158147 playground.Application[495]: Mouse pointer is over the widget
158225 playground.Application[495]: Mouse pointer is over the widget
158303 playground.Application[495]: Mouse pointer is over the widget
```

The features of the `HoverButton` widget are as follows:

◆ Contains text and/or icon, similar to a button

◆ Event interval is configurable

◆ Allows repetition of activities in a timer

qx.ui.form.RepeatButton

`RepeatButton` is a special button, repeatedly fires the `execute` event. This `RepeatButton` starts firing an event when the user presses the button and continuously fires until the user releases the button. Similar to the `HoverButton`, this `RepeatButton` also provides the properties like `interval` to fire the event and other properties.

One of the best uses of the `RepeatButton` is seen at the ends of the scroll bars. On clicking this button, the scroll bar scrolls until the button is released. Slider uses these `RepeatButton` buttons internally.

The following is a sample code snippet to demonstrate the `RepeatButton`:

```
var button = new qx.ui.form.RepeatButton("Hello World");
button.addListener("execute", function(e) {
  this.debug("Button is Pressed");
}, this);
this.getRoot().add(button, {left: 10, top : 10});
```

The GUI's look for the preceding code is as follows:

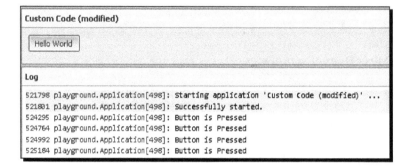

The features of the `RepeatButton` widget are as follows:

- ◆ Supports mouse
- ◆ Displays text and/or icon
- ◆ Adjustable event interval

qx.ui.form.Slider

The `Slider` widget is the classic widget for controlling a bounded value. It lets the user move a slider handle along a horizontal or vertical groove. It translates the handle's position into an integer value within the defined range. This widget is used to select a value from a range, for example, percentage selection in an application.

The features of the `Slider` widget are as follows:

- ◆ Mouse support
- ◆ Horizontal or vertical orientations.
- ◆ Configurable steps

Time for action – adding widgets into Team Twitter

As we have learnt the `basic` and `form` widgets, let's update the Team Twitter widgets to add the `basic` or `form` widgets in the layout that we created in the previous chapters.

1. Let's create the necessary widgets for the `TweetSearchWidget`. Let's code the `initLayout` method to create and add the widgets into the layout, the required widgets for searching, and the links for user login and user signup forms. This will enhance the `TweetSearchWidget.js` class under `C:\teamtwitter\source\class\teamtwitter\ui`.

First, create the widgets as per the following screen requirement and update the class. Even if you cannot get it right, try it by yourself first without seeing the code mentioned in the code files. By doing so, you'll apply the concepts that you learnt in the earlier sections. Feel free to refer to the earlier sections when you need any help on the concepts:

Once you update the code, you can build the client application, generate a web application, deploy the web application, and check the web application as we did in the previous chapter.

After you attempt this, compare your code with the `978-1-849513-70-8_05_02.txt` file under `Chapter 5` folder in the support files for this book. If you missed anything, update your class by referring to this code file. The methods in the `TweetSearchWidget` class are mentioned and explained as follows:

- ❑ `_initLayout`: Creates the layout for the form.
- ❑ `signIn`: Displays the **Login** form.
- ❑ `signUp`: Displays the **Sign Up Form**.
- ❑ `hideSignUpAndSignIn`: Hides the **Sign In** and **Sign Up** links. This function is called after the user logs in.
- ❑ `showSignUpAndSignIn`: Shows the **Sign In** and **Sign Up** links. This function is called after the user logs out.
- ❑ `getSearchText`: Returns the search text entered by the user.
- ❑ `searchTweets`: Searches the tweet based on the search text, team, selected tags, and selected users.

Again, build the client application, generate a web application, deploy the web application, and check the web application. Do this whenever you make changes and whenever you want to see the changes in the application.

2. Once the user clicks on the **Sign Up** link, the user registration window should appear. Let's create the necessary widgets and update the `UserSignUpForm.js` class under `C:\teamtwitter\source\class\teamtwitter\ui`.

First, try by yourself to create the widgets, as per the following screen requirement, and update the class:

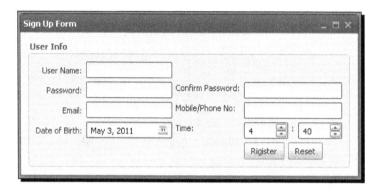

Once you update the code, you can build the client application, generate a web application, deploy the web application, and check the web application as we did in the previous chapter.

Once you deploy the rebuilt application, reload the application in the browser and click on the **Sign Up** link in TweetSearchWidget. It should display the user registration window.

After you attempt this, compare your code with the one in the 978-1-849513-70-8_05_03.txt file under Chapter 5. If you missed anything, update your class by referring to this code file. The following are the methods in the UserSignUpForm class:

- _initLayout: Creates the layout for the form. The execute listener is added for registerBtn to add the user

- resetForm: Resets the form

Register a few users using the registration form in the Team Twitter application.

3. Once the user clicks on the **Sign In** link, a login form should appear. Let's create the necessary widgets and update the UserLoginForm.js class under C:\ teamtwitter\source\class\teamtwitter\ui.

First, try by yourself to create the widgets, as per the following screen requirement, and update the class:

Once you update the code, you can build the client application, generate a web application, deploy the web application, and check the web application as it is mentioned in the previous chapter.

Once you deploy the rebuilt application, reload the application in the browser, click on the **Sign In** link in TweetSearchWidget, and it should display the **Login** form.

After you attempt this, compare your code with the code in the code files. If you missed anything, check the following code, and update your class. This code is also available in the 978-1-849513-70-8_05_04.txt file under Chapter 5. If you missed anything, update your class by referring to this code file. The methods in the UserLoginForm class are as follows:

- _initLayout: Creates the layout for the form
- loginUser: Logs in the user
- openUserSignUpForm: Closes the **Login** form and opens the user **Sign Up Form**
- focusOnUserName: Focuses on the username field in the **Login** form

4. Once you register a few users, all the users have to be displayed as a list in the UserListWidget. Let's update the following UsersListWidget.js class under C:\teamtwitter\source\class\teamtwitter\ui. We have to load all the users from the database and display it in the list. You can use the respective RPC call to get the user list for a team.

First, try by yourself to create the widgets, as per the following screen requirement, and update the class. The list should allow multi selection. When you search the tweets, you will see that the tweets are retrieved on the basis of the selected users:

Just to give you a hint, the creation of a `List` widget is shown in the following code snippet. Try updating `UsersListWidget`:

```
this._userList = new qx.ui.form.List();
this._userList.setSelectionMode("multi");
this._userList.addListener("changeSelection", this.
userClicked);
this.add(this._userList);
```

After you attempt this, compare your code with the `978-1-849513-70-8_05_05.txt` file under `Chapter 5`. If you missed anything, update your class based on this code file.

5. Once the user logs in to the application, he/she should be allowed to tweet on a particular tag and a user can even attach a YouTube video ID to attach the YouTube video to the tweet.

    First, try by yourself to create the widgets, as per the following screen requirement, and update the class:

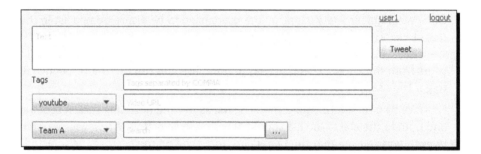

    This screen is created by adding text area, labels, text fields, and buttons into the layout that we created in the previous chapter in the `TweetInput.js` file under `C:\teamtwitter\source\class\teamtwitter\ui`.

    After you attempt this, compare your code with the `978-1-849513-70-8_05_06.txt` file under `Chapter 5`. If you missed anything, update your class by referring to this code file.

6. The next step is to create the `Tags` widget. All the tweet tags have to be displayed in a flow layout, as shown in the following screenshot. Each tag should be associated with a checkbox, so that you can filter the tweets based on the selected tags. Let's update the `TagsWidget.js` class under `C:\teamtwitter\source\class\teamtwitter\ui`.

    First, try by yourself to create the widgets, as per the following screen requirement, and update the class:

Just to give you a hint, creation of the `CheckBox` widget is shown in the following code snippet, which should be repeated in a for loop for all the tags in the database:

```
var tag = new qx.ui.form.CheckBox(result[i][0] + " (" + result[i]
[1] + ")");
tag.setValue(true);
tag.addListener("changeValue", _this.tagClicked, this);
_this.mainPanel.add(tag);
```

After you attempt this, compare your code with the code in the `978-1-849513-70-8_05_07.txt` file under `Chapter 5`. If you miss anything, update your class by referring to this code file.

What just happened?

We have learnt the various interface defined in the `qx.ui.form` package and also learnt about various `form` widgets and their usage. We have developed different widgets for the Team Twitter application using some of the `form` widgets.

Let's learn about some special widgets to add more functionality to the applications.

Special widgets

Other than the `basic` and `form` widgets, the qooxdoo framework provides the most useful widgets and controls in order to develop applications with good functionality in lesser time. Framework reduces or saves the developer's time by avoiding the creation of controls such as date chooser, color picker, and so on, and simplifies the code. This allows the developers to concentrate more on the business logic than on creating the custom widgets.

Let's have a look at some of the special widgets supported in the qooxdoo framework. Some of the special widgets are `popup`, `tooltip`, and `control`.

The popup widgets

The `popup` widgets are displayed over the application page and are rendered above the existing content. The best examples for the `popup` widgets are `Menu`, `ComboBox`, `SelectBox`, and `tooltip`.

Basically, `popup` is a composite container with the configurable layout. You can add multiple widgets into the `popup` widget and the pop-up is displayed over the existing content. The pop-up is normally hidden when the user is not pointing to the required place, such as a menu. This behavior is controllable through the `autoHide` property. With the `bringToFront` and `sendToBack` properties, the `zIndex` property of the `popup` widget could be controlled in relation to other visible `popup` widgets.

The classes for the user-defined `popup` and `tooltip` widgets are shown in the following screenshot:

qx.ui.popup

The `qx.ui.popup` package provides the following classes for the `popup` widget:

♦ `qx.ui.popup.Popup`: The `Popup` class is used to display the `popup` widget on top of the existing content in the application

♦ `qx.ui.popup.Manager`: The `popup.Manager` is a singleton class and is used to manage multiple instances of a `popup` widget and its states

The tooltip widgets

qooxdoo provides a set of classes to manage the `tooltip` widgets.

qx.ui.tooltip

The `qx.ui.tooltip` package provides the following classes for the `tooltip` widget:

♦ `qx.ui.tooltip.ToolTip`: The `ToolTip` class provides additional information for widgets when the user hovers over a widget. This tool tip information can contain plain text, icons, and/or complex HTML code. Tool tip is shown for a particular time period and automatically hidden after the time elapses.

♦ qx.ui.tooltip.Manager: The tooltip.Manager is also a singleton class and is used to manage the tool tips of all widgets. This class will display the tool tip of a particular widget and hide all other tool tips associated with other widgets. Tool tip is shown only when a user hovers over a widget.

The following code snippet demonstrates the popup and tooltip widgets' creation and display:

```
var button = new qx.ui.form.Button("Open Popup");
this.getRoot().add(button);

// popup creation
var popup = new qx.ui.popup.Popup(new qx.ui.layout.Canvas());
popup.add(new qx.ui.basic.Atom("Hello World #1", "icon/32/apps/media-
photo-album.png"));

button.addListener("click", function(e)
{
// displaying the popup by placing it to mouse
popup.placeToMouse(e);
popup.show();
}, this);

// tooltip creation
var tooltip = new qx.ui.tooltip.ToolTip("Opens a popup");
//associating the tooltip to button widget
button.setToolTip(tooltip);
```

The GUI look for the preceding code is as follows:

A tooltip widget is displayed when a user places the cursor on the button. A popup widget is displayed when the user clicks on the button. The popup widget can be placed at a point using the API placeToPoint() or it can be placed at the mouse pointer's position using the API placeToMouse().

The control widgets

qooxdoo provides a collection of high-level GUI controls such as `ColorSelector`, `DataChooser`, `ColorPopup`, and so on. These controls provide rich functionalities to the application.

qx.ui.control.ColorPopup

The `qx.ui.control.ColorPopup` widget contains a palette of colors. You can use this widget to choose a color from the basic colors for any purpose in your application. You can also preset a color in the `ColorPopup` widget. This class is a subclass of the `popup` class and it inherits all the features of a `popup` class. The `ColorSelector` will be hidden when the user clicks on any other area in the application. `ColorPopup` allows selection of a color. Once you select a color, the pop-up will automatically hide and return the selected color. If the basic colors are not enough, you can launch the `ColorSelector` from the `ColorPopup` widget.

The following code snippet demonstrates the usage of `ColorPopup`:

```
var mypop = new qx.ui.control.ColorPopup();
mypop.setValue("#23F3C1");
mypop.show();
```

The GUI look for the preceding code is as follows:

qx.ui.control.ColorSelector

`ColorSelector` control allows you to choose any possible color, either through the **Hex**, **RGB**, or **HSB** values. You can also use the visual control to choose a color, as you can see in the following screenshot. This control looks very similar to the typical color selector in any of the native applications.

The following code snippet demonstrates the usage of `ColorSelector`:

```
var selector = new qx.ui.control.ColorSelector();
this.getRoot().add(selector, {left: 20, top: 20});
```

The GUI look for the preceding code is as follows:

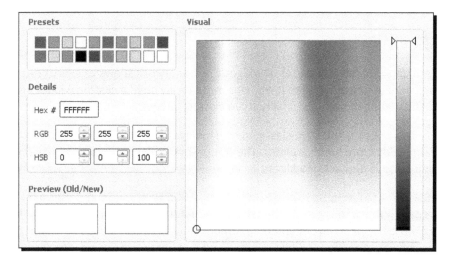

qx.ui.control.DateChooser

The `DateChooser` control is a calendar component that allows you to choose a date. It has a navigation bar to change the month. It displays columns for the calendar week and displays the days of a month.

The following code snippet demonstrates the usage of `DateChooser`:

```
var chooser = new qx.ui.control.DateChooser();
this.getRoot().add(chooser, {left : 10, top : 300});
```

The GUI look for the preceding code is as follows:

We have learnt about the classes used for the `popup` and `tooltip` widgets. We have also learnt the useful controls that provide rich functionalities to the applications and save time in development.

For more samples on the `popup` and `control` widget, have a look at the qooxdoo demos in the demo browser.

Custom widgets

Even though qooxdoo has a large set of widgets, its framework allows to inherit the existing widgets and adding functionality to it. So, a user can easily build a custom widget just by inheriting and adding more functionality to an existing widget.

`qx.ui.core.Widget` is the base class and every widget extends this widget directly or indirectly and adds more functionalities. The framework itself reuses most of the simple widgets and builds a new set of widgets.

For example, `qx.ui.form.Spinner` extends `qx.ui.core.Widget` and uses a text field and two repeat buttons to create the functionality of a spinner. The layout used for the `Spinner` class is the `Grid` layout and the methods modifying this layout are made private, so that the layout cannot be modified outside, and it maintains the same look throughout the application.

The most required method to override the widget is `_createChildControlImpl(id)`. This method is used to create any of the children, based on the ID and return value of the child widget.

A user can override the method, as shown in the following code snippet:

```
// overridden
_createChildControlImpl : function(id, hash)
{
  var control;

  switch(id)
  {
    case "textfield":
      control = new qx.ui.form.TextField();
      control.setFilter(this._getFilterRegExp());
      control.addState("inner");
      control.setWidth(40);
      control.setFocusable(false);
      control.addListener("changeValue", this._onTextChange, this);
```

```
      this._add(control, {column: 0, row: 0, rowSpan: 2});
      break;

  case "upbutton":
    control = new qx.ui.form.RepeatButton();
    control.addState("inner");
    control.setFocusable(false);
    control.addListener("execute", this._countUp, this);
    this._add(control, {column: 1, row: 0});
    break;

  case "xxx":
//..........
    break;
  }

  return control || this.base(arguments, id);
},
```

There are some other methods predefined to get the created child widget. A user can use them and override them to provide extended functionality:

- getChildControl(id, notCreate): Gets the new or existing child widget with the id given, based on the notCreate Boolean value

- _showChildControl(id): Used to show the child control

- _excludeChildControl(id): Hides and excludes the child control

- _isChildControlVisibile(id): Returns the true value, if the child control is visible

- _getChildren(): Returns all the children in an array

- _add(), _addAt(), _addBefore(), _addAfter(): Adds a widget to the children array, based on the configured layout

- _remove(): Removes the widgets from the children array

- _setLayout(): Configures the layout

- _getLayout(): Returns the configured layout

A user can configure the theme for the custom widget, which you will see in *Chapter 9, Working with Themes*.

Time for action – adding a custom widget to Team Twitter

1. Copy the user identity image, `identity.png`, from the support files for this book to the following location: `C:/teamtwitter/source/resource/teamtwitter`. And add the following asset information in the `Application.js` file under `C:/teamtwitter/source/class/teamtwitter`. The updated `Application.js` is available as the `978-1-849513-70-8_05_08.txt` file under `Chapter 5`.

```
/*
************************************************************
#asset(teamtwitter/*)
************************************************************
*/
```

2. Let's create a custom widget for our tweet, which actually should show the user image, tag name, tweet date, time, and the username.

Create the `CTweet.js` file under `C:\teamtwitter\source\class\teamtwitter\ui`. First, try by yourself to create the custom widget, as per the following screen requirement, and update the class. Follow the custom widget creation in qooxdoo:

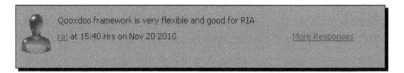

Just to give you a hint, the `_createChildControlImpl` implementation template is illustrated in the following code snippet. Fill in the blanks with the proper controls, add them to the widget container in the layout created in the previous chapters, and make sure that you define the properties section:

```
//overridden
_createChildControlImpl : function(id, hash) {
    var control;
    switch(id) {
  case "userImg":
    //create user image and add to the widget layout
    // _____
    break;
  case "tweetUser" :
    // create user label and add to the widget layout
    // _____
    break;
```

```
    case "tweetLog" :
      // create time label and add to the widget layout
      // _____
      break;
    case "more":
      // create responses label and add to the widget layout
    // _____
      break;
      }
      return control;
},
```

After you attempt this, compare your code with the `978-1-849513-70-8_05_09.txt` file under `Chapter 5`. If you miss anything, update your class by referring to this code file.

3. Similar to the preceding widget, you can write one more custom widget that can show the video widget. To do this, create the `CVideoTweet.js` class under `C:\teamtwitter\source\class\teamtwitter\ui`, and you can either extend the `CTweet` class or you can write your own widget from scratch.

    First, by yourself, try to create the custom widget, as per the following screen requirement, and update the class. Follow the custom widget creation, as we mentioned in step 2:

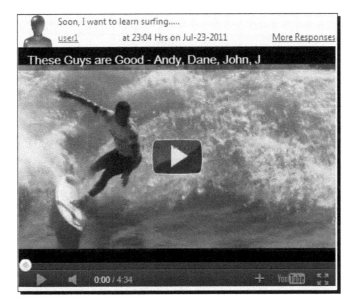

Just to give you a hint, a YouTube video widget can be added just by embedding the object code into an `Html` class, as mentioned in the following code snippet:

```
this.videoHTML = new qx.ui.embed.Html("");
control = this.videoHTML;
this._add(this.videoHTML, {row: 2, column : 0, colSpan : 4});
```

You can create the object code based on the YouTube sharing code, substitute the video ID that is entered by the user, and set it to the control, as mentioned in the following code snippet:

```
this.videoHTML.setHtml('<object width="425" height="315"><param
name="movie" value="http://www.youtube.com/v/' + value +
'?version=3&amp;hl=en_US"></param><param name="allowFullScreen"
value="true"></param><param name="allowscriptaccess"
value="always"></param><embed src="http://www.youtube.com/v/' +
value + '?version=3&amp;hl=en_US" type="application/x-shockwave-
flash" width="425" height="315" allowscriptaccess="always"
allowfullscreen="true"></embed></object>');
```

After you attempt this, compare your code with the `978-1-849513-70-8_05_10.txt` file under `Chapter 5`. If you miss anything, update your class by referring to this code.

4. Now, we need to display the tweets in a widget. Let's implement the `TweetsDisplayWidget` for that. We need to fetch the tweets based on the team, selected tags, selected users, and the tweet search text. For each tweet, either create a `CTweet` or a `CVideoTweet` widget, set the tweet information, and add it to the layout created in the previous chapter.

Update the `TweetsDisplayWidget.js` class under `C:\teamtwitter\source\class\teamtwitter\ui` to implement the `loadTweets` method.

Just to give you a hint, the following code checks one tweet and creates either the `CTweet` or `CVideoTweet` widget. You have to do the following for each tweet that you fetched:

```
var tweetData = result[i];

var tweet = null;
if (tweetData[4] != null && tweetData[4] != "") {
  tweet = new teamtwitter.ui.CVideoTweet();
  tweet.setVideoId(tweetData[4]);
} else {
  tweet = new teamtwitter.ui.CTweet();
}
```

```
tweet.setTwtData(tweetData[0]);
tweet.setUserName(tweetData[1]);
tweet.setTime(tweetData[2]);
tweet.setDate(tweetData[3]);
_this.add(tweet);
```

After you attempt this, compare your code with the `978-1-849513-70-8_05_11.txt` file under `Chapter 5`. If you miss anything, update your class by referring to this code file.

Generate the web application using the following command:

```
C:\teamtwitter-server>ant dist
```

Deploy the updated Team Twitter web application:

```
C:\teamtwitter-server>ant deploy
```

Good enough! Now, our application is ready. You can access your Team Twitter URL in the browser and enjoy tweeting across the team. Now try adding users, tags, and tweets.

What just happened?

We have learnt how to create custom widgets from the basic widgets, and we have created a couple of custom widgets for our Team Twitter application. This custom widget is reused many times in our application.

Inline widgets

Inline widgets are a kind of small qooxdoo application, which can be integrated in any of the existing HTML pages. Till now, we created standalone qooxdoo applications, whereas here we will try to use the qooxdoo inline applications inside the HTML-dominated pages.

When a portal has many classic HTML pages, migration of a whole portal into a standalone RIA application takes maximum time and development effort. So, in this kind of environment, inline applications are very useful.

An inline application can be created with the Python `create-application.py` tool with the `-t` attribute as `inline`. This tool is available inside the `tool` folder.

```
C:\qooxdoo-1.2-sdk\tool\bin> create-application.py -n <name> -t inline
```

Let's create a sample inline application, say `dateChooser`, using the following command:

```
C:\qooxdoo-1.2-sdk\tool\bin> create-application.py -n dateChooser -t inline
```

This command creates a sample application skeleton using an `Application` class, as shown in the following code snippet:

```
/**
 * This is the main application class of your custom application
"dateChooser"
 */
qx.Class.define("datechooser.Application",
{
  extend : qx.application.Inline,

  members :
  {
    /** This method contains the initial application code and gets
called during startup of the application
     * @lint ignoreDeprecated(alert)
     */
    main : function() {
      // Call super class
      this.base(arguments);

      // Enable logging in debug variant
      if (qx.core.Variant.isSet("qx.debug", "on"))  {
        // support native logging capabilities, e.g. Firebug for
Firefox qx.log.appender.Native;
        // support additional cross-browser console. Press F7 to
toggle visibility qx.log.appender.Console;
      }
      /*
        Here is the actual application code...
      */
    }
  }
});
```

A user can integrate the qooxdoo widget either by positioning absolutely at a pixel or by adding the widget in the page flow using an existing **Document Object Model (DOM)** node (just like a `div` tag), where these DOM nodes act as islands for the qooxdoo widgets.

The code for absolute positioning is as follows:

```
// add a date chooser widget
var dateChooser = new qx.ui.control.DateChooser();
// add the date chooser widget to the page
this.getRoot().add(dateChooser, { left : 100, top : 100 });
```

The code for positioning at a DOM node is as follows:

```
// create the island by connecting it to the existing
// "dateChooser" DOM element of your HTML page.
// Typically this is a DIV as in <div id="dateChooser"></div>
var dateChooserIsle = new qx.ui.root.Inline(document.
getElementById("dateChooser"));
// create the date chooser widget and add it to the inline widget
(=island)
var dateChooser = new qx.ui.control.DateChooser();
dateChooserIsle.add(dateChooser);
```

The skeleton look on compiling is shown in the following screenshot:

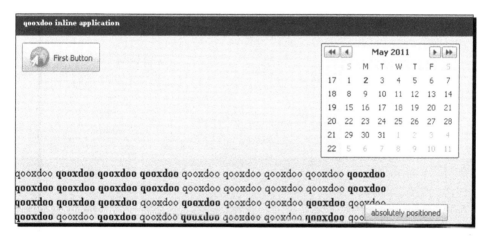

We have learnt how to create inline widgets in qooxdoo and how to add them to the
HTML pages.

The table widget

The `table` widget allows you to display the records in rows and columns. Each row is a record and all the columns in a row are the properties of that record. For example, you can display the list of employee records in a table. qooxdoo provides many classes to provide functionalities such as store the table data, render the cell, edit the cell, and so on.

All the table-related classes are under the package `qx.ui.table`. The class hierarchy of the `table` classes is as follows:

Class hierarchy

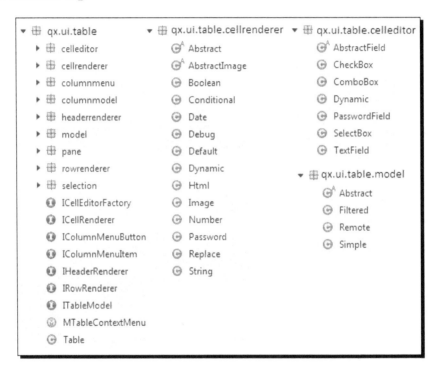

The `qx.ui.table.Table` class is the `table` widget class. By default, all the cells are rendered as text initially when the table is displayed, and on double-clicking a cell, the cell value goes into edit mode if it is allowed to edit, and the default cell editor is the `TextField` widget. The `qx.ui.table.cellrenderer` package provides various renderers for the cell and the default cell renderer is `qx.ui.table.cellrenderer.Default`. Only if you want to change the default cell renderer to a custom renderer, such as `Image` or `Date` for a cell, can you create an instance of one of these renderers and set it as a cell renderer for that cell.

Similarly, the `qx.ui.table.celleditor` package provides various editors for the cell and the default cell editor is `qx.ui.table.celleditor.TextField`. Only if you want to change the default cell editor to a custom renderer such as `CheckBox`, or `ComboBox` for a cell, can you create an instance of one of these editors and set it as the editor for that cell. The `qx.ui.table.rowrenderer.Default` renders alternate rows in two different colors. You can restrict the row selection to a single row selection or to a set of continuous rows or multiple sets of rows with intervals. This is set through the options in the `qx.ui.table.selection.Model` class.

qooxdoo allows you to control the cell editing options at each column level and, by default, all columns are not editable. qooxdoo supports sorting on the columns, based on the records in the table model and, by default, all the columns are enabled for sorting. The table model is used to store the table data. The `qx.ui.table.model` package provides various table models and the most-used and normal table model is `qx.ui.table.model.Simple`.

Table construction

The following code snippet demonstrates the creation of the table model, setting the column options, creation of the table, and customization of column rendering:

```
// get the data for the table
var rowData = this.getRecords();

// create the table model, set the data, and set the column options
var tableModel = this._tableModel = new qx.ui.table.model.Simple();
tableModel.setColumns([ "Employee ID", "Bonus", "Joining Date",
"Trainee" ]);
tableModel.setData(rowData);
tableModel.setColumnEditable(1, true);
tableModel.setColumnEditable(2, true);
tableModel.setColumnSortable(3, false);

// create the table and set the table model
var table = new qx.ui.table.Table(tableModel);
table.set({
width: 600,
height: 400,
  decorator : null
  });

//allow multiple row selection
table.getSelectionModel().setSelectionMode(
qx.ui.table.selection.Model.MULTIPLE_INTERVAL_SELECTION);
```

```
//customize the column rendering
var tcm = table.getTableColumnModel();
// Display a checkbox cell renderer in column 3
tcm.setDataCellRenderer(3, new qx.ui.table.cellrenderer.Boolean());

// Display icon in the header using header renderer for column 2
tcm.setHeaderCellRenderer(2, new        qx.ui.table.headerrenderer.
Icon("icon/16/apps/office-calendar.png", "Joining Date"));
```

In the preceding code, we have allowed editing for the columns 1 and 2, and we have disabled sorting on column 3. We have set the selection of multiple sets of rows with intervals. We have set the checkbox renderer for column 3 and icon for the column 2 header.

The GUI look for the preceding code is as follows:

Employee ID	Bonus	Joining Date	Trainee	
83	985,505.46	12/8/10	☐	
81	957,390.69	1/8/11	☐	
52	907,006.8	1/26/11	☐	
13	900,631.72	3/6/11	☑	
49	899,186.41	3/6/11	☑	
91	803,942.81	12/25/10	☑	
39	801,633.32	3/19/11	☑	

100 rows

Remote table model

A simple table model stores all the records in the model class and renders only the visible records, based on the available space for the table and the position of the scroll bar. If the number of records is huge, retrieving all the data at a time and loading all the data in the table model takes time and it is not a good idea. To handle the huge data with good performance, either you could use the pagination technique to display one page at a time or retrieve the data on demand as you scroll. To support the second option, qooxdoo provides the RemoteTableModel class. This table model class loads only the data that has to be displayed and the data nearer to that displayed data. On the scroll action, the required set of data is retrieved asynchronously in the background and displayed in the table. The old data that was used most recently is unloaded as the cache in the table model gets filled.

Features of the remote table model are as follows. It:

◆ Allows editing and sorting of cells at the column level

◆ Allows various row selection options

◆ Supports customization of cell and header rendering

◆ Supports different table models including the `RemoteTableModel` class allowing the hiding and showing of the columns in the table

We have learnt about the `table` widget, the related classes for rendering and editing the cells, and model classes for storing the table data. We have learnt how to construct the table widget using the classes in the `qx.ui.table` package.

The tree widget

The `tree` widget allows the display of the hierarchical structure. The first item is a root element. A user can add multiple folders or files, and a folder can again contain multiple folders or files, similar to the root node. Each and every folder or a file is termed as a node. Expanding and collapsing of these nodes is handled automatically, and the `tree` widget gives flexibility to do some activities on expanding and collapsing by firing events such as `changeOpen`, `changeOpenSymbolMode`, and `changeModel` events on the node (`TreeFolder`).

Class hierarchy

All the tree-related classes are under the `qx.ui.tree` package. The following screenshot displays the class hierarchy of the tree classes:

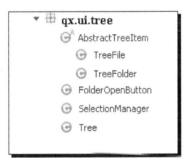

The tree-related classes are:

◆ `qx.ui.tree.Tree`: This is the class for constructing a visual tree structure

◆ `qx.ui.tree.TreeFolder`: This is the class used for creating a folder node

◆ `qx.ui.tree.TreeFile`: This is the class used for creating leaf nodes

The API classes used to create a tree can be easily understood with the following **Unified Modeling Language (UML)** diagram:

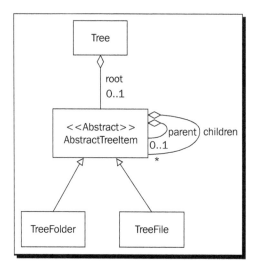

Tree construction

The following steps describe how to construct a tree:

1. Create a tree reference:

   ```
   var tree = new qx.ui.tree.Tree();
   ```

2. Create the `TreeFolder` node and set this as the root node for the tree:

   ```
   var root = new qx.ui.tree.TreeFolder("root");
   tree.setRoot(root);
   ```

3. Create the child nodes, either by using `TreeFolder` or `TreeFile` and add them to the root node in a hierarchy:

   ```
   // creating folder children
   var ch1 = new qx.ui.tree.TreeFolder("Folder1");
   var ch2 = new qx.ui.tree.TreeFolder("Folder2");

   // Create leaf nodes
   var ch1_1 = new qx.ui.tree.TreeFile("File1");
   var ch1_2 = new qx.ui.tree.TreeFile("File2");
   ch1.add(ch1_1, ch1_2);

   // add children to root node
   root.add(ch1, ch2);
   ```

4. Add the tree into a container:

```
this.getRoot().add(tree);
```

The GUI look for the preceding code is as follows:

We have learnt about the `tree` widget and the tree-related classes and learnt to create the `tree` widget. We have also learnt how to construct the `tree` widget by using the classes in the `qx.ui.tree` package.

The treevirtual widget

The `treevirtual` widget allows you to create a virtual tree that looks like a tree and provides the table features to store the data in columns, dynamically filling the tree with contents.

Class hierarchy

All the virtual tree-related classes are under the package `qx.ui.treevirtual`. The following screenshot displays the class hierarchy of the classes under the `treevirtual` widget:

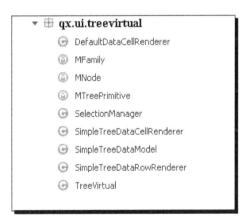

The `TreeVirtual` class also provides most of the implementations for the events such as `treeClose`, `treeOpenWhileEmpty`, `treeOpenWithContent`, and so on, and most of the methods to access data in terms of the tree are added into the class by adding mixins such as `qx.ui.treevirtual.MNode` and `qx.ui.treevirtual.MFamily`.

This widget is very useful when the user is displaying hierarchical data to show in columns, for example, to show the filesystem tree. If the user is interested in showing the file permissions and last updated time for the files, then each row needs two more columns. To have a clear understanding of this widget, check the sample code and the diagram in the following section.

TreeVirtual construction

The following steps describe how to construct a virtual tree:

1. Create a virtual tree reference with the columns defined:

   ```
   // tree
   var tree = new qx.ui.treevirtual.TreeVirtual(
     [
       "Tree",
       "Permissions",
       "Last Accessed"
     ]);
   ```

2. Retrieve the data model to create the folder (branch) or file (leaf) nodes:

   ```
   var dataModel = tree.getDataModel();
   ```

3. Add a root branch, use the `addBranch` on the data model, and specify the parent node as null to add as a root node:

   ```
   var te1 = dataModel.addBranch(null, "Desktop", true);
   ```

4. Create child nodes either as branches or leaf nodes and add them to the root node in a hierarchy:

   ```
   // creating a branch children
   te1_1 = dataModel.addBranch(te1, "Workspace", true);
   // creating a leaf node
   var te = dataModel.addLeaf(te1_1, "Windows (C:)");
   ```

5. Set the column data:

   ```
   dataModel.setColumnData(te, 1, "-rwxr-xr-x");
   dataModel.setColumnData(te, 2, "2007-01-30 22:54:03");
   ```

6. Call a `setData()` method on `datamodel`.

   `dataModel.setData();`

7. Add the tree into the container

   `this.getRoot().add(tree);`

The GUI look for the preceding code is as follows:

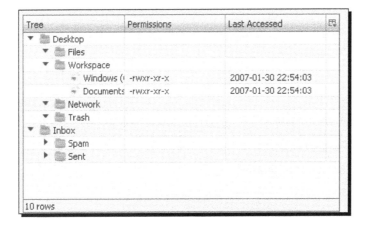

We have learnt about the `treevirtual` widget and the use of this widget. We have learnt how to construct the `treevirtual` widget by using the classes under the `qx.ui.treevirtual` package.

Pop quiz

1. Widgets layout can be modified

    a. True

    b. False

2. qooxdoo supports rich text in label, only if the rich property is set to true

    a. True

    b. False

3. To create a custom widget, the user class

    a. Should extend `qx.ui.Widget` only

    b. Can extend any of the predefined widgets

    c. Should implement `qx.ui.form.IForm`

4. Type of widgets that allow embedding inside of a normal HTML page

   a. Basic widgets

   b. Special widgets

   c. Inline widgets

   d. Custom widgets

5. Widgets useful for taking input in a numeric range

   a. Spinner

   b. TextField

   c. Slider

   d. a and c

   e. all of the above

6. qooxdoo widgets are

   a. Browser compatible

   b. Have mouse and keyboard support

   c. Auto-sizing

   d. Event mechanism

   e. All the above

   f. None

7. Which widget is useful to show inline help when a user points to the widget

   a. Popup

   b. ToolTip

   c. Status

   d. Label

8. Which widget is useful to show a list of data and allows a user to select multiple items

   a. List

   b. ComboBox

   c. SelectBox

   d. table

9. Which widget is better to use for displaying hierarchical data

    a. tree

    b. treevirtual

    c. table

    d. List

10. qooxdoo allows controlling cell editing options at _____ level

    a. Column

    b. Cell

    c. Row

    d. Table

11. The default cell editor for a cell in the table is

    a. qx.ui.table.celleditor

    b. qx.ui.table.celleditor.boolean

    c. qx.ui.table.celleditor.textfield

    d. qx.ui.table.celleditor.dynamic

12. To display rows in different colors, a renderer should be added at the _____ level

    a. Column

    b. Cell

    c. Row

    d. Table

13. To allow a user to select multiple choices for a question, you should use

    a. Radio buttons

    b. Radio buttons in a RadioGroup

    c. Radio buttons in RadioButtonGroup

    d. multiple checkboxes

14. If you want to allow the user to either select or enter text, you should use

    a. SelectBox

    b. ComboBox

    c. list

    d. TextField

Summary

In the previous chapters, we learnt more about qooxdoo framework support, various features, basic class hierarchy, different layout managers, containers, and so on. In this chapter, we explored the qooxdoo widgets.

In particular, we:

- Got an idea about the different types of widgets available in the qooxdoo framework
- Learnt about various basic widgets such as `Label`, `Image`, and `Atom`
- Explored the form widgets and the form API
- Learnt how to create a custom widget
- Learnt more widgets such as `tree`, `table`, and so on and the controls such as `ColorPopup`, `DateChooser`, and so on
- Learnt how to make use of special widgets to add rich functionalities to the application

We have applied the learning from this chapter in our Team Twitter application. We created a new sign up form and created a custom widget to show tweet information. Now, we have knowledge about most of the qooxdoo-provided widgets and their usage.

In the next chapter, we will explore more on form handling, creating simple forms, and validating form data and the most advanced features like pooling, data binding, and so on.

6
Working with Forms and Data

In simple words, the qooxdoo framework makes form handling as simple and as generic as possible.

The qooxdoo framework provides multiple components right from retrieving the data to displaying the information on the screen. With the use of object orientation, the qooxdoo framework separates the functionalities into multiple components such as data store, model, data controller, and view.

In *Chapter 4, Working with Layouts and Menus*, we learnt how to choose the layout manager and how to pick the container for a screen requirement in the application. In *Chapter 5, Working with Widgets*, we went through different widgets and their respective classes. We learnt how to create various widgets based on their purposes and how to use them. We understood the widget's class hierarchy in the `qx.ui.form` package. Altogether, in the previous two chapters, we learnt most of the basic graphical user interface development.

In this chapter, we will learn the built-in capabilities that the qooxdoo framework provides for the form and data handling. These features are really useful for the applications and they are readily available in the framework. It saves lot of time in the application development.

This chapter mainly concentrates on retrieving the data from the data store, storing the data in the model, updating the information in the view (widget) using the controller, validating the user entered data, resetting the form, and so on. We will also learn how to pool the widgets in qooxdoo framework. With pooling, you can create the widget once and reuse it.

By binding a widget to another widget, on changing first widget's value, the qooxdoo framework keeps the other widget visually updated always and reduces maximum efforts of the developers. You do not have to code to do activities such as registering an event for one widget, retrieving the value on the change event, and updating the value on the other widget. All these activities are performed automatically by the qooxdoo framework if you bind these two widgets. This feature is known as **data binding**.

In this chapter, we will concentrate on the following topics:

- Form handling—covers validation, resetting, and rendering
- Object pooling
- Data binding—covers model, controllers, and stores

Form handling

Let's step into the `qx.ui.form` package again to know more on the easier ways to reset the form, validate all the widgets on a single call or instantaneously upon changing focus out of the widget, and render a form.

We have already learnt how to create the form widgets and render them in the layout. Now, we will validate the introductory statement "qooxdoo framework makes form handling as simple and as generic as possible". qooxdoo provides a class, `qx.ui.form.Form`, to support this functionality. The generic activities that qooxdoo provides for the form objects are:

- Validation
- Resetting
- Rendering or handling form layout
- Serialization

Validation

Once a user entered the values into the input widgets of the form, the data should be validated before saving it. The qooxdoo framework provides the best ways to do this and highlights the widgets that have invalid user-entered values, clearly by making the borders red.

The qooxdoo framework provides the `qx.ui.form.validation.Manager` class for this feature. The methods and events available in this class are divided into three groups. They are as follows:

♦ **Validation**: The methods and events available for validation are:

- ❑ `getValid()/isValid()`: This method returns the valid state of the manager.

- ❑ `validate()`: This method initiates the validation.

- ❑ `validator`: This is a property to store the `validator`. To validate synchronously, you can set a function reference and to validate asynchronously, you can set an instance of `qx.ui.form.validation.AsyncValidator`. The default value is `null`.

- ❑ `complete`: It is an event, invoked on completion of the validations for all the items.

- ❑ `changeValid`: It is an event, invoked on change of the valid state of form.

♦ **Form item management**: The method under this group is `add(formItem, validator, context)`, which adds a form item, corresponding validator, and the context of the validator.

The form item should handle any invalid state and it should have an invalid message, which is displayed if the user-entered value is invalid. Manager requires access to the value of the form item. So, a value property should exist for the form item. In brief, a form item has to implement the following interfaces:

- ❑ `qx.ui.form.IForm`

- ❑ One of following interfaces:

    - ❑ `qx.ui.form.IBooleanForm`

    - ❑ `qx.ui.form.IColorForm`

    - ❑ `qx.ui.form.INumberForm`

    - ❑ `qx.ui.form.IDateForm`

    - ❑ `qx.ui.form.IStringForm`

The validator function can be specified in the `validator` parameter whereas `context` is an optional argument whose default value is `null`.

`Reset()` is another method under this group. It resets all the form items.

♦ **Invalid messages**: The method and property under this group are as follows:

- ❏ `getInvalidMessages()`: This method returns all the invalid messages in an array

- ❏ `invalidMessage`: This property says why a form validation failed

In the previous chapter, we went through various form items. You can add most of the form items into the validation manager as most of them implement at least two interfaces, which matches the earlier-mentioned criteria. So, we understood everything that is required for a validation manager to validate. Now, let's learn how to write code for the validators.

In general, there are two different approaches in validation. The first approach is a client-side validation, which is synchronous, mostly. On the other hand, a server-side validation is asynchronous, in most cases.

Synchronous

Most of the client-side validations are done synchronously, for example, validating a field across common formats such as e-mail address, regular expressions, numeric or only character types, IP addresses (`127.0.0.1`), and non-empty fields.

♦ **Required field check**: Validation against an empty field is nothing but checking that a field is required. In qooxdoo, this is very easy. Just define the form item as a required field and add that to the validation manager, as shown in the following code snippet. The validation manager will take all the necessary steps to mark the field as invalid as soon as the validate method is invoked, if the text field is empty:

```
var manager = new qx.ui.form.validation.Manager();
var textfield = new qx.ui.form.TextField();
textfield.setRequired(true);
manager.add(textfield);
```

A sample GUI screen, expecting a URL is as follows:

♦ **Default validator**: Similar to the required field check, qooxdoo provides few default validators for specific input types such as e-mail address, data type check, URLs or regular expression, and so on. All the default validators are predefined as static utility functions under the `qx.util.Validate` class.

The following code snippet demonstrates how to use the default validators available in the `Validate` class:

```
Manager.add(textfield, qx.util.Validate.url());
```

Different validator functions available in the `qx.util.Validate` class are:

- ❑ `email()`: Validates an e-mail address
- ❑ `number()`: Validates a number
- ❑ `string()`: Validates a string
- ❑ `url()`: Validates a URL
- ❑ `inArray()`: Validates that the value is in the specified array
- ❑ `regExp()`: Validates the given regular expression

qooxdoo also allows developers to write their own functions for validation, as per the requirement.

◆ **Custom validator**: A custom validator is nothing but a function returning a Boolean value; either `true` or `false` based on the value check or it can throw a validation error containing a message to display as the invalid message. If the function throws a validation error, the invalid message will be displayed for the respective field. In case the function returns a Boolean value, `true` indicates that there is no validation error and `false` indicates that there is a validation error and displays the invalid message set for that field. You can also set the invalid message upfront in the `initLayout` when you create the field and just return the `true` or `false` value in the validator. qooxdoo displays the invalid message that is already set for that field. The validator function should have the arguments as `value` and `item` in the same order. The following code snippet illustrates the sample validator method:

```
myValidator : function(value, item) {
  if(<condition>){
    item.setInvalidMessage("invalid data");"
    return false;
  }
// or
  if( <condition>){
    throw new qx.core.ValidationError("invalid data");
  }
  return true;
}
// adding above function as validator for textfield.
manager.add(textfield, this.myValidator);
```

Asynchronous

An asynchronous request doesn't keep the user in the waiting state until the request is processed and replied. When a developer doesn't want the application to wait until the validation of the particular item or widget completes, the developer can write the validation to occur asynchronously. A subclass instance of `qx.ui.form.validation. AsyncValidator` is an asynchronous validator. The only difference in coding to the synchronous case is the wrapping of validator function in an `AsyncValidator`.

The following code snippet demonstrates an asynchronous validation:

```
manager.add(textField, new qx.ui.form.validation.AsyncValidator(
function(validator, value) {
    // here comes the async call
    window.setTimeout(function() {
    // callback the async validation
    validator.setValid(false);
  }, 1000);
}
));
```

Take a look at the following sequence diagram to get an insight on how the asynchronous validation is handled:

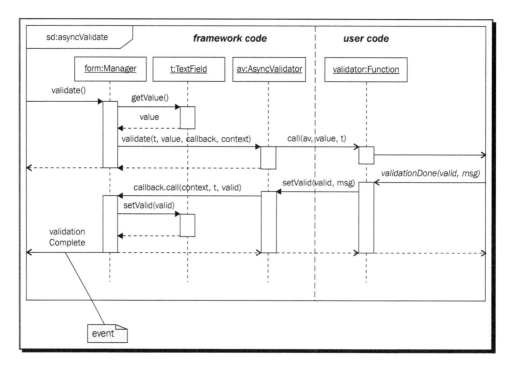

On invoking the `validate()` method, the manager calls the validator of each form item. Once this validation is completed, the manager fires the `validationComplete` event. The whole sequence goes, as shown in the preceding sequence diagram.

Till now, all the validators validate a single item in its own context. In a situation where we need to validate multiple items for mutually depending data, the validator can be set to the manager itself. This validator function should take the items array as an argument as we will be using in the Team Twitter application in the following *Time for action – enhancing the UserSignUpForm* section in this chapter.

Resetting

The resetting feature makes it easier to reset all the form items in a single method call. This resets all the form items to its initial values. This is more helpful when we are reusing the form. We can create the form once, use it, and then pool it for future use (the concept of pooling is explained in the *Object pooling* section). Whenever we get the object from the pool and display it, we need to reinitialize the whole form. This can be done in a single method call.

The qooxdoo framework provides the `qx.ui.form.Resetter` class for this feature. The `Resetter` class is very simple and it can handle all form items supplying a value property and all widgets implementing the single selection-linked list or select box.

The methods available in the `Resetter` class are:

◆ `add(item)`: Adds the item to the list of items by storing the current value of the item as the resetting value

◆ `redefine()`: Redefines the resetting values of all the items with their latest values

◆ `reset()`: Resets all the items with their stored reset values

◆ `redefineItem(item)`/`resetItem(Item)`: Redefines or resets the individual item

The following code snippet demonstrates resetting the form items on clicking the **Reset** button:

```
// create a textfield
var textField = new qx.ui.form.TextField("acb");
// create a checkbox
var checkBox = new qx.ui.form.CheckBox("box");
// create a list
var list = new qx.ui.form.List();
list.add(new qx.ui.form.ListItem("a"));
list.add(new qx.ui.form.ListItem("b"));
list.setSelection([list.getSelectables()[0]]);
```

```
// create the resetter
var resetter = new qx.ui.form.Resetter();
// add the form items
resetter.add(textField);
resetter.add(checkBox);
resetter.add(list);
// add a reset button
var resetButton = new qx.ui.form.Button("Reset");
resetButton.addListener("execute", function() {
resetter.reset();
});
```

The qooxdoo Form class, `qx.ui.form.Form`, also takes advantage of the `qx.ui.form.Resetter` class and reduces the developers' efforts further. You don't have to create an instance of the `Resetter` class and add form items into it separately. You just have to create the form instance, which will provide all the generic activities. We'll see this in the code snippet from our Team Twitter application. This will be demonstrated at the end of this section.

Rendering

The qooxdoo framework provides renderers, which give additional functionalities in addition to the basic layouts for the forms. You can use these renderers for the forms instead of building the form using multiple layout managers. These renderers add a group of widgets at once with a title instead of adding them one-by-one. You can add the related widgets grouped together with a title. All the classes related to the renderer are in the `qx.ui.form.renderer` package:

The class hierarchy of the renderers is shown in the following diagram:

qooxdoo provides an interface, `qx.ui.form.renderer.IFormRenderer`, which has the following methods:

♦ `addItems(items : qx.ui.form.IForm[], names : String[], title : String) : void`: This method adds a group of form items with the corresponding names. The names are displayed as hints for the user telling them what to do with the form item. The title is optional and can be used as grouping for the given form items.

♦ `addButton(button : qx.ui.form.Button) : void`: This method adds a button into the form layout.

qooxdoo framework provides three different implementations for the `IFormRenderer` interface, namely, single column, double column, and single column with placeholder. Let's see each one of them in brief.

Single column

The single column renderer defines the vertical layout and renders the label and corresponding input widgets in a row. While displaying a label, it adds a colon at the end of every label and adds an asterisk to every required field-related label.

The `qx.ui.form.renderer.Single` class is used by default, which is inherited from the `AbstractRenderer` class, where this `AbstractRenderer` class takes the form object from the constructor and configures it by itself. So if you need to set some additional information on your renderer before adding the widgets, be sure to do that before calling `this.base(arguments, form)`.

Using this single column renderer is very easy; just create the form, add all the items to the form, pass this form into the renderer, and add the renderer object to the panel:

```
// create the form and add it to the document
var formView = new qx.ui.form.renderer.Single(form);
this.add(formView);
```

Double column

The double column renderer has the same features as the already-introduced single column renderer, but renders the form items in two columns. The class defined for this purpose is `qx.ui.form.renderer.Double`.

Using the double renderer is very similar to the single renderer and is illustrated in the following code snippet:

```
// create the form and add it to the document
var formView = new qx.ui.form.renderer.Double(form);
this.add(formView);
```

Single column with placeholder

The single column with placeholder renderer displays the input fields in a single column and in addition to that, it displays the placeholder in the input widgets. These placeholders act as hints on the input fields. The class defined for this purpose is `qx.ui.form.renderer.SinglePlaceHolder`.

This class is more of a demonstration class to show how easily you can implement your own renderer. The only limitation with this renderer is that it doesn't support all the fields but supports adding the fields with the placeholder property.

The following code snippet demonstrates the use of the single column with the placeholder renderer:

```
// create the form and add it to the document
var formView = new qx.ui.form.renderer.SinglePlaceHolder(form);
this.add(formView);
```

Serialization

User-entered data is serialized before it is sent across the network to the server. The qooxdoo framework ensures that it works well with form widgets and corresponding data binding components. First, the values are retrieved from the widgets and set into the model and then the model is serialized. In qooxdoo, you don't have to create separate model classes for each form. Serializing the form data is very simple. Let's go through the following steps to achieve this:

1. Create form widgets, as shown in the following code snippet:

```
// create the ui
var name = new qx.ui.form.TextField();
var password = new qx.ui.form.PasswordField();
```

2. Create the model object, as shown in the following code snippet:

```
// create the model
var model = qx.data.marshal.Json.createModel({name: "a", password: "b"});
```

3. Create the form controller and bind the form widgets' data to the model (we will go through the form controller in detail in the *Data controller* section):

```
// create the controller and connect the form items
var controller = new qx.data.controller.Object(model);
controller.addTarget(name, "value", "name", true);
controller.addTarget(password, "value", "password", true);
```

4. Serialize the data as follows:

```
// serialize
qx.util.Serializer.toUriParameter(model);
```

The final result is `name=a` and `password=b`, as the initial values of the model are a and b.

Time for action – enhancing the UserSignUpForm

1. Let's apply the concepts of form handling in one of the widgets (`UserSignUpForm`) of the Team Twitter application. You will come to know how easily you can develop forms and how effective the form features are. Update the `UserSignUpForm.js` class under `C:\teamtwitter\source\teamtwitter\ui` and use the form features instead of doing everything, such as rendering, validating, and so on, by yourself.

   Add the elements of the widget into the form instead of adding it through a grid layout. The following code snippet gives you a hint on the creation of the form and addition of elements to it:

```
var form = new qx.ui.form.Form();
form.addGroupHeader(this.tr("User Info"));
var userNameField = new qx.ui.form.TextField();
userNameField.setRequired(true);
form.add(userNameField, this.tr("User Name"));
var emailField = new qx.ui.form.TextField();
emailField.setRequired(true);
form.add(emailField, this.tr("Email"), qx.util.Validate.email());

// Similarly add all the widgets in to the form
// _____
```

   Once you add the elements into the form, set the single or double renderer. As per the `UserSignUpForm` widget requirement, we need to render the elements in two columns, each column should display a label and the respective field. So, we can use the double renderer.

The following code snippet creates the double renderer for the form and adds the renderer to the layout of the widget.

```
var formView = new qx.ui.form.renderer.Double(form);
this.add(formView);
```

Our form is ready with all the fields. Now, we can perform the validations on the fields.

2. Let's add validation to our Team Twitter signup form. The possible validations include checking that the password and confirm password values are the same, the date field is a valid date, the e-mail is valid, and the mobile number is a numeric value. You don't have to create the validation manager and add all the fields. Form already has the validation manager and adds all the form fields into the validated manager. You just have to set the context and the validator method.

Update the `UserSignUpForm.js` class under `C:\teamtwitter\source\teamtwitter\ui` for the validation, as shown in the following code snippet:

```
_initLayout : function() {
  // ..... after adding all fields into the form
  // set the validator method for the form
  var manager = form.getValidationManager();
  manager.setContext(this);
  manager.setValidator(this.formValidator);
  // .....
},


formValidator : function(items){
  if(items[2].getValue() != items[3].getValue()){
    items[3].setValid(false);
    items[3].setInvalidMessage(this.tr("Not matching with password
Field. Re enter"));
    return false;
  }
  return true;
}
```

3. Perform the validation on the click event for the **Register** button.

Use the following code snippet inside the register button's execute button listener.

```
manager.validate();
if(manager.isValid()) {

  // make an rpc call to store the user information into db.
}
```

4. Let's implement the `execute` listener method for the **Reset** button. You don't have to create an instance of the `Resetter` class. The form already has the `Resetter` instance and adds all the form fields into the `Resetter`. All you have to do is invoke `form.reset()`, when you want to reset.

Use the following code snippet to reset the form:

```
resetBtn.addListener("execute", function(){
  form.reset();
});
```

5. Build and view the signup form. You can test and verify the data validation.

A form with invalid data shows the data validation error message, as shown in the following screenshot:

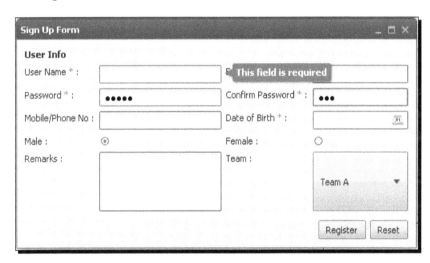

After you attempt this, you can refer the code provided in the `978-1-849513-70-8_06_01.txt` file under `Chapter 6` available with the support files for this book. This code file uses some more features, which will be explained in the *Time for action – enhancing the UserSignUpForm* again section.

What just happened?

We got to know the features provided by the qooxdoo framework for form handling such as validation, resetting, and rendering. With all these features, we can build robust applications in a short time. We refactored the `UserSignUpForm` widget by using the `Form` class and the form features that we learnt.

Object pooling

Object pooling is the concept of reusing the created instances instead of destroying and recreating. Object creation and laying out the screen is a slightly time consuming process. To improve the performance of our application, you can pool the created instances, layouts, and so on, and reuse the pooled objects whenever you need them again. This minimizes the amount of browser memory usage by reusing window instances after they have been closed. However, it could equally be used to pool instances of any `Object` type (except singletons).

It is the client's responsibility to ensure that the pooled objects are not referenced or used from anywhere else in the application.

In qooxdoo, pooling objects is very simple and can be done with the `qx.util.ObjectPool` class. This class provides different methods, which are listed as follows:

- `poolObject(Object obj)`: This method places an object in a pool of objects of its type.
- `getObject(clazz)`: Returns an existing instance of the required class type in the pool. If the instance is not available, a new instance will be created, pooled, and this method will return the newly-created object.

Note that once an instance has been pooled, there are no means to get that exact instance back. The instance may be discarded for garbage collection if the pool of its type is already full. It is assumed that no other references exist to this object, and that it will not be used at all while it is pooled.

Size is an integer property to represent the number of objects for each class that is pooled. The default value for this is `null`, which means infinity. The `setSize()`, `getSize()`, `resetSize()`, and `initSize()` methods are available to access this property.

We got to know the concept of object pooling in the qooxdoo framework. This can be used to improve the performance of the application if certain widgets are repeatedly used at different places.

Data binding

Data binding is a functionality that allows connecting data from a source to a target. qooxdoo provides the best and simplest ways to transfer data between the server and the client. The entire topic can be divided into a low-level part, called **single value binding**, and some higher-level concepts involving stores and controllers.

Data binding includes five major components and is best summarized by the following diagram:

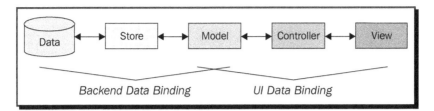

- ◆ **Data**: This part is nothing but the raw data and can be a plain local file, database data, a regular web server, or even a web service. All sources of data are possible, depending on the implementation of the actual store.

- ◆ **Store**: The store component is responsible for fetching the data from its source and for including it into a data model of an application. Framework provides a JSON store, which creates the data into a JSON format, which we will go through in detail in the *Data store* section in this chapter. Most of these concepts are defined in two packages, namely, `qx.data.store` and `qx.data.marshal`.

- ◆ **Model**: This model holds data and acts as an integration point between store and controller. Almost all models are plain qooxdoo classes holding the data in properties, which are configured to fire events on every change. But there is no need to manually write our own model classes for every data source you want to work with. The stores provide a smart way to automatically create these classes during runtime.

- ◆ **Controller**: The main task of the controller components is to connect the data in the model to the view components (widgets). This controller actually binds the data with the widgets. The qooxdoo framework provides different controllers for object, form, list, and tree under the `qx.data.controller` package.

- ◆ **View**: The view component is a widget in qooxdoo terms and it can be any one among the big list of qooxdoo widgets, depending on the type of controller. qooxdoo's data binding is not limited to some predefined data bound widgets.

The class hierarchy for the data binding is shown in the following screenshot:

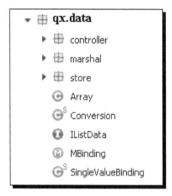

The qx.data.Array class is a complementary array class, defined for data binding purposes. This class mainly fires events when items are added or removed. This class implements IListdata, where IListdata defines a minimum of functionality with which the controllers need to work.

The first and foremost basic concept is single value binding.

Single value binding

The single value binding feature connects one property to another by binding or tying the properties together. The only requirement is that the property should fire an event on every value change. So, on every value change, the new value will be assigned to the tied property. qooxdoo's single value binding feature simplifies the whole implementation of adding a listener for the original property, and changing the tied property inside the listener. Instead, just use a bind() method on the widget.

The connection is always in one direction, and still the reverse is also possible by creating one more binding. But the developer has to take care to not form the loops. This is the basic concept of all the controllers.

For achieving this binding, we need source, source property, target, and target property. All these are the inputs for our bind() method, available in the qx.data. SingleValueBinding class and the method is of the static type. So, a user can call the method directly with the following class name:

```
qx.data.SingleValueBinding.bind (Object: source, String: source
property, Object: target, String: target property, map: options);
```

But single value binding has a limitation, too. Both properties should have the qooxdoo getter and setter methods, as usual. The source property also needs to fire change events on every change of its value.

For the best usability, the `bind()` method is defined in the `qx.core.Object` class, which is the base class for all qooxdoo classes. This bind method again calls the same static bind method, defined in the `SingleValueBinding` class, by specifying the source object as `this`.

Property binding

By default, every property in a class will have the getter and setter methods. So, these can be directly binded, and are shown clearly in the following code snippet:

```
var label1 = new qx.ui.basic.Label();
var label2 = new qx.ui.basic.Label();
label1.bind("value", label2, "value");
```

In the preceding code snippet, every change of the value property of `lable1` will automatically synchronize the value property of `lable2`.

Event binding

One can bind a data event with a property, as shown in the following code snippet, and the method call is completely similar to the property binding. The only change is, instead of the source property name, the developer has to give the event name.

```
var textField = new qx.ui.form.TextField();
var label = new qx.ui.basic.Label();
textField.bind("input", label, "value");
```

In the preceding code snippet, when the user enters some characters in the text field, these characters can be viewed in the label, too.

Hierarchical data binding

It is also possible to bind the hierarchy of properties as a source. The parent child relationship in the hierarchy is denoted by a dot in the property chain. For example, If object a has a `child` property, which references to object b, then object b has a string property named `abc` and the `abc` property has to be tied to another property. It should be done as shown in the following code snippet:

```
qx.data.SingleValueBinding.bind(a, "child.abc", textfield, "value");
```

Array binding

This is possible only with the qooxdoo array, which is defined under the `qx.data.Array` data package. Let's bind array elements with a label's content:

```
// bind the first array element to a label's value
a.bind("array[0]", labelFirst, "value");
// bind the last array element to a label's value
a.bind("array[last]", labelFirst, "value");
```

One can use any numeric value in the brackets or the string value `last` which maps to `length-1`. Till now, we have seen different possible sources to bind to a target. Also, we have some options to set while binding—to validate and to convert to some other format.

Options map

The options map is a `Map` object; with three valid keys that refer to three callback functions to perform some operations such as conversion, validation, and so on:

- `converter`: Converts the value to a user-defined format. This converter is a function with two arguments, one is the data to convert and another is the corresponding model object. This model object is available only when the controller is used. The function should look as follows:

```
function (data, modelObj){
    // do some thing…….
    return convertedData;
}
```

- `onUpdate`: This is a callback function called upon a successful update on the `target` object. The function takes three parameters and the function should look as follows:

```
function (source, target, data){
    // do some thing…….
}
```

- `onSetFail`: This function gets called upon the update's failure.

```
function (e) {
    // function on fail
}
```

Including this `bind` method, the `SingleValueBinding` class has many more managing and logging methods. They are as follows:

- `getAllBindings()` returns all the bindings in a map
- `getAllBindingsForObject(sourceObject)` returns all the binding to the source object

- ◆ removeAllBindings() removes all the bindings in the application
- ◆ removeAllBindingsForObject(object) removes all the bindings of the object given
- ◆ removeBindingFromObject(bindingId) removes the particular binding from the source object
- ◆ showBindinginLog(object, id) logs the binding
- ◆ showAllBindingsInLog() logs all the bindings

Data controller

Controller connects a view component to a set of data stored in a model. The qooxdoo framework provides four different controllers for different view components. The different controllers are listed as follows:

- ◆ Object controller (qx.data.controller.Object)
- ◆ List controller (qx.data.controller.List)
- ◆ Form controller (qx.data.controller.Form)
- ◆ Tree controller (qx.data.controller.Tree)

The class hierarchy of the controller is under the qx.data.controller package:

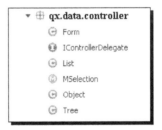

Controllers do contain a selection array, which contains the currently selected model items. When using this selection array, there is no need to deal with view widgets such as ListItems. It is also possible to change the array in place and add/remove something from the selection. As it is a data array, you can use all the methods defined for the array to manipulate the selection of the corresponding controller.

Object controller

This Object controller is a very simple and lightweight controller. Object controller binds one model object containing one or more properties with the view objects quite easily. Every property in the model can be bound to one or more targets properties. The bindings will be for atomic types (Number, String, Map, and so on) only.

A sample code snippet to explain the `Object` controller with the basic `SingleValueBinding`, which we learnt earlier, is as follows:

```
// create two sliders
var slider1 = new qx.ui.form.Slider();
var slider2 = new qx.ui.form.Slider();
// create a controller and use the first slider as a model
var controller = new qx.data.controller.Object(slider1);
// add the second slider as a target
controller.addTarget(slider2, "value", "value");
```

The features of the `Object` controller are as follows:

◆ It manages the bindings between the model properties and the different targets

◆ There is no need for the user to take care of the binding IDs

◆ It can create a bi-directional binding (read-/write-binding)

◆ It handles model changing, which means adding the old targets

List controller

The `List` controller is responsible for synchronizing every list-like widget with a data array. It does not matter if the array contains atomic values such as strings or complete objects where one property holds the value for the label and another property holds the icon's URL.

The currently supported list widgets are:

◆ `qx.ui.form.SelectBox`

◆ `qx.ui.form.ComboBox`

◆ `qx.ui.form.List`

The following code snippet shows how to bind an array of strings to a list widget:

```
// create the model
var model = new qx.data.Array(["a", "b", "c", "d", "e"]);
// create a list widget
var list = new qx.ui.form.List();
// create the controller
var listController = new qx.data.controller.List(model, list);
```

Features of the `List` controller are as follows:

◆ It synchronizes the model and the target

◆ Labels and icons are "bindable"

◆ It takes care of the selection

- It passes on the options used by the bindings
- It allows filtering too and user-defined filtered function

Form controller

The Form controller is responsible for connecting a form to a model and vice versa. The same created model can also be used for serialization. Internally, each and every form widget binds with the model using the qx.data.controller.Object class.

The following code snippet uses a controller and creates a model object with the data entered in the form:

```
// form
var form = new qx.ui.form.Form();

// add the form items
var nameTextfield = new qx.ui.form.TextField();
nameTextfield.setRequired(true);
nameTextfield.setWidth(200);
form.add(nameTextfield, "First Name", null, "firstName");
form.add(new qx.ui.form.TextField(), "Last Name", null,
"lastName");
form.add(new qx.ui.form.TextField(), "Company");
form.add(new qx.ui.form.TextField(), "Email");
form.add(new qx.ui.form.DateField(), "Date");

// buttons
var saveButton = new qx.ui.form.Button("Save");
saveButton.setWidth(70);
form.addButton(saveButton);
var cancelButton = new qx.ui.form.Button("Cancel");
cancelButton.setWidth(70);
form.addButton(cancelButton);

// create the view
groupBox.add(new qx.ui.form.renderer.Single(form));

// binding /////////////////////////
var controller = new qx.data.controller.Form(null, form);
var model = controller.createModel();
```

Features of the Form controller:

- Connects a form to a model (bi-directional)
- Creates a model for a given form

Tree controller

The `Tree` controller is responsible for tree widgets. The supported widget is `qx.ui.tree.Tree`. The major responsibility is creating and adding the folders or leaves to the target tree, based on the model given.

The code snippet to explain the tree controller usage is as follows:

```
var nodes = [];
for (var i = 0; i < 50; i++) {
  nodes[i] = new demobrowser.demo.data.model.Node();
  nodes[i].setName("Item " + i);
  nodes[i].setName2("Thing " + i);
  // if its not the root node
  if (i != 0) {
    // add the children in some random order
    nodes[parseInt(Math.random() * i)].getChildren().
push(nodes[i]);
  }
}

// create the tree
var tree = new qx.ui.tree.Tree();
tree.setSelectionMode("multi");
this.getRoot().add(tree, {left: 10, top: 100});
tree.setWidth(250);
tree.setHeight(300);

// bind the widget to the data with the controller
var treeController = new qx.data.controller.Tree(nodes[0],
tree, "children", "name");

// open the root node
tree.getRoot().setOpen(true);
```

The features of the `Tree` controller are as follows:

- It synchronizes the model and the target
- Labels and icons are "bindable"
- It takes care of the selection
- It passes on the options used by the bindings

Data stores

The main purpose of the store components is to load data from a source and convert that data into a model. The task of loading data and converting the data into a model has been split up. The store itself takes care of loading the data but delegates the creation of model classes and instances to a marshaler.

The class hierarchy is shown in the following screenshot:

The classes responsible for the loading and converting the data are as follows:

- `qx.data.store`: Responsible for fetching data
- `qx.data.marshal`: Responsible for parsing data into qooxdoo classes and objects
- `qx.data.store.Json`: Class used for fetching the JSON data from a URL
- `qx.data.marshal.Json`: The loaded data will be parsed and saved into qooxdoo objects, with actual data as the properties in the object

JSON store

The JSON store takes a URL, fetches the given data from that URL, and converts the data using the JSON marshaler to qooxdoo model instances, which will be available in the model property after loading. The state of the loading process is mapped to a state property. For the loading of the data, a `qx.io.remote.Request` will be used in the store. After setting the URL during the creation process, the loading will begin immediately.

The following code snippet shows how to use the JSON data store:

```
var url = "json/data.json";
var store = new qx.data.store.Json(url);
store.getModel();
```

JSONP store

The JSONP store is based on the JSON store, but uses a script tag for loading the data. Therefore, a parameter name for the callback and a URL must be specified. After setting the URL and the callback parameter name during the creation process, the loading will begin immediately.

The following code snippet shows how to use the JSONP data store.

```
var url = "json/data.json";
var store = new qx.data.store.Jsonp(url, null, "CallbackParamName");
```

YQL store

YQL is the Yahoo! Query Language. YQL is an SQL-like language that lets you query, filter, and join data across Web services. Based on the JSONP store, qooxdoo offers a YQL store, where you can specify the YQL queries and qooxdoo handles the rest. This store lets you fetch the data over the Internet, based on the query.

The following code demonstrates how to fetch some twitter messages:

```
var query = "select * from twitter.user.timeline where
id='wittemann'";
var store = new qx.data.store.YQL(query);
```

Time for action – enhancing the UserSignUpForm again

In the previous chapter, when we wrote the `userSignUpForm` class, we handled all the fields individually. It requires a lot of coding to add the fields individually on the layout, to gather the data from the fields individually before sending the data to the server, and so on. In this chapter, we have already used the form and the features such as renderer, resetter, and validator in the *Time for action – enhancing the UserSignUpForm* section.

1. Let's use the form controller now to gather the data generically from all the fields in the form and send the data to the server through an RPC call.

   In the `UserSignUpForm.js` class, update the register button's executing listener, after the validation is completed successfully:

   ```
   var controller = new qx.data.controller.Form(null, form);
   var model = controller.createModel();
   var user = qx.lang.Json.parse(qx.util.Serializer.toJson(model));
   ```

2. Now, let's perform the user registration call to the server through an RPC call. Pass the user model that you got in step 1.

Update the `UserSignUpForm.js` register button's executing listener, after gathering the user model.

```
var rpc = new qx.io.remote.Rpc();
rpc.setCrossDomain(false);
rpc.setTimeout(10000);
var webURL = "http://localhost:8080/teamtwitter/.qxrpc";
rpc.setUrl(webURL);
rpc.setServiceName("teamtwitter.ui.handler.TweetHandler");
//rpc.setServiceName("qooxdoo.test");
var _this = this;
rpc.callAsync(function(result, ex, id){
  if (ex == null) {
    alert(result);
    _this.close();
  } else {
    alert("Async(" + id + ") exception: " + ex);
  }
}, "registerUser", user);
```

3. Now, compile and deploy the Team Twitter web application into Tomcat and check the registration screen.

What just happened?

qooxdoo separates out the different functionalities in data binding into different components and provides a pretty neat design. We got to know the various components provided by the qooxdoo framework for the data binding process. These concepts help us to implement certain functionalities very easily by spending very little effort. We enhanced the `UserSignUpForm` widget to make use of the form controller, serialized the data in the JSON format, and sent it to the server through RPC.

Pop quiz

1. qooxdoo form features is/are

    a. Resetter

    b. Validation

    c. Renderer

    d. All the above

2. The validation class that helps in validating all the items of a form asynchronously is

    a. `qx.ui.form.validation.Asyncvalidator`

    b. `qx.ui.form.validation.Validator`

    c. `qx.ui.form.validation.Manager`

    d. `qx.ui.form.Form`

3. Validation functions provided by the qooxdoo framework are in the class

    a. `qx.ui.form.validation.Asyncvalidator`

    b. `qx.ui.form.validation.Validator`

    c. `qx.ui.form.validation.Manager`

    d. `qx.ui.form.Form`

4. Resetter resets all the added widgets with its initial values of the widgets

    a. true

    b. false

5. The allowed form widgets in the `SinglePlaceHolder` renderer are

    a. `TextField`

    b. `SelectBox`

    c. `ListItem`

    d. `TextArea`

    e. `Spinner`

    f. `Button`

    g. `Both a and d`

6. Which process is carried out on the data before passing the data over the network to the server

    a. Validation

    b. Data binding

    c. Controlling

    d. Serialization

7. The process of tying a source property to a target property is

    a. Data binding

    b. Serialization

    c. Data stores

    d. Marshalling

8. With data binding, you can

    a. bind a property to a property

    b. bind an event to a property

    c. bind a hierarchical property to a property

    d. bind an array element to a property

    e. all of the above

9. Converting the model data into qooxdoo objects is the responsibility of

    a. `SingleValueBinding`

    b. Data controller

    c. Data store

    d. Marshal

10. Fetching data from a URL is the responsibility of

    a. `SingleValueBinding`

    b. Data controller

    c. Data store

    d. Marshal

Summary

In the previous chapters, we explored the various qooxdoo-provided widgets, forms, and so on.

In this chapter, especially, we covered slightly more advanced features:

- We learnt about the qooxdoo form object and its handling
- We learnt easy and simple ways to create a form and to validate form data
- We got an idea on serializing form data
- We got good ideas on data handling, converting model objects to view controls, fetching data from a URL, and so on

We have applied the learning from this chapter in our Team Twitter application. We created a new signup form with validations and used the double renderer to have a nice signup form. By now, we learnt more about application creation or development.

From the next chapter onwards, we will start learning about application testing and debugging of any issues. We will explore qooxdoo-provided features for debugging and logging, as well as different debugging tools available for debugging the qooxdoo applications.

7
Testing and Debugging

This chapter explains the qooxdoo framework support for the unit testing and integration tests. It also explains logging and debugging qooxdoo applications using Firebug and IE developer tools.

Up to the last chapter, we have learnt how to develop the graphical user interface using the qooxdoo framework. In this chapter, we will learn to write and run unit test cases for the qooxdoo classes, to write and run integration test cases for qooxdoo applications, to log messages in qooxdoo applications, and to use debugging tools on qooxdoo applications. We will learn tools provided by the qooxdoo framework for testing and also a few external tools for debugging the qooxdoo applications.

In this chapter, we will cover the following topics:

- **Unit testing**:
    - Generating unit test setup
    - Writing, building, and running unit tests

- **Integration testing**:
    - Writing integration tests
    - Running integration tests

- **Debugging**:
    - Logging statements in qooxdoo code
    - Tracing through AOP

- ❑ Introduction to the Firebug add-on
- ❑ Placing breakpoints, inspecting objects, and interactive debugging
- ❑ IE developer tools

The qooxdoo framework provides a lot of support for testing and encourages having automated tests for the qooxdoo applications. We will learn how to test and debug qooxdoo applications.

Unit testing

The qooxdoo framework provides a set of classes and internal tools for unit testing the qooxdoo classes. Unit testing is nothing but cross-checking the implementation of the source code in terms of small units, to see whether each unit is satisfying and performing its basic intention or requirement. A unit is the smallest testable part of an application and, in object-oriented programming, the smallest unit is considered as a method.

It is the developer's responsibility to make sure that any new changes do not affect the working code. Creating some unit tests and continuously executing them identifies software breakage at an early stage. The qooxdoo framework provides a good environment to create unit test cases easily. The `testrunner` tool is also provided to run the test cases. The qooxdoo framework provides a separate package named `qx.dev.unit`, with a set of classes, where these classes provide an interface to qooxdoo's unit test framework.

The class hierarchy for unit testing is shown in the following screenshot:

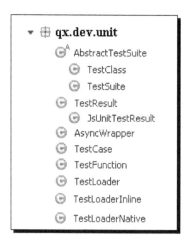

On creating a new application, the qooxdoo framework generates a `DemoTest.js` test class file under `<application-home>/source/class/application-name/test`, which contains a couple of sample test cases, namely, `testSimple` and `testAdvanced`:

The generated `DemoTest.js` test class looks like this:

```
qx.Class.define("teamtwitter.test.DemoTest",
{
  extend : qx.dev.unit.TestCase,

  members :
  {
    /**
     * Here are some simple tests
     */
    testSimple : function()
    {
      this.assertEquals(4, 3+1, "This should never fail!");
      this.assertFalse(false, "Can false be true?!");
    },

    /**
     * Here are some more advanced tests
     */
    testAdvanced: function ()
    {
      var a = 3;
      var b = a;
      this.assertIdentical(a, b, "A rose by any other name is still a
rose");
      this.assertInRange(3, 1, 10, "You must be kidding, 3 can never
be outside [1,10]!");
    }
  }
});
```

To create more unit test classes, create classes extending the `qx.dev.unit.TestCase` class and add methods with names starting with *test*. You can place all the unit test classes under the `<application-home>/source/class/application-name/test` directory. You can use assertion methods inherited from the `TestCase` class to ease the implementation process. The `qx.dev.unit.TestCase` class is the base class for all unit tests and contains all the assert methods required for unit testing.

The unit test framework provides certain methods, namely, the `setup()` and `tearDown()` methods, to set up certain things before the test case and to clear certain things after the test case. Both of these methods are optional; you can override the respective method and write your code.

Framework exceptions are used to communicate the test results back to the test runner. If it does not throw any exception, the test is successful. Throwing an exception from the test method signals a failure. Return values from the test methods are not evaluated.

Developers can test the AJAX calls also, by using asynchronous test cases, where the test cases have to be wrapped under the `AsyncWrapper` class. This `qx.dev.unit.AsyncWrapper` class stores the information needed to instruct a running test to wait until either the test case function successfully completes or an exception is thrown.

Once you write the unit test cases, you need to compile the test cases and generate the updated `TestRunner` application before running the unit test cases. The following command generates the updated `TestRunner` application:

```
C:/teamtwitter> generate.py test
```

If you have the unit tests only testing the qooxdoo UI classes, you can run the Test Runner by opening `index.html` under the `test` directory. The `DemoTest` and `TagsWidgetTest` classes can be run without deploying the application, by opening the following file in the browser:

```
file:///C:/teamtwitter/test/index.html#
```

If you have any test case calling the server to test any function, you need to deploy the application to test those test cases. As we have added a couple of test cases to test the handler functionalities, we need to run the test against the deployed version of the application. The `LoginUserTest` class can be run only in the deployed version:

```
http://localhost:8080/teamtwitter/test/index.html#
```

Time for action – performing unit test

1. Generate the unit test setup for the Team Twitter application by running the `generate.py` script with the option `test`. Open a command prompt and change your current directory to the Team Twitter application home directory and run the following command:

   ```
   C:\teamtwitter> generate.py test
   ```

This command creates the entire test environment, which includes the resources and scripts required, as shown in the following screenshot:

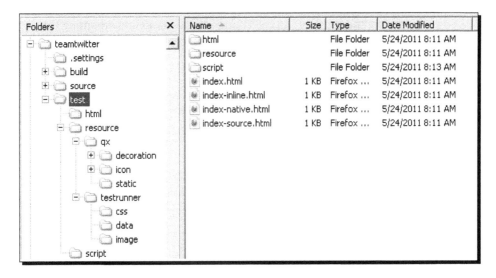

- ❑ test: This directory contains the unit test environment for the application. This whole directory content is generated when you run the generate.py test command.

- ❑ resource: This directory contains the resource files. It contains the resources required for the testrunner tool.

- ❑ script: This directory contains the JavaScript files required for the TestRunner application. This directory has two JavaScript files, namely, testrunner.js and tests.js. You do not have to touch these files. These are used to render the testrunner tool, which will execute the unit tests written for the application.

- ❑ index.html: This HTML file brings up the testrunner tool for the application. It reads all the unit test cases written for the application and displays those cases in the tool for execution.

2. Let's write couple of unit test classes for our Team Twitter application. Let's create a test class to test our tags widget with some static values. Create the `TagsWidgetTest.js` class under `C:\teamtwitter\source\teamtwitter\test`, extending the `qx.dev.unit.TestCase` class and implementing the `testTagsWidget` method, as mentioned in the following code snippet:

```
testTagsWidget : function() {
var tagsWidget = new teamtwitter.ui.TagsWidget();
var tags = "Java;Javascript;qooxdoo;Spring;Eclipse;Database;Or
acle;SQL;PLSQL;RIA;Photography;Tools;Travel;Hiking;TV Shows;";
tagsWidget.setDelimitedTags(tags);
var tagsArray = tagsWidget.getTagsArray();
var valueArray = tags.split(";");
for (var i=0; i<tagsArray.length; i++) {
this.assertInArray(tagsArray[i], valueArray, "Not a valid
tag");
}
}
```

After your attempt, you can compare your code with the code in the `978-1-849513-70-8_07_01.txt` file under `Chapter 7` folder in the support files for this book.

3. Now, let's write a test case for our user login form. Here, let's have two test cases to check for a valid user, and another for checking an invalid user. As this is a server call to check for users against the database, it is better to write these as asynchronous test cases. Create the `LoginUserTest.js` class under `C:\teamtwitter\source\class\teamtwitter\test`, extending the `qx.dev.unit.TestCase` class and implementing the `testLoginUser` and `testLoginInValidUser` methods, as mentioned in the following code snippet. The test code assumes that there is already a user `raj`, with the password `raj`. Before running this test, register a user with the same details, or update the test code with an existing user's details, as shown in the following code:

```
testLoginUser : function() {
var rpc = new qx.io.remote.Rpc();
rpc.setCrossDomain( false );
rpc.setTimeout(10000);
var webURL = "http://localhost:8080/teamtwitter/.qxrpc";
rpc.setUrl(webURL);
rpc.setServiceName("teamtwitter.ui.handler.TweetHandler");
var _this = this;
```

```
      rpc.callAsync(function(result, ex, id){
        _this.resume(function() {
          if (ex == null) {
            _this.assertNotEquals(result, 0, "InValid User");
          }
        }, this);

      }, "loginUser", "raj", "raj");
      this.wait(10000);
    },

  testLoginInValidUser : function() {
    var rpc = new qx.io.remote.Rpc();
    rpc.setCrossDomain( false );
    rpc.setTimeout(10000);
    var webURL = "http://localhost:8080/teamtwitter/.qxrpc";
    rpc.setUrl(webURL);
    rpc.setServiceName("teamtwitter.ui.handler.TweetHandler");
    var _this = this;
    rpc.callAsync(function(result, ex, id){
      _this.resume(function() {
        if (ex == null) {
          _this.assertEquals(result, 0, "Allowed to login with
wrong password");
        }
      }, this);

    }, "loginUser", "raj", "wrongpassword");
    this.wait(10000);
  }
```

Note that the `wait` method should always be the last call in the asynchronous wrapper method, as this informs the test runner to wait for a resume call. You can find this code in the `978-1-849513-70-8_07_02.txt` file under Chapter 7.

The preceding two user login test cases gets validated against the database, for which the data in the database should be populated before running test cases.

4. Let's redefine the test cases defined in step 3 by writing the `setup()` method to create an `rpc` instance, and the `teardown()` method to clear the `rpc` instance, as mentioned in the following code snippet. Once you add the `setup()` and `teardown()` methods, you can remove the repetitive `rpc` instance creation in each test case. You can use `setup()` and `teardown()` for such purposes. Before invoking any test case, Test Runner will call `setup()` and, after invoking any test case, Test Runner will call the `teardown()` method.

```
members :
{
  rpc : null,

  setUp : function() {
    this.rpc = new qx.io.remote.Rpc();
    this.rpc.setCrossDomain( false );
    this.rpc.setTimeout(10000);
    var webURL = "http://localhost:8080/teamtwitter/.qxrpc";
    this.rpc.setUrl(webURL);
    this.rpc.setServiceName("teamtwitter.ui.handler.
TweetHandler");
  },

  tearDown : function() {

    this.rpc = null;
  }
}
```

5. We need to deploy the source version of the Team Twitter application to enable us to debug and write the test cases. If we want to deploy the source version of the application, we need to deploy the qooxdoo SDK along with the application.

Copy the qooxdoo SDK directory to the `teamtwitter` application directory (`C:/teamtwitter/qooxdoo-1.2-sdk`).

Update the reference in `C:/teamtwitter/config.json`. As you have the qooxdoo SDK right under the Team Twitter application, you can just mention the qooxdoo SDK directory name:

```
"let" :
  {
    "APPLICATION"  : "teamtwitter",
    "QOOXDOO_PATH" : "qooxdoo-1.2-sdk",
    // ...
}
```

Update the reference in `C:/teamtwitter/generate.py`, as follows:

```
QOOXDOO_PATH = 'qooxdoo-1.2-sdk'
```

Update the reference in `C:/teamtwitter-server/build.properties`, as follows:

```
applicationName=teamtwitter
deployDir=C:/apache-tomcat-7.0.14/webapps
qooxdooDir=C:/teamtwitter/qooxdoo-1.2-sdk
clientApplicationDir=C:/teamtwitter
qooxdooSDKName=qooxdoo-1.2-sdk
```

6. Let's update the `build.xml` file to add a few more targets required for testing and debugging. As we wrote one test class to test UI and one test class to test the handler functionalities, we need to run the test cases on the deployed version. Add couple of targets in the `build.xml` file, to generate the test runner and to deploy the test runner inside the deployed web application, as mentioned in the following code snippet:

```
<target name="client.generate-test">
  <exec executable="python" dir="${clientApplicationDir}">
    <arg value="generate.py" />
    <arg value="test" />
  </exec>
</target>
<target name="deploy.client.test" depends="client.generate-test">
  <copy todir="${deployDir}/${applicationName}/test">
    <fileset dir="${clientApplicationDir}/test">
    </fileset>
  </copy>
</target>
<target name="deploy.sdk">

  <copy todir="${deployDir}/${applicationName}/${qooxdooSDKName}">
    <fileset dir="${qooxdooDir}">
    </fileset>
  </copy>
</target>
```

In addition to that, update the `build.xml` file to copy the source version and build version of the Team Twitter application, and the test runner setup in the `copy.web` target. Also, add a target to deploy SDK under the Team Twitter web application. As this task not required every time, add this target seperately to avoid copying the huge directory every time. The updated `build.xml` file is available as a support file, named `978-1-849513-70-8_07_03.txt` under `Chapter 7`, for this book.

As we are deploying the source version and build version of the Team Twitter application, add a file, `index.html`, under `C:/teamtwitter-server/webapp`, just to have links to the source version and the build version of the application. The `index.html` file is available as a file named `978-1-849513-70-8_07_04.txt` under `Chapter 7`.

7. Now, let's clean the Team Twitter deployment and redeploy the Team Twitter web application. To do this, stop the Tomcat server, delete the `teamtwitter` directory under the `C:/apache-tomcat-7.0.14/webapps` directory, run the following targets in the ANT `build.xml` to regenerate the Team Twitter web application, and deploy it on the web server:

```
C:\teamtwitter-server>ant clean
C:\teamtwitter-server>ant dist
C:\teamtwitter-server>ant deploy
C:\teamtwitter-server>ant deploy.sdk
C:\teamtwitter-server>ant deploy.client.test
```

Start the Tomcat server now.

8. Open the URL `http://localhost:8080/teamtwitter/test/index.html#` and run the tests:

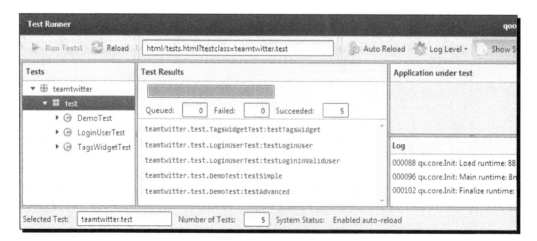

What just happened?

We have learnt the qooxdoo framework support for the unit tests. We have generated the unit tests setup for the application, written a few unit tests, and run those unit tests in the deployed location.

Integration testing

qooxdoo always encourages testing. It provides a few tools to help the developers and testers to write integration testing. In qooxdoo 1.3, the qooxdoo team experimented with a few features and tools for the GUI automation testing. These features and tools were outside of SDK until qooxdoo 1.4. In qooxdoo 1.4, the qooxdoo team integrated those features and tools into qooxdoo SDK. Let's see how to set up the environment, write integration tests, and run the automation tests on the GUI.

We will make use of the features available in qooxdoo 1.4, instead of setting up each component separately. As of now, we'll create a separate application in qooxdoo 1.4 to write the integration tests and run them against the Team Twitter application created in qooxdoo 1.2. We'll cover the migration of the application to a newer version of qooxdoo in *Chapter 11*, *Miscellaneous*.

Integration test setup

JavaScript is the programming language for qooxdoo. It encourages you to write the GUI automated tests also in JavaScript, following the qooxdoo object-oriented programming syntax. qooxdoo uses the Mozilla Rhino JavaScript framework and runs the scripts on the Selenium RC server. The following diagram explains the flow of the test code execution:

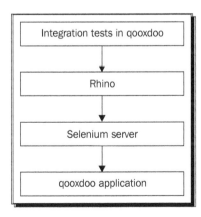

Writing test cases

You should write all the automated test cases in the `teamtwitter_tests.simulation` package, where `teamtwitter_tests` is the application's namespace or package. When you generate an application in qooxdoo, it generates the simulation package for the application namespace and generates the `DemoSimulation` class, as shown in the following code snippet:

```
qx.Class.define("teamtwitter_tests.simulation.DemoSimulation", {
  extend : simulator.unit.TestCase,
  members :
  {
    /** Check if a widget is present (part of the DOM) */
    testButtonPresent : function()
    {
      this.assertNotNull(this.getSimulation().getWidgetOrNull("qxh=qx.
ui.form.Button"), "Button widget not present!");
    },
    /** Click a button and check if an alert box pops up */
    testButtonClick : function()
    {
      this.getQxSelenium().qxClick("qxh=qx.ui.form.Button");
      this.assertEquals("true", String(this.getQxSelenium().
isAlertPresent()));
    }
  }
});
```

All the simulation test classes must inherit `simulator.unit.TestCase`, to make use of the assert statements, to check any details in the test.

Simulator API documentation

The `simulator` component of the qooxdoo framework provides a few APIs to write the automated tests in JavaScript. The qooxdoo API document does not contain the simulator APIs. Let's generate the API for the simulator component:

`C:\qooxdoo-1.4.1-sdk\component\simulator>generate.py api`

After generating the API, you can access the simulator API in the browser, using the location `file:///C:/qooxdoo-1.4.1-sdk/component/simulator/api/index.html#simulator`. For more details, refer to the *Time for action – performing integration test* section, in this chapter.

Simulator class hierarchy

The class hierarchy of the simulator component is shown in the following screenshot:

The main API classes you'll be using most of the time are as follows:

- `simulator.Simulation`: Simulates the automated GUI test of a qooxdoo application using `QxSelenium`. Provides access to the AUT's log messages and any exceptions caught by qooxdoo's global error handling. Also supports event testing.

- `simulator.QxSelenium`: Adapter between the qooxdoo simulator and the Selenium Java Client Driver. If `simulator.threadsafe` is set in the qooxdoo configuration, it uses `com.thoughtworks.selenium.grid.tools.ThreadSafeSeleniumSessionStorage`; otherwise, it uses `com.thoughtworks.selenium.QxSelenium`. This class extends `DefaultSelenium` and adds additional qooxdoo related methods.

- `simulator.unit.TestCase`: This is the base class for integration tests. It provides different assert methods to check the values within the jobs and also the `fail()` method to force a test case fail. This class has the instance of both `Simulation` and `QxSelenium` classes. You just have to extend this class to write a new test class and you can access the `Simulation` and `QxSelenium` classes, through this class.

Selenium Java Client Driver API documentation

In addition to the simulator API provided by the qooxdoo framework, refer to the Selenium Java client driver API, at the following location:

```
file:///C:/selenium-remote-control-1.0.3/selenium-java-client-
driver-1.0.1/javadoc/index.html.
```

Locating strategy

To locate the widget to perform the automated tests, first, the widget has to be identified. There are different strategies to identify the widget. But, it is not as easy as using normal web GUI automation tools.

Selenium locators

The Selenium locators are:

◆ **ID locators**: Widgets are identified based on the id property of the widget. Recent versions of qooxdoo do not assign the id property to the widget. If you want to use the ID locator strategy, the developer should set the ID for each widget, as shown in the following code snippet:
```
registerButton.getContainerElement().getDomElement().id =
"registerButton";
```

◆ **XPath locators**: This strategy is not well suited to the qooxdoo applications, as the DOM structures of qooxdoo applications may change during the runtime, as the content is generated dynamically.

◆ **DOM locators**: Same issues as XPath locators.

◆ **CSS locators**: Same issues as XPath locators.

So, the ID strategy may only work, if you put in the effort to set the id property for each widget.

qooxdoo locators

The following locating strategies are specifically designed for the qooxdoo applications:

◆ **qxh locators**: This locator searches the widget in a hierarchy. It uses syntax similar to the XPath locators, but differs significantly. This locator has a series of location steps separated by the forward slash (/) character. No leading or trailing / is allowed. All searches begin from the root object. Each of the following search steps searches the result of the previous location step. There is no restriction that each locator step should result in a single match. If there are multiple children matches to the search condition, the first match wins. You can specify each location step in one of the following ways:

- ❑ qxh=`<string>`—Searches for the JavaScript property on the current object. The following locator step looks for the JavaScript `mytoolbar` property on the current object:

  `qxh=mytoolbar`

- ❑ qxh=`<classname>`—Searches for the instance of the given class on the child widgets of the root object or on the child widgets of the result from the previous locator step. The following locator step looks for the instance of `qx.ui.form.Button`:

  `qxh=qx.ui.form.Button`

- ❑ qxh=`child[n]`—Searches for the nth child widget of the result from the previous locator step. The following qxh locater searches for the third child widget:

  `qxh=child[3]`

- ❑ qxh=`[@attrib{=val}]`—Searches for the child that has a qooxdoo or JavaScript property `attrib`, with the value `val`. You can use regular expressions to match the property value:

  `qxh=[@label="RegisterButton"]`
  `qxh=[@label=".*Label$"]`

- ❑ qxh=`<wildcard_operator>`—Special token (`*`) acts as a wildcard operator. This will recursively search all the levels in the hierarchy until the next locator step is matched. The following locator step searches all the levels in the hierarchy, from root object, for the widget with a label property with the value `Sign Up`. As it searches all the levels recursively, it is not an effective search and takes more time:

  `qxh=*/[@label="Sign Up"]`

Try to avoid using only one locator step that has a wildcard search directly from the root object. But, you can use this for relatively few levels of search and mix with specific locators, as mentioned in the following example:

`qxh=*/[@label="Section 3"]/[@page]/*/[@label="First Button"]`

This searches recursively from the root for an object with label `Section 3`, and then, assuming it is a `ButtonView` widget, which has a page property, navigates to the corresponding page, where it again searches recursively for an item with label `First Button`. This is much more effective than searching the entire object space with `*/[@label="First Button"]`.

- ❑ qxh=<specific operators>—Three special operators at the beginning of a locator specify which object space to search:

  - ❑ app: Signifies the object space down from qx.core.Init.getInstance().getApplication()

  - ❑ inline: Signifies the object space down from the root widget of a "qooxdoo isle" in an inline application

  - ❑ doc: Signifies the object space down from the application's root widget, that is, qx.core.Init.getApplication().getRoot()

- ◆ **qxhv locators**: The qxhv= locator searches in the widget hierarchy in a manner similar to the qxh locator, except that it searches only visible widgets that have the visibility property set to visible. Sometimes, it may give unexpected results. One of the scenarios is the root node of the qx.ui.tree.Tree class being set to invisible, in many of the qooxdoo applications. The qxhv locator will never find any descendants of the tree's root node, even though they are visible in the GUI.

- ◆ **qxidv locators**: The qxidv= locator searches for an HTML element and finds the related qooxdoo widget, only if the widget is visible.

- ◆ **qxhybrid locators**: The qxhybrid= locator allows you to combine different locator strategies separated by &&. Each sub locator applies the locator strategy on the DOM element returned by previous locator. The first locator in the locator series can be any of the qooxdoo locators or Selenium locators and the following locators can be any of the qooxdoo locators or XPath locators. The qxhybrid locator is used especially if you assign the id property for the container elements and if you don't assign the id property for the child form elements.

  qxhybrid=users&&qxh=[@label=Foo]

  This locator searches first for the widget with the id property set to users, and then uses the qxh locator to search for any child widgets with the Foo label.

Time for action – performing integration test

1. Let's set up the software required for the integration testing. qooxdoo 1.4 integrates some of qooxdoo's internal tools into the SDK itself, so let's download qooxdoo 1.4 SDK from http://sourceforge.net/projects/qooxdoo/files/qooxdoo-current/1.4.1/ and extract it to the C:/ directory.

   Download the Mozilla Rhino framework from http://www.mozilla.org/rhino/download.html (download version 1.7R1 or later). Extract the ZIP file to the C:/ directory.

Download the Selenium RC server from the following URL (download version 1.0.3):

```
http://code.google.com/p/selenium/downloads/
detail?name=selenium-remote-control-1.0.3.zip&can=2&q=
```

Create a `selenium-remote-control-1.0.3` directory under `C:/`, and extract the ZIP file to it.

2. The normal practice is to write the automated test cases in the Team Twitter application code itself. As we have used qooxdoo 1.2 for the Team Twitter application and have not migrated yet, let's create a separate application for the automated test cases. You can run the tests against the Team Twitter application developed in qooxdoo 1.2. You can maintain the test cases in a separate code base, if the quality assurance team writes these test cases. In that case too, you can create a separate application for the test cases.

   Let's create a qooxdoo application for writing the automated test cases. In the command prompt, go to `C:\qooxdoo-1.4.1-sdk\tool\bin` and run the following command:

```
create-application.py --name teamtwitter_tests --out C:\
```

 If you are already using qooxdoo 1.4 for the application, and you want to maintain the automated test cases in the application code base, you don't have to create a separate application. Skip this step and use your Team Twitter application for test cases, instead of the `teamtwitter_tests` application.

3. As qooxdoo integrated the simulator component in the SDK itself, it provides a couple of jobs, namely, `simulation-build` and `simulation-run`, in the generator tool.

   As we use two external tools, Rhino and Selenium, we need to configure qooxdoo for those tools.

   The qooxdoo application has all the configurations required for the `generate.py` tool in the `config.json` file. This basically inherits the `application.json` configuration from the qooxdoo framework. If you want to set some configuration or override some configuration, you can do that in the `config.json` file for the application. Let's set a few details for the external tools in the `teamtwitter_tests` configuration.

Edit the `config.json` file in the `C:\teamtwitter_tests` directory:

```
"let" :
  {
    "APPLICATION"   : "teamtwitter_tests",
    "QOOXDOO_PATH"  : "../qooxdoo-1.4.1-sdk",
    "QXTHEME"       : "teamtwitter_tests.theme.Theme",
    "API_EXCLUDE"   : ["qx.test.*", "${APPLICATION}.theme.*",
"${APPLICATION}.test.*", "${APPLICATION}.simulation.*"],
    "LOCALES"       : [ "en" ],
    "CACHE"         : "${TMPDIR}/qx${QOOXDOO_VERSION}/cache",
    "ROOT"          : ".",
   "SIMULATOR_CLASSPATH" : ["../selenium-remote-control-1.0.3/
selenium-java-client-driver-1.0.1/selenium-java-client-driver.
jar", "../rhino1_7R3/js.jar"]
  },

  "jobs" :
  {
  "simulation-run" :
  {
    "environment" :
    {
    "simulator.testBrowser" : "*firefox3",
    "simulator.selServer" : "localhost",
    "simulator.selPort" : 4444,
    "simulator.autHost" : "http://localhost",
    "simulator.autPath" : "/${APPLICATION}/source/index.html"
    }
  }
  }
```

Add the `SIMULATOR_CLASSPATH` value in the `let` section. This configures the libraries for Rhino and Selenium Java Client. Make sure you add the comma (,) at the end of the previous line.

Add the `jobs` section and set the details for the `simulator-run` job. Make sure that you add a comma after the `let` section.

It configures the environment for Selenium. If you want to test in Internet Explorer, you can set the `simulator.testBrowser` value to `*iexplore`. You can set the application details in the `simulator.autHost` and `simulator.autPath` values. If you writing the automated test cases in the application code base itself, these settings will work. If you are testing these test cases against an application running on some other machine, you can set the details in these parameters.

4. The job `simulation-build` generates the simulation application based on the written automated tests. After adding new test cases or modifying existing test cases in the simulation package, you need to execute this job before running the automated test cases:

```
C:\teamtwitter_tests>generate.py simulation-build
```

If you see the application directory `C:\teamtwitter_tests`, you will see a new `simulator` directory. These generated scripts are used to execute the test cases when you run the `simulation-run` job.

5. You need to provide the qooxdoo simulator user extension file to the Selenium server while starting. I would suggest you create the `start.bat` batch file under `C:/selenium-remote-control-1.0.3/selenium-server-1.0.3`, with the following content:

```
java -jar selenium-server.jar -userExtensions C:/qooxdoo-1.4.1-
sdk/component/simulator/tool/user-extensions/user-extensions.js
```

Go to `C:\selenium-remote-control-1.0.3\selenium-server-1.0.3` and start the Selenium server, using the `start.bat` file that you created just now:

```
C:\selenium-remote-control-1.0.3\selenium-server-1.0.3>start.bat
```

> Make sure that you set the following environment variables:
> PATH: `C:\Program Files\java\jdk1.6.0_26\bin`
> JAVA_HOME: `C:\Program Files\java`

6. Let's build the `inspector` component in the qooxdoo framework and deploy it in Tomcat:

```
C:\qooxdoo-1.4.1-sdk\component\inspector>generate.py build
```

Copy the build version of inspector as the inspector web application in Tomcat. To do this, copy the build directory of `inspector` component to the `webapps` directory of Tomcat, and rename the directory from `build` to `inspector`.

Stop Tomcat and then start it again, using the following command:

`C:\apache-tomcat-7.0.14\bin>startup.bat`

Check whether you can access the Team Twitter application from the browser. Enter the URL `http://localhost:8080/teamtwitter/`:

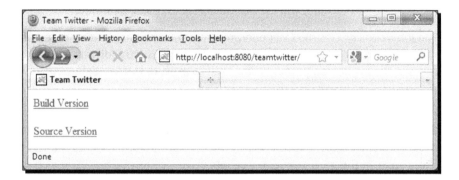

You can access the build version to use the application, and the source version to debug the application. The build version is optimized by the qooxdoo framework and used for production deployment. The source version refers to the qooxdoo SDK and loads all the JavaScript to allow the developer to debug the JavaScript code of the application.

Open the Inspector application and enter **/teamwitter/** in the textbox at the top-right corner:

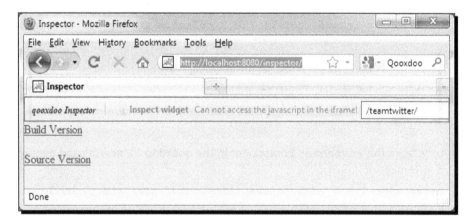

 We used Firefox 3.6 to test this application.

7. Let's try the operations that we want to test in the Inspector application. Inspector provides the hierarchical locator for all the inspected widgets. Sometimes, it is not robust, as the DOM structure might change at runtime. You should try the default locator generated by the Inspector a few times; if it does not always work, you should use one of the qooxdoo locator strategies and tweak the locator generated by the Inspector to make sure it works all the time. Once you get the hang of the locators, as you write many integration test cases, you might write the test cases using one or many locator strategies directly, without the help of the `inspector` component. But, the `inspector` component is very useful to inspect the widget, to find out the widget properties, to find out the widget hierarchy, and also to know the hierarchical locator path. Inspector allows you to debug the locating strategies and see which locator step is the issue and change the locator strategy for that particular locator step.

Open the Inspector application and access the `/teamtwitter/build/index.html` page, as shown in the following screenshot:

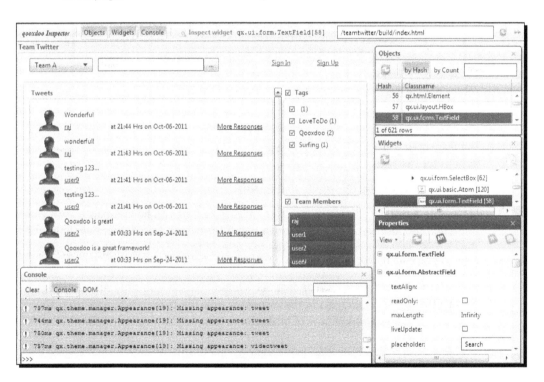

Click on the **Selenium** button in the **qooxdoo Inspector** toolbar displayed at the top. It displays the **Selenium** window of the `inspector` component. Click on the **Options** icon at the top-right corner of the **Selenium** window, click on the **Use default URI button**, and click on the **OK** button, as shown in the following screenshot:

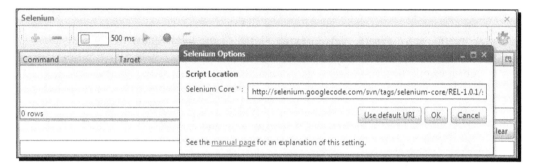

 If you do not have Internet access to connect to the default source, or if you do not want to connect to the external source, you can host the Selenium core in your local web server and configure it in the **Selenium** window.

After configuring the Selenium core location, all the icons will get enabled in the Selenium window.

Click on the **Record** icon (the red circle) to automatically record the commands for the inspected widgets. Then, start inspecting the widgets to perform the necessary actions for the tests.

Now, let's register, log in, tweet, and log out.

8. Let's write a test case to register a user. Make sure that you have executed the *Time for action* sections of *Chapter 6, Working with Forms and Data*, where we enhanced the `UserSignUpForm` class to use the features of the `Form` class. The integration testing is performed on that version.

Click on the **Record** icon, click on **Inspect widget**, and click on the required widget. Inspect the following widgets in the Inspector, edit the commands, and enter the values in the **Selenium** window of Inspector:

Widget	Command	Value
Sign Up	qxClick	
User Name in Sign up form	qxType	user1
Email in Sign up form	qxType	user1@gmail.com

Widget	Command	Value
Password in Sign up form	`Type`	`Test`
Confirm Password in Sign up form	`Type`	`test`
Register button in Sign up form	`qxClick`	

Try running those steps in Inspector, update the qxh locators with different location strategies, find out the correct strategy that works always, and convert it into a test case method. Create a simulation test class by extending it from `simulator.unit.TestCase`. Create the TeamTwitter.js class under the `C:/teamtwitter_tests/source/class/teamtwitter_tests/simulation/` folder and add the `testRegister()` method, following the Simulator API and Selenium Java client API. Restrict the use of `child[n]` locators.

9. Let's write a test case to log in as the user that we created in the previous test case. Inspect the following widgets in the Inspector, edit the commands, and enter the values in the **Selenium** window of Inspector:

Widget	Command	Value
Sign In	`qxClick`	
User Name in the login form	`qxType`	`User1`
Password in the login form	`Type`	`t`
Sign In button in login form	`qxClick`	
Text Area in Tweet Input widget	`qxClick`	

Add the `testLogin()` method to the Team Twitter test class.

10. Let's write a test case to tweet after login. Inspect the following widgets in the Inspector, edit the commands, and enter the values in the **Selenium** window of the Inspector:

Widget	Command	Value
Text Area in Tweet Input widget	`qxType`	`Testing 123...`
Tweet Button		

Add the `testTweet()` method to the Team Twitter test class.

11. Let's write a test case to log out. Inspect the following widget in the Inspector:

Widget	Command	Value
logout	`qxClick`	

Add the `testLogout()` method to the Team Twitter test class.

After your attempt, you can compare your code with the code in the `978-1-849513-70-8_07_05.txt` file under `Chapter 7`. Before running the Team Twitter automated GUI tests, configure the qooxdoo framework for the Team Twitter application details in the `config.json` file, under `C:\teamtwitter_tests`:

```
"jobs" :
  {
  "simulation-run" :
  {
    "environment" :
    {
    "simulator.testBrowser" : "*firefox3",
    "simulator.selServer" : "localhost",
    "simulator.selPort" : 4444,
    "simulator.autHost" : "http://localhost:8080",
    "simulator.autPath" : "/teamtwitter/build/index.html"
    }
  }
  }
```

12. Always, before running the automated GUI tests in qooxdoo, run the `simulation-build` job to make sure the generated simulator setup picks up the latest test cases:

    `C:\teamtwitter_tests>generate.py simulation-build`

    Then, run the test cases by running the `simulation-run` job:

    `C:\teamtwitter_tests>generate.py simulation-run`

    ```
    ========================================================================
        EXECUTING: SIMULATION-RUN
    ========================================================================
    >>> Initializing cache...
    >>> Running Simulation...
    >>> Loading Simulator...
    >>> Load runtime: 125ms
    >>> Simulator run on Thu, 06 Oct 2011 16:09:18 GMT
    >>> Application under test: http://localhost:8080/teamtwitter/
    build/index.html
    >>> Platform: Windows 7
    ```

```
>>> User agent: Mozilla/5.0 (Windows; U; Windows NT 6.1; en-US;
rv:1.9.2.23) Gecko/20110920 Firefox/3.6.23
>>> PASS    teamtwitter_tests.simulation.TeamTwitter:testRegister
>>> PASS    teamtwitter_tests.simulation.TeamTwitter:testLogin
>>> PASS    teamtwitter_tests.simulation.TeamTwitter:testTweet
>>> PASS    teamtwitter_tests.simulation.TeamTwitter:testLogout
>>> Simulator run finished in: 2 minutes 22 seconds.
>>> Main runtime: 142140ms
>>> Finalize runtime: 0ms


C:\teamtwitter_tests>
```

What just happened?

We have downloaded necessary software and set up the environment for integration testing. We have explored the `simulator` and `inspector` components in the qooxdoo framework. We learnt different widget-locating strategies used by the `simulator` component and used the Inspector application to identify the locators for the widgets. Based on the locators that are identified by the Inspector, and by tweaking the location strategy, we wrote the test cases for the Team Twitter application and ran those test cases through the `simulator` component.

Debugging

Debugging is a process of going through the code, analyzing it, and identifying the defect in the code. Analysis can be done either with the logs or by checking the code, line by line, while it is executing the function. To check the logs, first of all, you should add the debugging statements in the code. The qooxdoo framework supports different log levels, such as, `debug`, `info`, `warn`, and `error`. Based on the log level set, qooxdoo generates the log messages.

If you cannot pinpoint the Issue on the code, you can do active debugging by placing breakpoints in the code and checking the code execution in the flow. There are different tools available to help us to debug the JavaScript in the browser. Firebug is one of the most popular add-ons for the Mozilla Firefox browser, and IE developer tools is one of the more popular tools for Internet Explorer.

Whenever you get an error for an operation, the first thing to check is the log. Normally, the production application runs with error log levels. You can check if the application generates an error log for that operation. Sometimes, the issue may be straightforward and easily interpretable from the error log. If you cannot interpret directly from the error log, and if you need more detail, you can run the application in debug mode and get the log messages at the debug level, too.

Logging statements in qooxdoo code

Similar to log4j, the qooxdoo framework includes four different logging methods, and all these logging methods are defined in the `qx.core.Object` class. Therefore, these methods are directly available for use inside any class, as any class can be inherited from the `qx.core.Object` class.

The logging methods are:

- `debug(String message)`: Fine-grained informational events that are most useful to debug an application
- `info(String message)`: Informational messages that highlight the progress of the application at coarse-grained level
- `warn(String message)`: Potentially harmful situations
- `error(String message)`: Error events

Debug level is the lowest log level—it produces all log messages till the debug-level; the error level is the highest log level—it produces only the error log messages.

To use these methods, one can call the method directly with `this` reference and the argument as either a string message or an object; if an object is passed, its dump will be displayed.

```
this.debug("Value of x:" + x);
```

Console object

The `console` is an object attached to the `window` object in the web page. In Firebug for Firefox, the object is attached only if the **Console** panel is enabled. The `console.log()` method allows one to inspect the object that is passed.

In contrast to the `debug()` method, the developer can pass any object to `console.log()`. Firebug allows the developer to inspect the object in a structured way. This is much easier to navigate than to skim through pages of source output.

The `console` object supports the following patterns in string formatting:

Pattern	Type
%s	String
%i	Numeric formatting (not yet supported)
%f	Floating point number (numeric formatting is not yet supported)
%o	Object hyperlink
%c	Style formatting

In addition to the log method, the `console` object provides many more methods, such as, `debug`, `info`, `warn`, `error`, and so on.

You can measure the time taken for certain operations by using the `time()` and `timeEnd()` methods. For example:

```
console.time("operation1");
------
console.timeEnd("operation1");
```

If you want detailed reports in the JavaScript profiler, you can use the `console.profile()` and `console.profileEnd()` methods.

Trace

The `trace` method logs the current stack trace, by using the defined logger. This can be useful to inspect from which method the current function was called.

qx.dev.Debug

Including all the earlier mentioned methods, qooxdoo provides the `qx.dev.Debug` class—a static class with some static methods to debug an object recursively or up to a certain level of recursion:

```
var myTest = {a:1, b:[2,3], c:4}
qx.dev.Debug.debugObject(myTest)
```

This will display the following output:

```
------------------------------------------------------------
1665905: Object, count=3:
a: 1
b: Array
0: 2
1: 3
c: 4
------------------------------------------------------------
```

Variant qx.debug

A developer normally wants to have some debugging statements in the development cycle, but these debugging statements should not get delivered in the build version. To control this, the qooxdoo framework provides a variant named qx.debug. Possible values for this variant are on and off. By default, it is set to on in the source version, and to off in the build version. You can make use of this variant while writing the debug statements in the code, as follows:

```
If (qx.core.variant.isSet("qx.debug","on")) {
  This.debug("x : " + x);
}
```

Miscellaneous

qooxdoo provides some more good features to debug the disposal of the objects and remote AJAX communication just by setting some properties, such as qx.disposerDebugLevel, qx.ioRemoteDebug, and qx.ioRemoteDebugData. All these properties can be defined in config.json on the particular jobs. For example, qx.disposerDebugLevel takes an integer value, which specifies 1 as to provide debug information for all the qooxdoo objects and 2 as to provide some of the non qooxdoo objects, too. As the debug level value increases, more debug information is printed.

```
{
"jobs" :
  {
  // existing jobs ...
  "source-disposerDebug" :
    {
    "desc" : "source version with qx.disposerDebugLevel, for
    destruct support",
    "extend" : [ "source" ],
    "settings" :
      {
      "qx.disposerDebugLevel" : "1"
      }
    }
  }
}
```

Introduction to Firebug

Firebug is advanced, powerful, and the most popular web development tool. There is an add-on for the Mozilla Firefox browser. For other browsers, Firefox Lite can be used. Firebug provides multiple tabs, such as **console**, **HTML**, **CSS**, **Script**, **DOM**, and so on, to support many features. It has many configuration parameters to configure what types of errors are to be displayed and which are to be ignored.

The best features provided by Firebug are as follows:

- ◆ Quickly find errors in JavaScript, CSS, and so on.
- ◆ Inspect HTML and modify style and layout in real-time.
- ◆ Use the most advanced JavaScript debugger available for any browser. This allows step-by-step debugging, similar to the debugging tools of an IDE.
- ◆ Accurately analyzes network usage and performance.
- ◆ Supports extending this Firebug to add your own features.
- ◆ Stack display of method calls at any break point.
- ◆ Excellent display of DOM and objects on watch.
- ◆ Provides a command line interceptor to run any JavaScript command.

For more information on Firebug, have a look at `getfirebug.com`.

Installing the Firebug add-on

If you are using the Mozilla Firefox browser, go to **Tools** | **Add-ons**. It pops up the **Add-ons** window. Click on the **Extensions** tab, check whether you have the **Firebug** (Web development Evolved) add-on already installed. If not, go to the **Get Add-ons** tab, search for **Firebug**, select the **Firebug** add-on, and add it to Firefox. Make sure you have Internet access, to enable Firefox to search for the add-on.

Alternatively, you can download the Firebug add-on (`firebug-x.y.z.xpi`) from the site `http://getfirebug.com/` and install it in Firefox.

IE developer tools

The IE developer tools provide similar functionalities for the Internet Explorer browser. From IE8, these tools is integrated with the Internet Explorer browser.

Tracing through AOP

qooxdoo supports aspect-oriented programming too. qooxdoo provides the base class `qx.core.Aspect` to attach functions (aspects) before or after each function call of all functions defined in a class.

The methods include:

- ◆ `addAdvice (Function funRef, String position, String type, String/ RegExp name)`: Adds the advice, where:
  - ❑ `funRef` is the function to be called before or after the function name given.
  - ❑ `position` tells when to call the function just mentioned. Possible values are `before` or `after`. The default value is `after`.
  - ❑ `type` is the function type. Possible values are `member`, `static`, `constructor`, `destructor`, `property` and `null` or `*`. The default is `null`.
  - ❑ `name`: Name of the function to be wrapped.
- ◆ `wrap (String fullName, function funRef, String type)`: Returns the wrapped function, where:
  - ❑ `fullName` is the full name of the function and includes the class name, too
  - ❑ `funRef` is the function to be wrapped
  - ❑ `type` is the type of the wrapped function

One can enable or disable the aspects by setting the variant `qx.aspects` to `on` or `off`, in the `jobs` description, under `variants`. Other possible variants are:

- ◆ `qx.client`: Specifies type of browser; this is an auto-detected variant
- ◆ `qx.debug`: You can turn `on` or `off` the debug statements; defaults to `on`
- ◆ `qx.dynlocale`: Dynamic locale switches `on` or `off`; defaults to `on`

The output log statements are displayed on the console.

Time for action – debugging

1. Web development tools, such as Firebug, provide lots of useful functionalities to debug the applications in real-time. You can place breakpoints, inspect the object, do interactive debugging, and so on. We will explore those features now. You should load the source version of the Team Twitter application to debug the application. You can do this by entering the following in your browser:

   ```
   http://localhost:8080/teamtwitter/source/index.html
   ```

2. In the Team Twitter application, after login, you have to remove the login form and display the tweet input section. In the `C:/teamtwitter/source/class/teamtwitter/ui/UserLoginForm.js` file, intentionally create an issue by changing the code in the `loginUser()` method, as mentioned in the following code snippet. Replace `_this.getLayoutParent().getLayoutParent().refreshLayoutAfterLogin();` with `_this.getLayoutParent().refreshLayoutAfterLogin();`.

Let's see how to debug and identify the issue. Rebuild the Team Twitter application and deploy it by running following commands:

```
ant dist
ant deploy
```

3. Let's debug the login operation in the Team Twitter application. Open the Team Twitter source version and enable all panels of Firebug. Firebug has many panels, namely, **Console**, **HTML**, **CSS**, **Script**, **DOM**, and **Net**. It also allows you to add a custom panel, if you want to extend Firebug. Some of the tabs are:

   ❑ **Console** tab: Displays JavaScript log messages. You can enter JavaScript commands after the **>>>** at the bottom of the **Console** tab. You can see the error for the issue in the following screenshot. It says **TypeError: _this. getLayoutParent().refreshLayoutAfterLogin is not a function**. Sometimes, these error messages will give a direct clue to fix the issue. Sometimes, you need to debug further in the **Script** tab. In this case, let's debug further in the **Script** tab to pinpoint the issue:

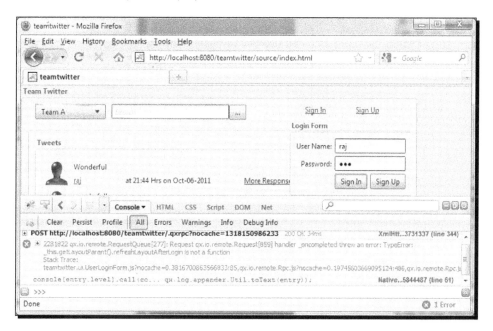

- ❑ **HTML** tab: Shows HTML as an indented hierarchy of DOM nodes, which you can open and close to see or hide child nodes. This even displays the structures that were generated in runtime.

- ❑ **CSS** tab: CSS inspector that allows you to view all loaded style sheets, to modify styles on the fly.

4. The **Script** tab shows the JavaScript files and the calling document. You can see the list of included JavaScript files and select one to view from this pane, by clicking on the drop-down list on the top of the Firebug window. You can select the drop-down list and type in to filter the list of JavaScript files. In the following screenshot, searching for **user**, it shows all the JavaScript files starting with "user". You can set the breakpoints and conditions under which the break points appear to examine the flow. To analyze the issue further, let's open the `UserLoginForm.js` file and add a breakpoint for the login operation to debug the issue:

Place a couple of breakpoints in the `userLoginForm.js` file, including the breakpoint at the exact line of error. When you log in now, the execution flow will stop at the breakpoint. You can use the debugging operations:

- ❑ **continue** (*F8*): Continues the flow and stops at the next breakpoint, if there is one

- ❑ **step into** (*F11*): Gets into the method to check the execution flow inside the method

- ❑ **step over** (*F10*): Goes to the next line of execution

- ❑ **step out** (*Shift + F11*): Comes out of the current method and stops on the next line

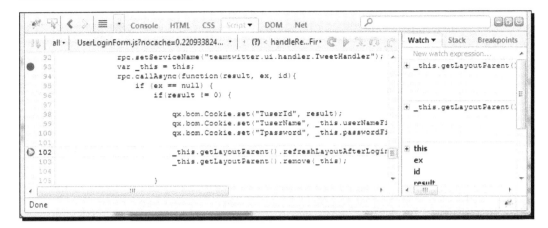

As the error in the preceding screenshot is complaining about the function, the function might have been called on a wrong reference.

5. After reaching the exact error location, let's inspect the references in the **Watch** window. Inspect a few references in the **Watch** section. Inspection of **_this. getLayoutParent()** shows this as **qx.ui.container.Composite**. You are supposed to call the refreshLayoutAfterLogin() method on teamtwitter. ui.MainWidget. It is confirmed that you are calling on a wrong reference. Now, you need to find the correct reference. Inspect different objects and references to find out the MainWidget class. The reference **_this.getLayoutParent(). getLayoutParent()** shows this as **teamtwitter.ui.mainWidget**:

Now replace the code line, `_this.getLayoutParent().refreshLayoutAfterLogin();` in the `UserLoginForm.js` file with `_this.getLayoutParent().getLayoutParent().refreshLayoutAfterLogin();`.

Rebuild the Team Twitter application and deploy and check it. You will find that the issue is resolved and the layout is refreshed, after login.

The **DOM** tab shows all the page objects and properties of the `window` object. As variables are properties of the `window` object, Firebug displays all JavaScript variables and their values.

The **Net** tab shows all the downloads, how long each resource took to download, the HTTP request headers, and the server response sent for each resource. The **XHR** sub tab available in the **Net** tab is very useful for AJAX debugging.

6. Let's trace the Team Twitter application throwing AOP. Add a couple of methods, in `Application.js`, that you want to call before and after the execution of the method:

```
beforeAdvice : function(e) {
  this.debug("before calling method:"+ e);
},

afterAdvice : function(e) {
  this.debug("after calling method:"+ e);
},
```

Set the following advices in `Application.js`:

```
qx.core.Aspect.addAdvice(this.beforeAdvice, "before", "*",
"teamtwitter.ui.*");
qx.core.Aspect.addAdvice(this.afterAdvice, "after", "*",
"teamtwitter.ui.*");
```

The updated `Application.js` is available as a file named `978-1-849513-70-8_07_06.txt` under `Chapter 7`.

Update the `C:/teamtwitter/config.json` file to enable the aspects:

```
"jobs" :
{
"source" :
{
  "require" :
  {
    "qx.Class" : ["aspects.Aop"]
  },
```

```
    "variants" :
    {
        "qx.aspects" : ["on"],
        "qx.debug" : ["on"]
    },
    "settings":
    {
        "qx.enableAspect" : true
    }
  }
}
```

The updated `config.json` is available as a file named `978-1-849513-70-8_07_07.txt` under `Chapter 7`

Rebuild the Team Twitter application and deploy and check it. You will see the tracing information in the console, as mentioned in the following screenshot:

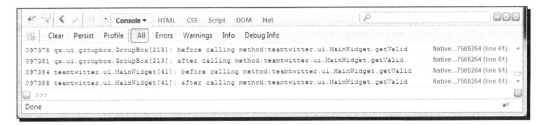

What just happened?

We have learnt the qooxdoo framework support for debugging the applications. We have also learnt various ways to write debug statements in the code and to prevent sending the debug messages in the production version. We have learnt to add aspects to the qooxdoo code. We have learnt how to install the Firebug add-on for the Mozilla Firefox browser, explored the development features supported by Firebug, and used those features to debug an issue in the Team Twitter application.

Pop quiz

1. Unit test case class should inherit from the class

    a. `qx.dev.unit.TestCase`

    b. `simulator.unit.TestCase`

    c. Either one

2. What are the components of the qooxdoo framework used in integration testing
    a. `testrunner`
    b. `simulator`
    c. `inspector`
    d. All of the above

3. The qooxdoo framework provides the following jobs to support integration tests
    a. `simulation-configure`
    b. `simulation-build`
    c. `simulation-run`
    d. All of the above

4. Integration test case classes should be under which namespace or package
    a. `aplication-namespace.test`
    b. `aplication-namespace.simulation`

5. The qooxdoo framework uses which client driver of Selenium RC server
    a. Java client driver
    b. Perl client driver
    c. Python client driver
    d. PHP client driver
    e. Ruby client driver

6. Which locator strategy is best for qooxdoo applications
    a. XPath locators
    b. DOM locators
    c. CC locators
    d. qooxdoo locators

7. Which is the lowest level in logging
    a. `info`
    b. `debug`
    c. `error`
    d. `warn`

8. What are the variants supported by the qooxdoo framework

    a. `qx.client`

    b. `qx.debug`

    c. `qx.aspects`

    d. `qx.dynlocale`

    e. All of the above

Summary

In this chapter, we have learnt how to perform unit test and integration test, and debug the qooxdoo applications. We tested and debugged our Team Twitter application.

We especially:

♦ Created the environment for unit test, wrote a few unit test classes, and ran those classes against the Team Twitter application

♦ Created the environment for integration test

♦ Learned the widget-locating strategy for qooxdoo applications

♦ Wrote few integration test classes and ran them against Team Twitter application

♦ Learned to write debugging statements in qooxdoo code

♦ Learned to add advices through AOP programming in qooxdoo

♦ Learned to use the powerful web development tool, Firebug

♦ Debugged an issue in the Team Twitter application using Firebug

We have learned about testing and debugging for qooxdoo applications and tried the concepts In our Team Twitter application. Now, we can debug and resolve issues and write test cases to validate any change in the application.

In the next chapter, we will learn to internationalize qooxdoo applications and make our application, Team Twitter, available in other languages including English.

8
Internationalization

This chapter explains the framework support for adapting qooxdoo applications to different languages and regions.

Up until the previous chapter, we have learnt to develop, debug, and test qooxdoo applications, and we even created our Team Twitter application and wrote some unit-test cases and automated-test cases. Now, it is time to learn to localize the application to multiple languages and regions. qooxdoo allows the translation of a new or an existing application to multiple languages, just by following some simple steps or an internationalization process. We will learn how to extract and translate messages into different languages and locales easily, without any code changes.

In this chapter, we shall cover the following topics:

♦ Introduction to qooxdoo internationalization
♦ Writing code for internationalization
♦ Writing PO files for various languages
♦ Running applications in multiple languages

Let us learn how to deliver qooxdoo applications in multiple languages and regions.

Internationalization

i18n is a standard industry abbreviation for internationalization (because there are 18 letters between i and n). Similarly, localization can be abbreviated as l10n.

Internationalization is a process of adapting the applications or software to different languages and regions. In qooxdoo, internationalization is divided into two distinct areas, namely, localization and translation.

Localization is the process of displaying the date (whether 03/28/1999 or 28/03/1999), time (the 24-hour or the A.M. /P.M. clock), number formats (decimal separator), and so on. Based on the region, qooxdoo supports all languages and locales, where locale defines the language, country, currency, time, and any specific variant preferences. en, en_US, and en_UK are three different locales that are used in English-speaking countries and differ, based on the regions. All these three locales inherit from the en locale, and each locale defines the deviation from the en locale. qooxdoo supports the fallback chain of locale settings; it looks up in the specific locale (that is, en_US), then in en, and then in C, which is the ancestor to all locales. To achieve the same, qooxdoo uses data from **Common Locale Data Repository** (**CLDR**).

Translation is the process of translating the visible text, such as labels, headings, help messages, and so on, into the specific language. qooxdoo provides tools to simplify the tasks in the process.

There are a few things we need to do to deliver the qooxdoo applications in multiple languages. We will see all those things one by one.

Writing code to use internationalization

qooxdoo framework makes the translation to other languages very easy by identifying all the localizable or translatable strings in the code and creates a separate .po file for each language, where the .po file allows for editing the localized strings.

To simplify the translation process, the framework provides a set of classes under the qx.locale package; it includes many of the static classes, such as, **String**, **Number**, **Key**, **Date**, a **Manager** class, and so on, to set or reset the language preferences or locale. The whole set of classes are listed in the following screenshot, for reference:

qx.locale.Manager

The `Manager` locale provides static translation methods, such as, `tr()`, `trn()`, and so on. It also provides general locale API to set or reset the locale, language, and so on. It mainly manages internationalization and changes the translation map, based on the change of the locale; for this purpose, manager has the methods, `addTranslation()`, `addLocale()`, and others.

The following code snippet will retrieve the information on all languages that are present in the application:

```
// log language and locale related info
var manager = qx.locale.Manager.getInstance();
this.info("Available locales:"+
  manager.getAvailableLocales());
this.info("Language:" + manager.getLanguage());
this.info("Locale:" + manager.getLocale());
```

The output of this code snippet will be:

Available locales: ["de", "en", "fr"]

Language: "en"

Locale: "en_us"

The `Manager` locale allows the developer to set the language or locale, add the translation map to a language, and so on. Refer to the API documentation for more information.

qx.locale.MTranslation

This is a mixin. It provides methods for marking the translatable strings in the classes. We can go through the methods in this mixin in detail in the later section.

qx.locale.String, qx.locale.Number, qx.locale.Date, and qx.locale.Key

All these are static classes. They provide methods to get: locale-dependent string formatting information (such as quotation signs), locale-dependent number formatting (such as decimal separators), locale-dependent date information (such as names of weekdays, A.M. /P.M., start of the week, and so on).

To know more on these classes, please go through the demo browser for localization. A set of statements are as follows for your reference:

```
info[(i++ * 2) + 1] = this.tr("Date format short:");
info[(i++ * 2) + 1] = qx.locale.Date.getDateFormat("short");
info[(i++ * 2) + 1] = this.tr("Date short:");
info[(i++ * 2) + 1] = (new qx.util.format.DateFormat
  (qx.locale.Date.getDateFormat("short"))).format(new Date());

info[(i++ * 2) + 1] = this.tr("Date format medium:");
info[(i++ * 2) + 1] = qx.locale.Date.getDateFormat("medium");
info[(i++ * 2) + 1] = this.tr("Date medium:");
info[(i++ * 2) + 1] = (new qx.util.format.DateFormat
  (qx.locale.Date.getDateFormat("medium"))).
  format(new Date());

info[(i++ * 2) + 1] = this.tr("Date format long:");
info[(i++ * 2) + 1] = qx.locale.Date.getDateFormat("long");
info[(i++ * 2) + 1] = this.tr("Date long:");
info[(i++ * 2) + 1] = (new qx.util.format.DateFormat
  (qx.locale.Date.getDateFormat("long"))).format(new Date());

info[(i++ * 2) + 1] = this.tr("Date format full:");
info[(i++ * 2) + 1] = qx.locale.Date.getDateFormat("full");
info[(i++ * 2) + 1] = this.tr("Date full:");
info[(i++ * 2) + 1] = (new qx.util.format.DateFormat
  (qx.locale.Date.getDateFormat("full"))).format(new Date());

info[(i++ * 2) + 1] = this.tr("Time format short:");
info[(i++ * 2) + 1] = qx.locale.Date.getTimeFormat("short");
info[(i++ * 2) + 1] = this.tr("Time short:");
info[(i++ * 2) + 1] = (new qx.util.format.DateFormat
  (qx.locale.Date.getTimeFormat("short"))).format(new Date());

info[(i++ * 2) + 1] = this.tr("Time format long:");
info[(i++ * 2) + 1] = qx.locale.Date.getTimeFormat("long");
info[(i++ * 2) + 1] = this.tr("Time long:");
info[(i++ * 2) + 1] = (new qx.util.format.DateFormat
  (qx.locale.Date.getTimeFormat("long"))).format(new Date());
```

```
info[(i++ * 2) + 1] = this.tr("Week start:");
info[(i++ * 2) + 1] = qx.locale.Date.getDayName("wide",
  qx.locale.Date.getWeekStart());

info[(i++ * 2) + 1] = this.tr("Format of %1:", 10000.12);
info[(i++ * 2) + 1] =
  qx.util.format.NumberFormat.getInstance().format(10000.12);
```

The result of this code is displayed, with all the locale-related information, as shown in the following screenshot. To view the information for different locales, use the Firebug console and run the locale set method on locale manager.

```
qx.locale.Manager.setLocale("fr");
```

On refreshing the browser, the information related to the `fr` locale is as shown in the following screenshot:

Let us get into the classes, in detail, to perform the translation.

A developer should identify the translatable strings using any of the following methods available in the `qx.locale.MTranslation` mixin. Only then can the qooxdoo framework recognize the strings to translate. Instead of hard coding the strings in the code, you should use one of the following methods while dealing with translatable strings.

The methods available in the mixin are:

- `tr(String msgId, Object varargs)`: Marks the message for translation, translates, and then returns a localized string object. The `toString()` method of the returned object performs the actual translation, based on the current locale. Variable arguments will be the parameter.

  For example, see the following code snippet:

  ```
  // this.tr usage
  var userNameLab = new qx.ui.basic.Label
    (this.tr("User Name:"));


  ...
  var passwordLab = new qx.ui.basic.Label(this.tr("Password:"));

  // this.tr with variable args
  alert(this.tr("Email address: %1, is not valid",
    emailField.getValue()));
  ```

  Variable arguments can be displayed easily, either by concatenating multiple strings or by formatting the string with the % character. As sentences in different languages can have different structures, it is always better to use the format string over string concatenation. This is why all the translation methods support format strings such as `Email address: %1, is not valid` as messages, and a variable number of additional arguments. The additional arguments are converted to strings and inserted into the original message. % is used as an escape character and the number following % references the corresponding additional argument. These variable arguments and formatting strings are common in all the translation methods available in this `MTranslation` mixin.

- `trn(String singularMsgId, String PluralMsgId, int count, Object varargs)`: Marks the messages for translation and translates and displays the message as per the count; if count is greater than 1, then it is a plural message, otherwise it is singular message. Having variable arguments is an optional parameter.

  For example, see the following code snippet:

  ```
  var count = 2;
  var label = new qx.ui.basic.Label(this.trn("Copied one file.",
    "Copied %1 files.", count, count));
  ```

- `trc(String hint, String msgId, Object varargs)`: Translates a message with an additional comment that can be used to add some contextual information for the translator. This meaningful comment, hopefully, helps the translator in finding the correct translation for the given string. Having variable arguments is an optional parameter.

  For example, see the following code snippet:

  ```
  var label = new qx.ui.basic.Label(this.trc("Helpful comment
    for the translator", "Hello World"));
  ```

- `marktr(String msgId)`: Marks the message to translate and returns the original message.

  For example, see the following code snippet:

  ```
  var label = new qx.ui.basic.label(this.marktr("Hello world"));
  ```

  By default, this `MTranslation` mixin is included in many classes. The classes that include the mixin by default are `qx.ui.core.Widget`, `qx.ui.table.columnmodel.Resize`, and `qx.application.AbstractGui`. So, if the user wants to identify the messages from any of the listed classes, they can directly accesses methods available in the `MTranslation` mixin. In other cases, just include the `MTranslation`, as shown in the following code snippet:

  ```
  qx.class.define("UserClass", {
    extend : qx.core.Object,
    include : qx.locale.MTranslation,

  ........

    members : {
      test : function() {
        this.tr("Good morning");
      }
    }
  }
  ```

Use the methods in our Team Twitter application to identify the translatable strings in the application, and generate the `.po` files for the desired languages, by following the steps in the next section.

Writing PO files for various languages

qooxdoo provides tools to identify all the marked strings and generate the PO files for all the languages that you support in your application. After generating the PO files, you can edit those PO files using one of the many po-aware editors.

Time for action – generating PO files for Team Twitter

1. Identify all the string literals that you want to localize, and mark them using the qooxdoo APIs. We will explain, here, with one of the widgets—UserSignUpForm—as an example, and you can do it yourself, for the rest of the widgets. Update the file `C:\teamtwitter\source\class\teamtwitter\ui\UserSignUpForm.js`, to mark the string that you want to localize, as mentioned in the following code snippet. This code is also available in the `978-1-849513-70-8_08_01.txt` file under Chapter 8.

```
_initLayout : function() {

    // setting a grid layout to the composite container
    this.setLayout(new qx.ui.layout.Grid(5,5));

    // creating the required fields with the headings as labels
    var userNameLab = new qx.ui.basic.Label
        (this.tr("User Name:"));
    var userNameField = new qx.ui.form.TextField();
    var emailLab = new qx.ui.basic.Label(this.tr("Email:"));
    var emailField = new qx.ui.form.TextField();
    var passwordLab = new qx.ui.basic.Label
        (this.tr("Password:"));
    var passwordField = new qx.ui.form.PasswordField();
    var confirmLab = new qx.ui.basic.Label
        (this.tr("Confirm Pass-word:"));
    var confirmField = new qx.ui.form.PasswordField();
    var contactNumLab = new qx.ui.basic.Label
        (this.tr("Mobile:"));
    var contactNumField = new qx.ui.form.TextField();
    var dobLab = new qx.ui.basic.Label(this.tr("DOB:"));
    var dob = new qx.ui.form.DateField();
    var genderLab = new qx.ui.basic.Label(this.tr("Gender:"));
    var radioGroup = new qx.ui.form.RadioButtonGroup();
    var male = new qx.ui.form.RadioButton(this.tr("Male"));
    radioGroup.add(male);
    var female = new qx.ui.form.RadioButton(this.tr("Female"));
    radioGroup.add(female);
    var remarksLab = new qx.ui.basic.Label(this.tr("Remarks:"));
```

```
var remarks = new qx.ui.form.TextArea();
var entryLab = new qx.ui.basic.Label(this.tr("Team:"));
var entryList = new qx.ui.form.SelectBox();
var lsItem = new qx.ui.form.ListItem("Team A", null, "1");
lsItem.setUserData("value", "1");
entryList.add(lsItem);

// creating the action buttons
var registerBtn = new qx.ui.form.Button(this.tr("Register"));
var resetBtn = new qx.ui.form.Button(this.tr("Reset"));
```

2. Configure the required languages in the LOCALES macro, inside the let section of your application's config.json file, thus:

```
"let" : {
  ........
  "LOCALES" : ["en", "fr", "de"]
}
```

3. Once we mark all the translatable strings, .po files have to be generated for each locale, where each .po file consists of locale-specific translated strings with the locale's key. These .po files can be generated by running the translation job in the generate.py as follows:

C:\teamtwitter\generate.py translation

Add the following target into our build.xml file, so that we can run from our ant build, directly. Update the C:\teamtwitter-server\build.xml file, thus:

```
<target name="client.generate-translation">
  <exec executable="python" dir="${clientApplicationDir}">
    <arg value="generate.py" />
    <arg value="translation" />
  </exec>
</target>
```

Now, you can run the target client.generate-translation, as follows:

C:\teamtwitter-server> ant client.generate-translation

This command generates .po files for all the languages specified in the config.json file in the LOCALES macro, within the global let section.

This adds English, French, and German translations to the project.

The generate translation command generates the locale-specific .po files. In this case, it generates en.po, fr.po, and de.po, under the source\ translation folder.

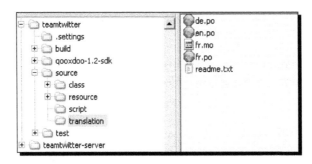

All the language-related .po files were created under the translation folder, for all the marked strings in the qooxdoo classes.

4. After generating the PO files, we need to edit them with the language-specific translations. These .po files are the actual files with all the translated messages. A developer can edit or add language-specific translated messages. As qooxdoo internally uses well-established tools and formats for internationalization ("getText" through polib), any po-aware editor, or a normal text editor, can be used to edit these .po files.

> If you use a normal text editor, you should make sure that the UTF-8 character set is used. If UTF-8 character set is not used, localization will not work properly. So, it is advisable to use a po-aware editor.

A sample .po file for French, opened in a text editor, is as follows:

```
#
msgid ""
msgstr ""
"Project-Id-Version: 1.0\n"
"Report-Msgid-Bugs-To: you@your.org\n"
"POT-Creation-Date: 2011-06-16 12:32+0500\n"
"PO-Revision-Date: 2011-06-16 12:32+0500\n"
"Last-Translator: you <you@your.org>\n"
"Language-Team: Team <yourteam@your.org>\n"
"MIME-Version: 1.0\n" "Content-Type: text/plain; charset=utf-8\n"
```

```
"Content-Transfer-Encoding: 8bit\n"
#: teamtwitter/ui/UserLoginForm.js:49
msgid "Login Form"
msgstr "Login Form"
#: teamtwitter/ui/UserLoginForm.js:54
msgid "User Name:"
msgstr "Nom d'utilisateur:"
#: teamtwitter/ui/UserLoginForm.js:57
msgid "Password:"
msgstr "Mot de passe:"
#: teamtwitter/ui/UserLoginForm.js:71
msgid "Sign In"
msgstr "Ouvrir une session"
#: teamtwitter/ui/UserLoginForm.js:72
msgid "Sign Up"
msgstr "Inscription"
#: teamtwitter/ui/UserSignUpForm.js:23
msgid "Sign Up Form"
msgstr "Inscription Formulaire"
#: teamtwitter/ui/UserSignUpForm.js:40
msgid "User Info"
msgstr "Infos utilisateurs"
#: teamtwitter/ui/UserSignUpForm.js:44
msgid "User Name"
```

Each translation string is a set of three-line blocks, and each block consists of a comment as the first line; this is a hint containing the class file and line number where the string is used. The second line holds the identifier we used in our application. The third line currently holds an empty string. This is the place where the translation should go for that specific string.

Some of the po-aware editors are:

- ❑ KBabel (Linux)
- ❑ Poedit (Linux, Windows, Mac OS X)
- ❑ LocFactory Editor (Mac OS X)

To translate our Team Twitter application, let us start translating the text using Poedit.

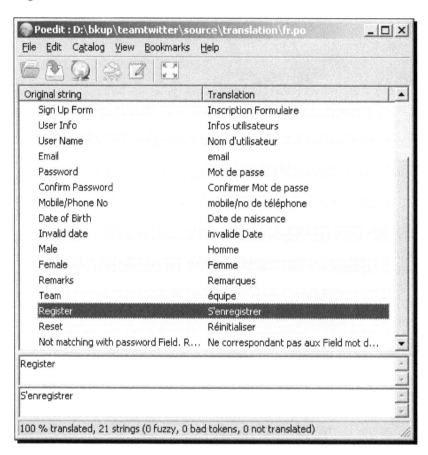

Poedit allows the user to load the languages in to translation DB and automatically translates the strings to a new language. Another way to translate is to manually edit the translated strings using any of the online translators, such as, Google Translate, Yahoo Babel Fish, and others.

After editing and saving the .po files, generate.py source run integrates the translations into the application's source version and generate.py build run integrates the translations into the application's build version. To get the effect of the new translations, it can be simply reloaded within the browser.

generate.py translation run generates .po files for the first time, and later on, the same command adds or merges the translatable strings in the existing .po files and similarly updates the de (German) language strings into de.po file.

5. Once you edit the PO files and regenerate the application source version, or build version, you can display the application in any of the locales that it supports. If your browser uses, by default, the locale you added, you should already see the application in the locale-specific language; otherwise, the developer can configure qooxdoo's qx.locale.Manager to switch the locale. A developer can set this locale in an application or use a Firebug console or IE developer console:

```
qx.locale.Manager.getInstance().setLocale("fr");
// or the locale you added
```

To dynamically change the languages in our Team Twitter application, we will add a list of all supported languages in a list at the top-right corner. When the user changes the language, the respective locale will be set to the locale `Manager` as shown in the following code snippet. Update the file `C:\teamtwitter\source\class\teamtwitter\Application.js`.

```
var langList = new qx.ui.form.SelectBox();
langList.add(new qx.ui.form.ListItem("English", null, "en"));
langList.add(new qx.ui.form.ListItem("French", null, "fr"));
langList.add(new qx.ui.form.ListItem("Italy", null, "it"));
langList.addListener("changeSelection", this.changeLanguage,
    this);

var layout= new qx.ui.layout.HBox();
layout.setSpacing(5); // apply spacing

var hBox = new qx.ui.container.Composite(layout);

hBox.add(new qx.ui.basic.Label(this.tr("Language:")));
hBox.add(langList);
hBox.set({
  alignX : "right",
  alignY : "middle"
});
doc.add(hBox, {
  left : 500,
  top : 0
});
doc.add(new teamtwitter.ui.MainWidget(), {
  left : 0,
  top : 25
});

changeLanguage : function(e) {
  var data = e.getData();
  qx.locale.Manager.getInstance().setLocale(data[0].
    getModel());
}
```

6. Compile, deploy, and run the application. A sample application screenshot, on selecting the French language, is as follows. We have demonstrated the internationalization only for the user registration form. So, change the language to **French** and check the signup link.

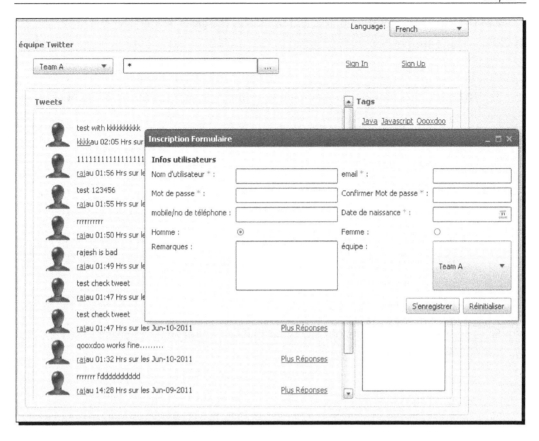

What just happened?

We learnt how to internationalize a qooxdoo application and localize the application for multiple languages. We followed the procedure and commands for internationalization and localized the Team Twitter application to different languages.

Pop quiz

1. The job available to generate or merge the `.po` files

    a. `generate.py build`

    b. `generate.py source`

    c. `generate.py translation`

    d. `generate.py localize`

2. The `marktr()` method marks and translates the given string

    a.   True

    b.   False

3. The mixin that provides functionalities to the `tr`, `trn`, `trc`, `marktr` functions is

    a.   `qx.locale.String`

    b.   `qx.locale.Number`

    c.   `qx.locale.MTranslation`

    d.   `qx.locale.Manager`

4. The `MTranslation` mixin was included, by default, in the classes

    a.   `qx.ui.core.Widget`

    b.   `qx.ui.table.columnmodel.Resize`

    c.   `qx.application.AbstracGui`

    d.   `qx.core.Object`

5. `.po` files that can be modified with normal text editors may be prone to UTF-8 character set issues

    a.   True

    b.   False

Summary

We learned a lot in this chapter about translation and localization.

Specifically, we covered:

- Built-in internationalization and location support in qooxdoo
- Editing PO files and online language translations
- We also localized our Team Twitter application to the French (`fr`) and German (`de`) languages

9
Working with Themes

This chapter explains the theme feature in qooxdoo framework. Themes enable you to change the look and feel of the application. You can use one of the themes available in the qooxdoo framework or you can customize the theme for your requirement. You don't need to know CSS, as the theme is configured in the qooxdoo classes. qooxdoo allows you to customize the styles through themes.

In the last chapter, we internationalized the Team Twitter application and localized it to multiple languages. Now, let us change the look and feel. In this chapter, we will explore the Themes feature, change the themes to the different available themes in qooxdoo framework, and then customize the theme for the Team Twitter application.

In this chapter, we will look at the following:

- ◆ `Meta` theme
- ◆ `Color` theme
- ◆ `Font` theme
- ◆ `Decoration` theme
- ◆ `Appearance` theme

Let us explore the theme feature of the qooxdoo framework.

Theme

qooxdoo allows you to keep the styles of the graphical user interface separately in the themes feature, so that the style can be changed at any point of time, by changing the theme and without needing to change the application code. The styles have to be defined in qooxdoo-specific syntax, which will be internally converted to DOM style for the application. For the style properties, you can refer to the respective classes. For instance, the possible font properties are defined in the `qx.bom.Font` class.

qooxdoo framework provides a set of classes to manage themes in the application and provides three different themes. It allows you to use one of them for your application (even at runtime), or to customize the theme for your application, and enables you to develop your own theme.

Class hierarchy of the theme package is shown in the following screenshot:

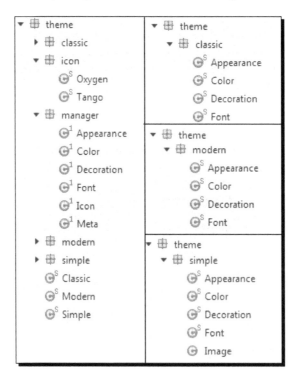

qooxdoo framework delivers three sets of themes, within the framework. They are the `Classic`, `Modern`, and `Simple` themes. The `Simple` theme is introduced in qooxdoo 1.4. The default theme set for any application is the `Modern` theme.

Meta theme

When you create a qooxdoo application, qooxdoo framework creates a namespace or package `<application-namespace>.theme`, with some auto-generated classes extending the `Modern` theme classes to the application theme. One can check the directory `teamtwitter\source\class\teamtwitter\theme` to see the classes **Appearance**, **Color**, **Decoration**, **Font**, and **Theme** created, as shown in the following screenshot:

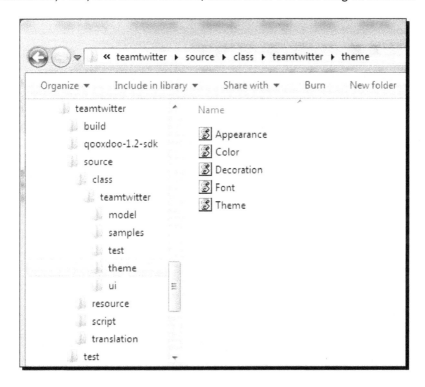

This theme allows you to define the `meta` configuration for each theme, namely, `Font`, `Color`, `Icon`, `Decoration`, and `Appearance`. Each theme plays a specific role in the application theme. As it allows you to configure all the themes in `meta` configuration, it is also called as the `Meta` theme.

The generated classes for `Font`, `Color`, `Decoration`, and `Appearance` classes extend respective classes from the package `qx.theme.modern`. The `theme` class sets the inherited classes in the `meta` configuration. The code snippets in the following sections show the generated theme classes for the application.

Theme

```
qx.Theme.define("teamtwitter.theme.Theme",
{
  meta :
  {
    color : teamtwitter.theme.Color,
    decoration : teamtwitter.theme.Decoration,
    font : teamtwitter.theme.Font,
    icon : qx.theme.icon.Tango,
    appearance : teamtwitter.theme.Appearance
  }
});
```

Font

```
qx.Theme.define("teamtwitter.theme.Font",
{
  extend : qx.theme.modern.Font,

  fonts :
  {
  }
});
```

Color

```
qx.Theme.define("teamtwitter.theme.Color",
{
  extend : qx.theme.modern.Color,

  colors :
  {
  }
});
```

Decoration

```
qx.Theme.define("teamtwitter.theme.Decoration",
{
  extend : qx.theme.modern.Decoration,

  decorations :
  {
  }
});
```

Appearance

```
qx.Theme.define("teamtwitter.theme.Appearance",
{
  extend : qx.theme.modern.Appearance,

  appearances :
  {
  }
});
```

You can change the theme from Modern to Classic by inheriting the classes from the package qx.theme.classic. In qooxdoo 1.4 SDK, you can also change your theme to the Simple theme, by inheriting the classes from the package qx.theme.simple.

Modern theme

The Modern theme is a graphically-rich theme, as shown in the following screenshot:

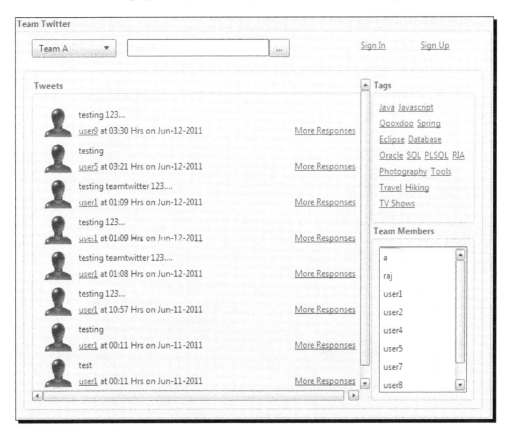

To customize or change the theme, you have to edit the `Font`, `Color`, `Decoration`, and `Appearance` classes, in the `teamtwitter.theme` package.

The following code snippet changes the `Font` class to use the `Classic` theme font. Similarly, you have to inherit the `Classic` theme classes for other classes in the theme package.

```
qx.Theme.define("teamtwitter.theme.Font",
{
   extend : qx.theme.classic.Font,

   fonts :
   {
   }
});
```

Classic theme

The `Classic` theme is a MS Windows-oriented theme, as shown in the following screenshot:

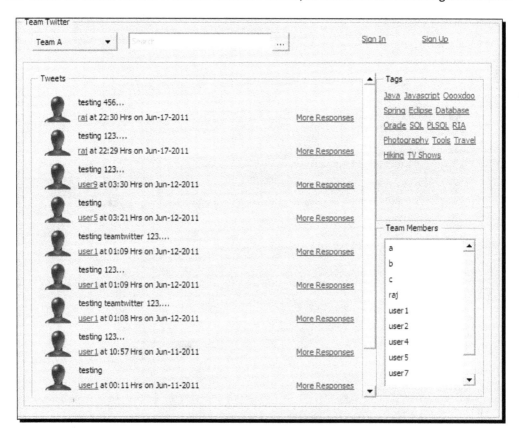

If you do not like a particular setting, either in the `Font`, `Color`, `Decoration`, or `Appearance` theme, in the theme that you are inheriting, you can simply override it by changing a setting in the application theme class. We will see that in the following sections.

When you create a custom widget, and you need to set the styles for the custom widget and its child controls, you can define those in the theme classes and let the qooxdoo framework apply the styles for you. This is something similar to defining styles in CSS and using them in the HTML element. But, here, you need to define in the theme classes.

If you want to create a unique theme for your application from scratch, you can do that as well. To do that, you need to define all the styles that are required by the qooxdoo framework, in your theme. You can take a look at the classes of one of the themes in the qooxdoo framework, and you can define your own style for all the configurations required for your framework. In addition to the required configurations for your framework to function, you can add your additional styles with your configuration keys and use them in your widgets.

Simple theme

The `Simple` theme is a lightweight theme and appears more like a website. It is available with qooxdoo 1.4 and is shown in the following screenshot:

You can change the theme at runtime, by calling the following API:

```
qx.theme.manager.Meta.getInstance().setTheme(qx.theme.Classic);
```

But changing the theme at runtime does not refresh the user interface perfectly, because of the heavy caching and optimization in the theme feature. It is advisable to set a specific theme for your application up front and to customize it as you wish.

Icon theme

qooxdoo provides two sets of icons in the qooxdoo framework. They are `qx.theme.icon.Oxygen` and `qx.theme.icon.Tango`. Based on the icon in the `meta` configuration of the theme, it uses the resources either from `qooxdoo-sdk/framework/source/resource/qx/icon/Oxygen` or from `qooxdoo-sdk/framework/source/resource/qx/icon/Tango`, as follows:

```
qx.Theme.define("teamtwitter.theme.Theme", {
  meta : {
    color : teamtwitter.theme.Color,
    decoration : teamtwitter.theme.Decoration,
    font : teamtwitter.theme.Font,
    icon : qx.theme.icon.Tango,
    appearance : teamtwitter.theme.Appearance
  }
}
```

Color theme

The `Color` theme defines all the colors used for various widgets in the framework. Each color is defined by a unique key and a value, either in Hex (for example, #A7A6AA), RGB (for example, 242, 242, 242), or in named colors (for example, white, black, and so on). The unique key can be used at the places where you want to set the color for any widget, in the qooxdoo framework and in your application.

The named colors in the qooxdoo framework are `black`, `white`, `silver`, `gray`, `maroon`, `red`, `purple`, `fuchsia`, `green`, `lime`, `olive`, `yellow`, `navy blue`, `teal`, `aqua`, `orange`, and `brown`. These named colors are defined in the class `qx.util.ColorUtil`.

Font theme

The Font theme defines all the font types or variants used in the framework. It is quite compact, as it defines a limited number of font types or variants. Both the Classic theme and Simple theme use the same font style for a particular font type or variant, in any OS, but the Modern theme uses different font styles for a particular font type or variant, based on the OS.

Decoration theme

Decorations are used to style the widget. In qooxdoo framework, decoration is an independent layer around the widget content, so that the decorations, such as background image, color, border, and so on, can be changed without any code change in the widget class.

The following schematic diagram illustrates the concept of decoration:

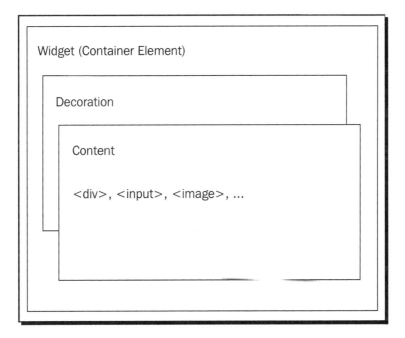

Decorations are set to the shadow and decorator properties of the widget. They could be applied separately or together; there is no dependency between them.

To make use of the decoration feature, you should avoid creating separate decorations inside the application code; instead, create the decorations property inside the theme and use it in the application code. This way, you can reuse the decorations for multiple widgets and also maintain an independent layer in the theme.

The following code snippet shows the definition for the selected `decoration` in the `Modern` theme:

```
qx.Theme.define("qx.theme.modern.Decoration",{
  aliases : {
    decoration : "qx/decoration/Modern"
  },

  decorations : {

      "selected" : {
      decorator : qx.ui.decoration.Background,
      style : {
        backgroundImage : "decoration/selection.png",
        backgroundRepeat : "scale"
      }
      },
  //--------
  //--------
  }
}
```

This code snippet has two sections, namely `aliases` and `decorations`.

Aliases

The `aliases` section has an entry for the decoration with the value `qx/decoration/Modern`. This adds an alias entry in the `AliasManager` class and verifies that the images are found by the `ResourceManager` class. If you look further in the `decorations` section, the `backgroundImage` property is set to `decoration/selection.png`. This entry uses the decoration alias defined in the `aliases` section. The `backgroundImage` property is finally resolved to `qx/decoration/Modern/selection.png`, in the resource section of the application.

Decorations

The `decorations` section defines all the decorations that can be used in the qooxdoo framework. Each decoration is defined against the decorator name, which is set to the `decorator` property of the widget. It is recommended to define the decorator in the `Decoration` theme and set the decorator in the `Appearance` theme, instead of setting it directly in the application code of the widget. By doing so, you maintain the theme of the application.

Each decoration definition in the theme contains two entries, namely, `decorator` and `style`.

Decorator

The decorator key defines which decorator to use. Qooxdoo framework provides a set of pre-defined decorator classes and mixins in the package qx.ui.decoration. You can specify one of the decorator classes or set of mixins, based on the decoration requirement.

In the earlier code snippet, the decoration definition for "selected" uses the decorator qx.ui.decoration.Background to set the background image of the selected item. This is used in the Appearance theme of qx.ui.form.ListItem. There are different decorators available for different purposes.

The class hierarchy of the decoration package is shown in the following screenshot:

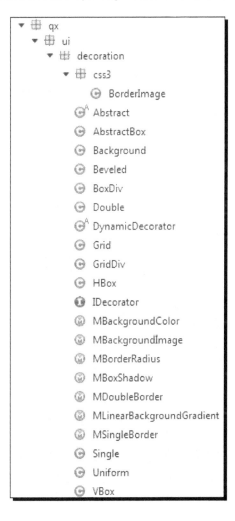

Available decorators in qooxdoo framework 1.4 are described as follows:

- **Background**: Renders a background image or color.

- **Uniform**: Similar to the **Background** decorator, but adds support for a uniform border that is identical for all edges.

- **Single**: Similar to the **Background** decorator, but adds support for separate borders for each edge.

- **Double**: Similar to the **Single** decorator, but with the ability to add two separate borders to each edge.

- **Beveled**: Pseudo (lightweight) rounded border with support for inner glow. May contain a background image/gradient.

- **HBox**: Uses three images in a row with a center image that is stretched horizontally. Useful for widgets, with a fixed height, that can be stretched horizontally.

- **VBox**: Uses three images in a column with a center image that is stretched vertically. Useful for widgets, with a fixed width, that can be stretched vertically.

- **Grid**: A complex decorator based on nine images. Allows much-customized styles (rounded borders, alpha transparency, gradients, and so on). Optionally makes use of image sprites to reduce image number.

If you want to write a custom decorator, you can either extend one of these decorators and customize it or write one yourself from scratch, adhering to the interface of a decorator.

In addition to all these decorators, qooxdoo supplies a set of mixins that supply separate features for decorators. All feature mixins can be used in combination to get an individual decorator. The mixins also include some of the following features that are not available in the standalone decorators:

- **MBackgroundColor**: For drawing a background color

- **MBackgroundImage**: For drawing a background image

- **MDoubleBorder**: For drawing two borders around a widget

- **MSingleBorder**: For drawing a single border

- **MBorderRadius**: For adding a CSS radius to the corners

- **MBoxShadow**: For adding a CSS box shadow to the widget (does not use the `shadow` property)

- **MLinearBackgroundGradient**: For drawing a linear gradient in the background

The last three mixins do not work cross-browser due to the fact that they rely on CSS properties that are not available in all browsers.

Style

The `style` key defines the values for the properties of the selected decorators or mixins. In the earlier code snippet, the style map sets the `backgroundImage` and `backgroundRepeat` properties of the decorator `qx.ui.decoration.Background`.

Writing new decorators

If the available decorators are not enough, you can write new decorators by implementing the following interface methods:

- ◆ `getInsets`: Returns a map of insets (space the decorator needs), for example, the border width.

- ◆ `getMarkup`: Returns the initial markup needed to build the decorator. This is executed by each widget using the decorator. This method may not be used by some decorators, and so is defined as an empty method.

- ◆ `init`: Normally used to initialize the given element using `getMarkup`, it is only executed once per widget.

- ◆ `resize`: Resizes the given element to the given dimensions. Directly works on the DOM to manipulate the content of the element.

- ◆ `tint`: Applies the given background color or optionally resets it to the locally-defined background color. This method may not be used by some decorators, and so is defined as an empty method.

The `resize` and `tint` methods are the most-executed or are called many times (for example, hover effects). Therefore, these method implementations should be light. The `getMarkup` and `init` methods are called only once. Most of the things should be done in these methods for performance reasons. Decorators are immutable; once they are used somewhere, you cannot change them. qooxdoo framework creates only one instance for each decoration configured. That instance is created on the first use.

Appearance theme

The `Appearance` theme describes the appearance of every widget, and its child widgets, to which a theme can be applied. As the basic styling is done through the `Decoration` theme, `Color` theme, `Font` theme, and `Icon` theme, the `Appearance` theme uses the definitions of all the other themes. It is the central meeting point where all other themes (`Decoration`, `Font`, `Color`, and `Icon`) get together. Whenever you want to customize a theme, the `Appearance` theme is the first place to look for the widget style. You can customize the style either in this theme itself or change the relevant item in the `Decoration` theme or `Color` theme. As we should know about all the other themes to understand the `Appearance` theme, we have covered them prior to this one.

The following code snippet shows a couple of appearance definitions in the Modern theme:

```
qx.Theme.define("qx.theme.classic.Appearance",
{
  appearances :
  {
  -------
  -------

    "menu-button" :
    {
      alias : "atom",

      style : function(states)
      {
        return {
          backgroundColor : states.selected ?
            "background-selected" : undefined,
          textColor : states.selected ? "text-selected" : undefined,
          padding : [ 2, 6 ]
        };
      }
    },

    "menu-button/icon" :
    {
      include : "image",

      style : function(states)
      {
        return {
          alignY : "middle"
        };
      }
    },

    "menu-button/label" :
    {
      include : "label",

      style : function(states)
      {
        return {
          alignY : "middle",
          padding : 1
        };
      }
    }
  -------
  -------

  }
});
```

All the appearance styles are defined under the appearances section of the Appearance theme. Each appearance is defined against a key, which is the selector to identify the appearance for the widget. This selector is basically matched with the appearance property of the widget.

Appearance selector (key)

For the widgets, the selector key is matched with the appearance property of the widget. This is not applicable to the child controls. For the child controls, the appearance property of the parent widget and the ID of the child control are used to match the selector key.

For the qx.ui.menu.Button widget, the appearance property is set to "menu-button", which is matched against the selector in the appearances. The Menu Button widget has four child controls, namely, icon, label, shortcut, and arrow. For these child controls, the appearance selector is a combination of the appearance property of the parent widget, that is, "menu-button", and the ID of the child control, that is, icon, label, and so on. Therefore, the appearance selector for the icon of the menu button is "menu-button/icon" and for the label of the menu button is "menu-button/label". The separator between the identifiers is the forward slash. This hierarchical selector continues to create multiple levels, as the child control contains another child control within it, for example, "tabview-page/button/label".

Another example is the Spinner widget. This widget contains a TextField property and two RepeatButton properties. These three properties are created as child controls with the IDs textfield, upbutton, and downbutton. Therefore, the selectors for these child controls are "spinner/textfield", "spinner/upbutton", and "spinner/downbutton", respectively.

For the appearance, you do not have to set anything explicitly on the widget. qooxdoo framework automatically matches the appearance property of the widget, or the hierarchical ID of the child control, with the appearance key in the Appearance theme and applies the appearance style to the widget. You need to make sure the corresponding appearance property is defined in the Appearance theme. Selectors for all the widgets and child controls must be defined in the Appearance theme of the application. Otherwise, a warning about the missing selectors is displayed.

Appearance entry (value)

The entry value in the appearances against the selector key can be defined in two different ways, namely, string (alias) and map.

Alias

The string value against the selector key is known as **alias**. This is basically a string that redirects to another selector in the appearances property.

The following code snippet explains the alias in the Appearance theme:

```
qx.Theme.define("qx.theme.classic.Appearance",
{
  appearances :
  {
  -------
  -------

    "label" :
    {
      style : function(states)
      {
        return {
          textColor : states.disabled ? "text-disabled" : undefined
        };
      }
    },

    "image" :
    {
      style : function(states)
      {
        return {
          opacity : !states.replacement && states.disabled ?
            0.3 : undefined
        }
      }
    },

    "atom" : {},
    "atom/label" : "label",
    "atom/icon" : "image"
  }
});
```

The atom widget has two child controls, namely, label and icon. It reuses the appearance style of generic Label and Image widgets. In the earlier code snippet, it uses the following alias to define the same:

```
"atom/label" : "label",
"atom/icon" : "image"
```

Appearance map

The map value against the selector key contains several key and value pairs. All the key and value pairs in the map are optional.

```
qx.Theme.define("qx.theme.classic.Appearance",
{
  appearances :
  {
  -------
  -------
    "spinner" :
    {
      style : function(states)
      {
        return {
          decorator : states.focused ? "focused-inset" : "inset",
          textColor : states.disabled ? "text-disabled" : undefined
        };
      }
    },

    "spinner/textfield" :
    {
      include : "textfield",

      style : function(states)
      {
        return {
          decorator : undefined,
          padding: [2, 3]
        };
      }
    },

    "spinner/upbutton" :
    {
      alias : "button",
      include : "button",

      style : function(states)
      {
        return {
          icon : "decoration/arrows/up-small.gif",
          padding : states.pressed ? [2, 2, 0, 4] : [1, 3, 1, 3],
          backgroundColor : states.hovered ?
            "button-hovered" : "button"
        }
      }
    }
  }
});
```

Style entry in the appearance map

Style entry is a method that returns a set of properties to be applied to the target widget. This method takes a few parameters. The `states` parameter is a map that contains the widget state keys, such as, `focused`, `disabled`, `hovered`, `selected`, and so on, and the Boolean value to indicate the state of the widget. This parameter is passed always to the style method, to react based on the state of the widget.

It is required that all the properties applied in one state be applied in all other states also.

The following snippet of code demonstrates an incorrect way of coding:

```
style : function(states)
{
  var result = {};
  if (states.hovered) {
    result.backgroundColor = "red";
  }
  // BAD: backgroundColor missing when widget isn't hovered!
  return result;
}
```

Instead, you should always define the `else` case and set it to `undefined`, as shown:

```
style : function(states)
{
  var result = {};
  if (states.hovered) {
    result.backgroundColor = "red";
  } else
  {
    //GOOD: There should be a setting for all possible states
    result.backgroundColor = undefined;
  }
  return result;
}
```

 The `undefined` value means that no value should be applied. When qooxdoo runs through the returned map, it calls the reset method for properties with a value of `undefined`. In most cases, it would also be perfectly valid to use `null` instead of `undefined`, but keep in mind that `null` is stored using the setter (explicit null), and so it overrides values given through the inheritance or through the `init` values. In short, this means that `undefined` is the better choice in almost all cases.

The include entry in the appearance map

`alias` applies all the styles of the referred appearance to the current appearance. In case you want to use most of the style from an existing appearance and slightly change one property, you can use an `include` key to use the styles of an existing appearance and, optionally, you can overwrite few properties in the style method of appearance.

In qooxdoo framework 1.4, for the `Modern` theme, there is an optional second parameter, `superStyles`, for the `style` method. This parameter is only available if an `include` key is specified in the appearance. This parameter contains the styles of the included appearance. This is very handy if you just want to overwrite certain properties, instead of completely writing the styles again. To overwrite a property in `superStyles`, declare that property in the `style` method and set the new value. To remove a property in `superStyles`, declare that property in the `style` method and set it to `undefined`.

You don't have to return the edited `superStyles`. Appearance manager in the qooxdoo framework automatically merges the `superStyles` parameter with the styles returned by the `style` method. On merging, the styles returned by the `style` method get precedence over the `superStyles` parameter; that is how it overwrites the values in `superStyles`.

You can just include an existing appearance without overwriting any styles in the `style` method. This has the same effect of referring to the appearance with `alias`. In this case, `alias` is the better choice, as it performs well compared to `include`.

The `include` entry does not affect child controls. It just affects the current selector.

The alias entry in the appearance map

Child control aliases are compared to the normal aliases mentioned earlier; they just define aliases for the child controls. They do not redirect the local selector to the selector defined by the alias.

An example to make this clearer is given as follows:

```
qx.Theme.define("qx.theme.modern.Appearance",
{
  appearances :
  {
    [...],
    "spinner/upbutton" :
    {
      alias : "button",
      style : function(states) {
```

```
            return {
              padding : 2,
              icon : "decoration/arrows/up.gif"
            }
          }
        },
        [...]
      }
    });
```

The result mapping would be similar to the following:

`"spinner/upbutton" => "spinner/upbutton"`

`"spinner/upbutton/icon" => "button/image"`

`"spinner/upbutton/label" => "button/label"`

As you can see, `spinner/upbutton` is kept in its original state. This allows one to just refine a specific outer part of a complex widget, instead of the whole widget. It is also possible to include the original part of the button in `spinner/upbutton`, as well. This is useful to override just a few properties, as seen in the following example:

```
qx.Theme.define("qx.theme.modern.Appearance",
{
  appearances :
  {
    [...],
    "spinner/upbutton" :
    {
      alias : "button",
      include : "button",
      style : function(states)
      {
        return {
          padding : 2,
          icon : "decoration/arrows/up.gif"
        }
      }
    },
    [...]
  }
});
```

The result mapping would be similar to the following:

`"spinner/upbutton"` => `"button"` + styles overridden in style method.

`"spinner/upbutton/icon"` => `"button/image"`

`"spinner/upbutton/label"` => `"button/label"`

When `alias` and `include` are identically pointing to the same selector, the result is identical to the alias string value mentioned against the selector key, as we mentioned in the alias section under *Appearance entry (value)* section in this chapter. Optionally, you can override a few properties in the style method of appearance.

Base calls

In the functions of qooxdoo classes, we call `this.base(<arguments>)` to call the overwritten function of the super class. Similarly, in the `Appearance` theme, you can enable the base flag to include the definitions of this selector key from the derived theme. In the following code snippet, the `myapp Appearance` theme extends the `classic Appearance` theme. For the `"spinner/textfield"` selector key, if you set `true` for the base flag, it includes all the definitions of the `"spinner/textfield"` selector key from the `classic Appearance` theme.

```
qx.Theme.define("myapp.theme.Appearance",
{
  extend : qx.theme.classic.Appearance,
  appearances : {
    [...],
    "spinner/textfield" : {
      base : true,
      style : function(states) {
        return {
          property : states.hovered ? value1 : value2
        };
      }
    },
    [...]
  }
}
```

So, user can define the appearance definitions through one of the following options:

◆ Define locally through style method

◆ Include the definitions through `include` key

◆ Enable base flag to include the definitions from the extended `Appearance` theme

While merging the definitions from these three definitions, the preference is given in the same order as it is mentioned above.

Performance

The appearance of each widget is rendered on change of the widget's state. As the appearance is updated every time a widget's state changes, the theme feature is quite expensive, and even a small variation has tremendous impact on the whole application's performance. So, the qooxdoo framework has taken more care and improved performance by implementing some impressive caching ideas.

The different caching techniques implemented in qooxdoo framework will be discussed now.

Appearance queue

This is the first and foremost improvement in theme handling. The improvement is made at the display level. It depends on the visibility of the widget and on the visibility of the parent widget. The qooxdoo framework queues up all the state changes of the visible widgets and of the widget placed in a visible parent widget, delays the updates until the widget gets visible again, and updates the screen once to avoid multiple updates. So, this queue minimizes the effect of multiple state changes when they happen one after another and combines all changes to a widget into one lookup in the theme.

For example, the `hovered` and `focused` state changes happen one after another. These two updates are queued and the screen is updated once instead of twice. This queue really improves the performance in heavy themes such as the `Modern` theme, because each click on the GUI influences a few widgets at once, and, in each widget, a few state changes at once.

Selector caching

Secondly, selector caching caches all the detected and validated selectors for all the widgets. As detection of the selector is quite complex with iterations up to the parent chain, the framework caches all the resulting selectors of each widget. The cached selector gets updated with any change in the `appearance` property of the widget. If the user sets the appearance directly in the code instead of defining the appearance inside the theme classes, qooxdoo framework has to redetect the selector with all iterations up to the parent chain. This is repeated every time when the code is executed, basically when the appearance is set.

So, the qooxdoo framework suggests not setting the appearance dynamically in the code and suggests the use of the `Appearance` theme, to make use of the selector cache. The system benefits more with child widgets, as these are never moved outside the parent, and the cached selector can be used for a lifetime, for child widgets.

Alias caching

The next one is alias caching. The support for aliases is resolved once per application load. So, after a while, all aliases are resolved to their final destination. This process is lazy and fills the redirection map with selector usage. This is a relatively complex process. So, this process of resolving all aliases is done only once and they are stored in the `Appearance` theme's `aliasMap` map object. The developer can have a look at this map for all the resolved aliases, just by typing `qx.theme.manager.Appearance.getInstance().__aliasMap` in the interactive `javascript` console of Firebug. It just contains the fully resolved alias (aliases may redirect to each other as well). The output looks similar to the following screenshot:

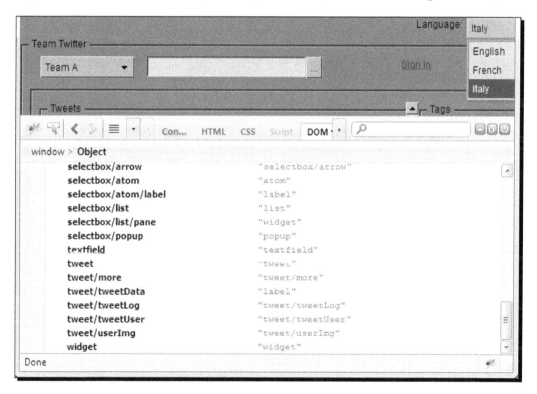

Result caching

The final caching implemented in the framework for themes is the result caching for a specific set of states. This may be the most massive source of performance tweaks in the system. On first usage, qooxdoo caches the appearance based on state. For example, the result of the button with the `hovered` and `focused` states. The result is used for any further requests for an `Appearance` theme with the identical set of states. This caching is, by the way, the most evident reason why the `appearance` property has no access to the individual widget. The result caching also reduces the overhead of the `include` and `base` statements, which are quite intensive tasks because of the map merge character with which they have been implemented. As with alias caching, result caching can be seen by typing the following in the interactive `javascript` console of Firebug—`qx.theme.manager.Appearance.getInstance().__styleCache`—where this style cache stores all the resulting styles of each widget. A sample style cache is shown in the following screenshot:

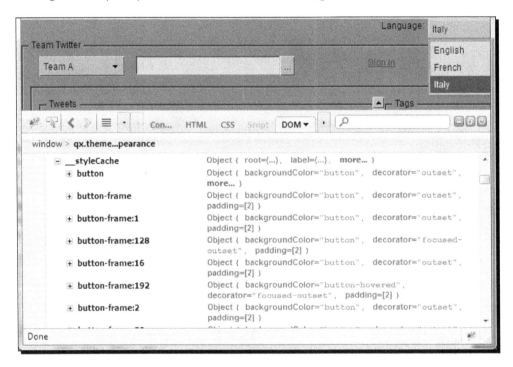

Time for action – customizing themes for Team Twitter

1. Update the Team Twitter theme classes under the following directory, to use the `Classic` theme:

`C:\teamtwitter\source\class\teamtwitter\theme`

`teamtwitter.theme.Font extends qx.theme.classic.Font`
`teamtwitter.theme.Color extends qx.theme.classic.Color`
`teamtwitter.theme.Decoration extends qx.theme.classic.Decoration`
`teamtwitter.theme.Appearance extends qx.theme.classic.Appearance`

Rebuild the application (`dist`), deploy it (`deploy`), and check the look and feel of the Team Twitter application.

2. Change the background color scheme for the Team Twitter application. You should know the correct keys to set the color used by the qooxdoo framework. A few keys may be different in different themes, based on the theme requirement. The `background` color is used to set the background color of the root pane and most of the container widgets. The `background-selected` color is used to set the background color of the selected item in the `List` or `SelectBox`.

The following code snippet sets a couple of background color theme configurations:

```
qx.Theme.define("teamtwitter.theme.Color",
{
  extend : qx.theme.classic.Color,

  colors :
  {
  "background" : "teal",
  "background-selected" : [0, 75, 75]
  }
});
```

Rebuild the application (`dist`), deploy it (`deploy`), and check the look and feel of the Team Twitter application.

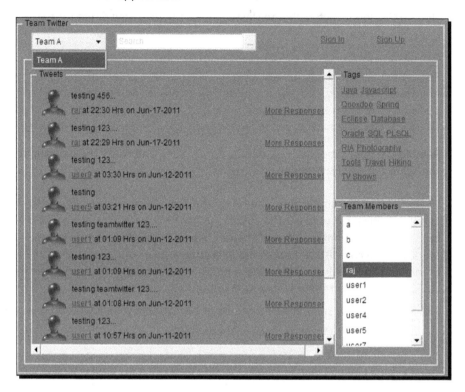

3. Increase the font size and change the font families in the `Font` theme for the Team Twitter application.

   The following code snippet overrides font definition for the `default` and `bold` font types or variants. The updated copy of the file `Font.js` is available as code file `978-1-849513-70-8_09_01.txt` under `Chapter 9` in the support files for this book.

```
qx.Theme.define("teamtwitter.theme.Font",
{
  extend : qx.theme.classic.Font,

  fonts :
  {
  "default" :
    {
      size : 12,
      lineHeight : 1.4,
      family : [ "Helvetica" ]
    },
```

```
      "bold" :
      {
        size : 13,
        lineHeight : 1.4,
        family : [ "Lucida Grande" ],
        bold : true
      }
    }
});
```

You can set values for all the properties in the qx.bom.Font class. The properties available are bold, color, decoration, family, italic, lineHeight, and size.

Rebuild the application (dist), deploy it (deploy), and check the look and feel of the Team Twitter application.

4. As the default qx.ui.groupbox.GroupBox border does not suit the Color theme, let us customize that in our decoration theme to match our color scheme. If you check the appearance theme for the qx.ui.groupbox.GroupBox, you will find that it uses the "groove" decorator. Let us customize that decorator.

    The following code snippet customizes the "groove" decorator:

```
qx.Theme.define("teamtwitter.theme.Decoration",
{
  extend : qx.theme.classic.Decoration,

  decorations :
  {
    "groove" :
    {
      decorator : qx.ui.decoration.Double,

      style .
      {
        width : 2,
        innerWidth: 1,
        color : ["border-dark-shadow", "border-light",
                 "border-light", "border-dark-shadow"],
        innerColor : ["border-light", "border-dark-shadow",
                      "border-dark-shadow", "border-light"]
      }
    }
  }
});
```

This code just changes the width of the "groove" decorator to 2, keeping the innerWidth as 1.

5. Update the `Color` theme further to change the colors to match the color scheme. Also, we will change the colors of the text fields and buttons to match the color scheme.

The following code snippet customizes the `Color` theme, again:

```
qx.Theme.define("teamtwitter.theme.Color",
{
  extend : qx.theme.classic.Color,

  colors :
  {
    "background" : "teal",
    "background-selected" : [0, 75, 75],

    "border-light" : "#00E1E1",
    "border-dark-shadow" : "#003232",

    „background-field" : „#96FFFF",
    „background-focused" : „#78FFFF",

    „button" : „#00C8C8",
    „button-hovered" : „#00A0A0"
  }
});
```

Rebuild the application (`dist`), deploy it (`deploy`), and check the look and feel of the Team Twitter application. After the customization, the screen of the Team Twitter appears as shown in the following screenshot:

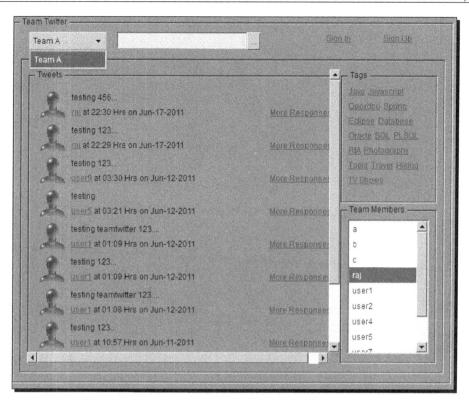

6. Let us update the appearance for the custom widget, `CTweet.js`, under `C:/teamtwitter/source/class/teamtwitter/ui`. We have already created the style in the inline code of our `CTweet` class. Now, we can move these styles into the theme, so that the style can be changed just by changing the theme instead of having to touch the code.

The following snippet of code shows the creation of child controls in the CTweet widget:

```
// overridden
_createChildControlImpl : function(id, hash)
{
  var control;
  switch(id)
  {
    case "userImg":
    //create user image
    var control = new
      qx.ui.basic.Image("teamtwitter/identity.png");
    control.set({
      width : 50,
      height : 50,
      scale : true
    });
    this._add(control, {row : 0, column:0, rowSpan : 2});
    break;

    case "tweetLog" :
    // create user label
    this.userLabel = new qx.ui.basic.Label("<a style = 'color:
      rgb(126, 26, 26);text-decoration:underline'>" +
      this.getUserName() + "</a>");
    this.userLabel.setRich(true);
    this.userLabel.setSelectable(true);
    this.userLabel.setCursor("pointer");
    this.userLabel.addListener("click", this.userNameClicked,
      this);
    // time label
    this.dateTimeLabel = new qx.ui.basic.Label(" at " +
      this.getTime() + " on "+ this.getDate());
    control = new qx.ui.container.Composite();
    control.setLayout(new qx.ui.layout.HBox());
    control.add(this.userLabel);
    control.add(this.dateTimeLabel);
    this._add(control, {row : 1, column:1});
    break;

    case "tweetData" :
    // creating the required fields with the headings as labels
    control = new qx.ui.basic.Label("");
```

```
    control.setRich(true);
    control.setSelectable(true);
    // adding the created fields
    this._add(control, {row : 0, column:1, colSpan : 2});
    break;

    case "more":
    // create responses label
    control = new qx.ui.basic.Label("<a style = 'color:
      rgb(126, 26, 26);text-decoration:underline'>
      More Responses</a>");
    control.set ( {
      rich : true,
      selectable : true,
      cursor : "pointer",
      alignX : "right"
    });
    control.addListener("click", this.moreClicked, this);
    this._add(control, {row : 1, column:2});
    break;
  }
  return control;
}
```

The above code is setting styles on the controls. It is recommended to set all styles in the themes, so that you maintain the styles on a separate layer.

The following code snippet shows the updated code that does not set styles directly in the code. It is better to separate the tweetLog child control into two, namely, tweetUser and tweetLog, so that separate styles can be used for those two child controls. The updated copy of the file CTweet.js is available as code file 978-1-849513-70-8 09_02.txt under Chapter 9 in the support files for this book.

```
_createChildControlImpl : function(id, hash) {
  var control;
  switch(id) {
    case "userImg":
    //create user image
    var control = new
      qx.ui.basic.Image("teamtwitter/identity.png");
    this._add(control, {row : 0, column:0, rowSpan : 2});
    break;

    case "tweetUser" :
    // create user label
```

```
      this.userLabel = new qx.ui.basic.Label("<a style =
        'text-decoration:underline'>" + this.getUserName() +
        "</a>");
      this.userLabel.set ( {
        rich : true
      });
      this.userLabel.addListener("click", this.userNameClicked,
        this);
      control = this.userLabel;
      this._add(control, {row : 1, column:1});
      break;

    case "tweetLog" :
    // time label
    this.dateTimeLabel = new qx.ui.basic.Label(" at " +
      this.getTime() + " on "+ this.getDate());
    control = this.dateTimeLabel;
    this._add(control, {row : 1, column:2});
    break;

    case "tweetData" :
    // creating the required fields with the headings as labels
    control = new qx.ui.basic.Label("");
    this._add(control, {row : 0, column:1, colSpan : 3});
    break;

    case "more":
    // create responses label
    control = new qx.ui.basic.Label("<a style =
      'text-decoration:underline'>More Responses</a>");
    control.set ( {
      rich : true
    });
    control.addListener("click", this.moreClicked, this);
    this._add(control, {row : 1, column:3});
    break;
  }
  return control;
}
```

To create these styles in the theme, the following changes are made to the Appearance theme. The updated copy of the file Appearance.js is available as code file 978-1-849513-70-8_09_03.txt under Chapter 9 in the support files for this book.

```
qx.Theme.define("teamtwitter.theme.Appearance",
{
  extend : qx.theme.classic.Appearance,
```

```
appearances :
{
  "tweet" : {
    style : function(states)
    {
      return {
        decorator : "tweet"
      };
    }
  },

  "tweet/userImg" : {
    include : "image",
    style : function(states)
    {
      return {
        width : 50,
        height : 50,
        scale : true
      }
    }
  },

  "tweet/tweetUser" : {
    include : "label",
    style : function(states)
    {
      return {
        textColor : "teamtwitter-link-text",
        cursor : "pointer",
        alignX : "right"
      }
    }
  },

  "tweet/tweetLog" : {
    include : "label",
    style : function(states)
    {
      return {
        alignX : "left"
      }
    }
  },

  "tweet/tweetData" : "label",
```

```
"tweet/more" : {
  include : "label",
  style : function(states)
  {
    return {
      textColor : "teamtwitter-link-text",
      cursor : "pointer",
      alignX : "right"
    }
  }
}
}
});
```

7. Now, add the decorator that is used in our Appearance theme. In the tweet appearance, we used a decorator to add the border for the tweet widget. The definition of that decorator should go into the Decoration theme, as mentioned in the following code snippet. The updated copy of the file Decoration.js is available as code file 978-1-849513-70-8_09_04.txt under Chapter 9.

```
"tweet" :
{
  decorator: qx.ui.decoration.Uniform,

  style :
  {
    width : 1,
    color : "border-tweet"
  }
}
```

8. During the process of customizing, we added a couple of colors in the Color theme, as mentioned in the following code snippet. The updated copy of the file Color.js is available as code file 978-1-849513-70-8_09_05.txt under Chapter 9 in the support files for this book.

```
"teamtwitter-link-text" : [126, 26, 26],
"border-tweet" : "#003333"
```

After these customizations in the themes, the screen of the Team Twitter application will appear as shown in the following screenshot:

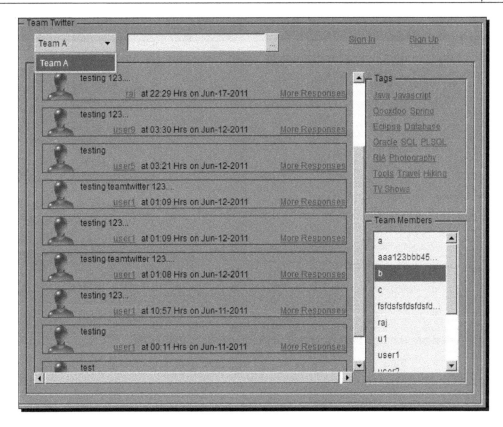

As said before, the Appearance theme is the first theme to start customization. To start customization, look for the selector key of the Appearance theme based on: the appearance value of the widget (for example, "button"), the hierarchical ID, or the parent widget's appearance value and the child control IDs (for example, "spinner/upbutton"). Once you have identified the selector key in the Appearance theme, you can either customize the style in the Appearance theme itself or change the relevant item in the Decoration theme or Color theme as required.

When you write a new appearance for your new custom widget, write the appearance first, and then write the decorations and colors, as required, or reuse the existing decorations and colors.

What just happened?

We learnt the theme feature of the qooxdoo framework. We have learned about the Meta theme and various themes in the theme system. We have also customized each theme—Icon theme, Color theme, Font theme, Decoration theme, and Appearance theme—for our Team Twitter application.

Pop quiz

1. What are the themes provided in qooxdoo framework 1.4

    a. Simple

    b. Classic

    c. Classy

    d. Modern

    e. Matt

2. Which theme is lightweight and looks like a website

    a. Simple

    b. Classic

    c. Classy

    d. Modern

    e. Matt

3. What are the icon sets provided in the qooxdoo framework

    a. Tango

    b. Simple

    c. Aqua

    d. Oxygen

4. What are the ways you can define a color in the Color theme

    a. Hex (for example, #A7A6AA)

    b. RGB (for example, 242, 242, 242)

    c. Named color (for example, white)

    d. All of the above

5. Which theme uses different font styles based on OS

    a. Simple

    b. Classic

    c. Classy

    d. Modern

    e. Matt

6. Which theme is the starting point to look for any customization

    a. `Icon`

    b. `Color`

    c. `Font`

    d. `Decoration`

    e. `Appearance`

7. Can you configure a decoration in the decoration theme just with the mixins

    a. Yes

    b. No

Summary

In this chapter, we have learnt about the themes feature in the qooxdoo framework and customized the theme for our Team Twitter application.

Specifically, we have covered:

- The class hierarchy of the `theme` package
- The `Meta` theme in qooxdoo
- The `Icon` theme—we came to know about the `Icon` themes that are supported by default in the qooxdoo framework
- The `Color` theme—we customized it for our Team Twitter application
- The `Font` theme—we customized it for our Team Twitter application
- The `Decoration` theme—we customized it for our Team Twitter application
- The `Appearance` theme—we customized it for our Team Twitter application

In the next chapter, we will learn some different ways to improve performance for the qooxdoo applications.

10
Performance

This chapter explains the various ways to analyze and improve the performance of the qooxdoo application. The qooxdoo framework provides certain features to support this.

Upto the previous chapter, we learnt about the qooxdoo framework and developed, debugged, tested, localized, and customized the themes of the qooxdoo application. In any typical application, performance is the key to success. In this chapter, we will learn various features that are provided by the qooxdoo framework to analyze and improve performance of the application.

In this chapter, we will cover the following topics:

- Memory management
- Object pooling
- Profiling
- Compile-time tuning
- Partitioning and lazy loading
- Good practices for performance

Memory management

Performance comes with better memory management; an inefficient memory management with lots of memory leaks causes serious problems and affects the performance to the maximum extent. It may lead to crashing of the application on continuous usage. To avoid that, a developer should make sure that the memory is managed properly, either internally by the qooxdoo framework or by making explicit calls in the code.

qooxdoo manages the browser memory very efficiently and takes care of most of the issues around object disposals. All the browsers, such as Internet Explorer (IE), Firefox, and Google Chrome, implement very good garbage-collector algorithms to collect all the out-of-scope garbage and release the memory for future use. One such famous algorithm is a "mark-and-sweep", either generational or non-generational algorithm. The whole point of implementing this garbage collector in the browser is to make the developer not worry about the object life cycle. If the developer still sees issues, then he might be using a wrong tool that doesn't free the connections to an object.

Normally, JavaScript automatically cleans up all the unused objects, as mentioned earlier, with the browser's in-built garbage collector. A browser usually differentiates the JavaScript objects to the DOM objects and sweeps out the objects with different garbage collectors for each. A problem arises when objects create links between the JavaScript objects and DOM objects. Another issue is of circular references, which cannot be easily resolved, especially if the algorithms depend on a reference counter.

qooxdoo solves this issue by including `dispose` or `destruct` methods, which can be overridden by each class. qooxdoo helps in differentiating the complex objects from the normal primitive types. A developer can explicitly dispose of the complex objects such as instances of `maps`, `arrays`, and other object instances, and doesn't have to dispose of primitive types such as strings, Booleans, and numbers.

A sample destructor is given as follows:

```
destruct : function()
{
  this._data = this._moreData = null;
  this._disposeObjects("_buttonOk", "_buttonCancel");
  this._disposeArray("_children");
  this._disposeMap("_registry");
}
```

The methods used are as follows:

- `_disposeObjects`: Disposes the objects (qooxdoo objects) under each key and finally deletes the key from the instance. Supports multiple arguments.
- `_disposeArray`: Disposes the array under the given key, but disposes all entries in this array first. It must contain instances of `qx.core.Object` only.
- `_disposeMap`: Disposes the map under the given key, but disposes all entries in this map first. It must contain instances of `qx.core.Object` only.

These methods dispose the objects of respective object types. To see the logs, a developer can set the `qx.disposerDebugLevel` variant with any of the integer values, where the higher integer value gives more debug statements or more verbose while disposing the objects. The default value for this is `0`. While using this property, make sure you have already enabled the `qx.debug` variant by setting it to `on`.

Part of the `config.json` to set the `variants` section of the `source` job is given as follows:

```
"jobs" :
{
  ---
  ---

  "source" :
  {

    "variants" :
    {
      "qx.disposerDebugLevel" : "9",
      "qx.debug" : ["on"]
    }
  }
}
```

A sample verbose log is shown in the following screenshot, with the `qx.disposerDebugLevel` set to 9, where all the objects were disposed. If the value is `1`, it shows all the not disposed objects. With the value `2`, it shows the non-qooxdoo objects too.

The output logs are as shown in the following screenshot. This was created while doing a soft shutdown of the application.

```
Console   Breakpoints   Locals   Watch   Call Stack
LOG: 040282 qx.core.ObjectRegistry: Disposed 14 objects
LOG: 014781 qx.core.Init: Load runtime: 14781ms
LOG: 015531 qx.core.Init: Main runtime: 750ms
LOG: 015937 qx.core.Init: Finalize runtime: 406ms
LOG: 048250 qx.core.ObjectRegistry: Disposed 872 objects
LOG: 007281 qx.core.Init: Load runtime: 7281ms
LOG: 007688 qx.core.Init: Main runtime: 407ms
LOG: 008063 qx.core.Init: Finalize runtime: 375ms
LOG: 030938 qx.core.ObjectRegistry: Disposed 944 objects
```

To understand more, let us take the window object. In the Team Twitter application, just open and close the signup window multiple times and check the final disposed object count. The number of objects might be in multiples of the actual objects. Every time the window is opened, a window object and its children are created. To resolve the memory issue, dispose the window and its children in the window close event. This can be done as shown in the following code snippet:

```
// add close event, call the dispose method, on close of the window.
this.addListener("close", function() {
  this.debug("window close method called.. ");
  this.close();
  qx.core.Init.getApplication().getRoot().remove(this);
  qx.event.Timer.once(function(){
    this.debug("calling dispose method.. ");
    this.dispose();
  }, this, 5);
}, this);
```

After adding this code, view the final disposed objects after opening the signup form multiple times. Observe the difference in the destroyed object count. To get a clearer picture of the current objects in the application, a developer can use the inspector (which is explained in *Chapter 7, Testing and Debugging* in the *Writing test cases* section) and observe the objects list on opening the window multiple times or observe the objects in qx.core.ObjectRegistry.getRegistry().

To test whether you added proper destructors, you can set the qx.disposerDebugLevel to 1 and qx.debug to on and try the operations in your application, as shown in the following code snippet:

```
"variants" :
{
  "qx.disposerDebugLevel" : "1",
  "qx.debug" : ["on"]
}
```

A typical log message looks as: Missing destruct definition for _abc in <classname>. These messages will help you to identify the items to dispose of. As we said before, make sure you dispose the complex objects such as maps, arrays, and other instances.

A developer can manually call the shutdown() method available in the ObjectRegistry in order to remove all the objects and carry out a soft shutdown of the application by using the following code snippet:

```
qx.core.ObjectRegistry.shutdown();
```

We have learnt the memory management in qooxdoo applications. We learnt how to explicitly dispose the widgets, array, map, and so on in the `destruct` function. We learnt the various settings to check the object's memory management.

Object pooling

Object pooling is a well-known technique to minimize the creation of objects that take a considerable amount of time in the construction and that consume heavy resources.

Creating complex widgets is very expensive as it takes maximum computation time and consumes much memory. Disposing of such widgets is also very cumbersome, and it is time-consuming to dispose of all the internal widgets of the complex widget. Furthermore, object disposing in JavaScript does not guarantee that the used memory is freed in a timely manner. Especially, IE is known to run the garbage collector only on certain events such as minimizing the browser window and so on. To reduce these timings, all the reusable objects should be pooled for better performance.

qooxdoo provides a utility class called `qx.util.ObjectPool` for managing objects in the pool. `ObjectPool` is mainly used to pool and reuse the window object or a well designed form object. However, it could also be used to pool instances of any type of the object except singletons.

While creating the object pool, the constructor takes the size and number of instances to maintain in the pool for each class type: `ObjectPool(integer size)`.

The methods available in `qx.util.ObjectPool` are as follows:

◆ `poolObject (object obj)`

This method puts an object into the pool. It is assumed that no other references exist to this object, and that it will not be used at all while it is pooled. Note that once an instance has been pooled, there is no means to get that exact instance back. The instance may be discarded for garbage collection if the pool of its type is already full.

◆ `getObject (class clazz)`

This method gets an object from the pool. It returns an instance of `clazz` from the pool; if not available in the pool, it creates a new object for the pool and returns the newly created object instance. Note that the pool determines which instance (if any) to return to the client. The client cannot get a specific instance from the pool.

We have learnt about object pooling in qooxdoo applications and learnt about the APIs to create and use an object pool.

Profiling

Profiler is a good tool to identify or measure each method call in the qooxdoo classes.

The profiler measures the time taken to execute a method and the total call count of the method. The qooxdoo framework provides this profiler by default and we need to enable this option, if required.

Enabling this profiling feature is very simple. As its implementation is based on the `aspects`, the developer should set the `qx.aspects` to on and include `qx.dev.Profile` in the first class in the `include` list, either by using the #use directive on the application or by including in the `let include` property. We have set the following line in the `Application.js`:

```
#use(qx.dev.Profile)
```

`qx.dev.Profile` is a static class and provides all the methods for profiling at a particular duration of time. As this has been implemented purely in the JavaScript, this profiler supports all the different browsers and it is a cross-browser tool. The different methods that are available and help in profiling are as follows:

◆ `start ()`: It starts profiling.

◆ `stop ()`: It stops profiling.

◆ `showResults (maxLength)`: It shows the results in a separate window. `maxLength` is an integer value and shows the given number of results. The default value is `100`. A sample result is shown in the following screenshot:

Name	Type	Own time	Avg time	calls
qx.util.Json.parse()	static	132ms	66.0ms	2
qx.bom.Label.getHtmlSize()	static	59.2ms	0.470ms	126
qx.bom.Label.__measureSize()	static	56.0ms	0.348ms	161
qx.bom.element.Dimension.getWidth()	static	51.0ms	0.317ms	161
qx.html.Element.flush()	static	47.9ms	12.0ms	4
qx.event.dispatch.Direct.dispatchEvent()	member	37.0ms	0.280ms	132
qx.ui.layout.Grid.renderLayout()	member	30.9ms	0.936ms	33
qx.ui.core.queue.Visibility.__computeVisible()	static	30.9ms	0.0242ms	1275
qx.ui.layout.Grid.__getOuterSize()	member	30.6ms	0.0906ms	338
qx.html.Element._copyData()	member	29.6ms	0.0874ms	339
qx.ui.core.queue.Appearance.flush()	static	27.0ms	3.86ms	7
qx.ui.core.queue.Layout.__getSortedQueue()	static	23.2ms	2.58ms	9
qx.html.Element()	constructor	21.0ms	0.0461ms	456
qx.html.Element._syncChildren()	member	21.0ms	5.25ms	4
qx.html.Element.__flush()	member	20.9ms	0.0594ms	352
qx.io.remote.RequestQueue._check()	member	20.5ms	5.12ms	4

Done

- ◆ getProfileData(): It returns the profile data as a JSON data structure, as shown in the following screenshot:

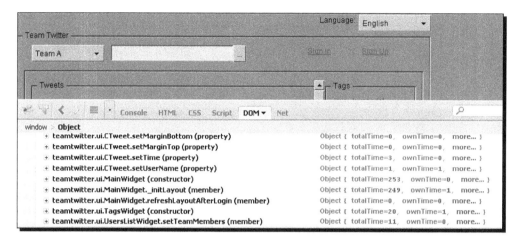

- ◆ normalizeProfileData(): It normalizes profiling data by subtracting the overhead of wrapping from the function's own time.

  Similar to the aspect's method after and method before, we can execute some code either profile after or profile before by using any of these methods.

- ◆ profileAfter/profileBefore(String fullFuncName, function func, String funcType, Arguments args, var returnValue):

  - ❏ fullFuncName: It is a full function name, including the class name and namespace.

  - ❏ func: It is the function to execute.

  - ❏ funcType: It is function type (default: null). It specifies the type of the wrapped function. It can have any one of these values: member, static, constructor, destructor, property, or *. The null value is handled in the similar way as the * value.

  - ❏ args: It is the arguments passed to the wrapped function.

  - ❏ returnValue: It is a return value of the wrapped function.

Finally, profiler data helps in finding the hot spots and time-consuming code. The developer can identify and reduce the complexities on the specific time-consuming code. But, this profiler has some limitations. To trust these statistics, the developer should be aware of the limitations and one has to re-calculate based on those limitations.

Limitations

The following are the limitations:

- The application is slowed down because profiling is done by wrapping each function. Profiling should always be turned off in production code before development.

- The profiler adds some overhead to each function call and this overhead is considered when calculating of the own time, but there can still be some inaccuracy.

- The Date() function used for time calculation has a granularity of about 10 ms on many platforms.

- Turning on profiling currently breaks in some browsers due to a very limited maximum recursion depth of some limited value. This is because the call stack is doubled.

There are some external debuggers which give the best statistical and profile information easily. Firebug is one such tool that allows finding the timing and profiling information very easily, without even changing any code or settings. Firebug has a separate profile button in the console tab. On clicking it for the first time, the profiling starts. On clicking it the next time, profiling ends and prepares and displays all the timing and method call count in a tabular format, as shown in the following screenshot:

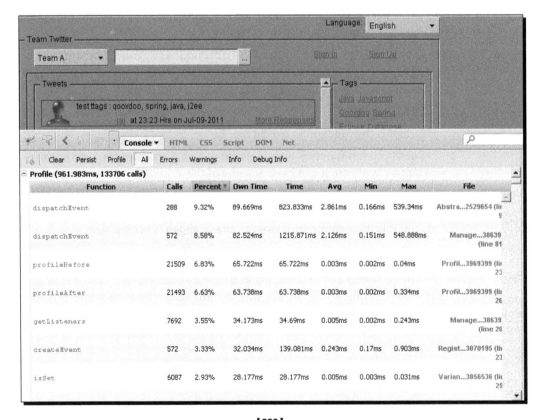

We have learnt how to profile the qooxdoo applications and to identify the time consuming methods, so that the developer can reduce the complexity and improve the performance of the application.

Compile-time tuning

qooxdoo provides certain jobs to tune the application for best performance while compiling the application itself. The jobs such as `lint`, which validates the JavaScript source code, and `log` with `classes-unused` set to the root package and identifies the unused classes in the package optimizing the classes, and so on.

Let us see the optimization that we can carry out at the qooxdoo application's compilation time.

Class optimizations

Currently, qooxdoo performs and allows optimization in four categories in the JavaScript classes while creating the build version.

The four categories are as follows:

Strings

String optimization reduces the repetitive references to the same string literal. qooxdoo framework extracts all the string literals inside the class definition, creates lexical variables, and replaces the strings with lexical variables.

Variables

Variable optimization mainly concentrates on the JavaScript's physical size, where all the long variable names are replaced with generated variable names with one or two characters. These variable name optimizations are performed on all the local and static lexical variables only, so that all the public variables remain with the same name and they can be used as they are. Depending on the original code, this can result in significant space being saved. This improves the data transfer time in the browser, resulting in quick page load.

Private

The private optimization is a bit tricky and mainly concentrates on restricting the private variables to the private scope only. This optimization is performed on all the private members of a class (member variable names beginning with __). Similar to the variable optimization, all those private variables are also replaced with shorter variable names and are substituted throughout the class.

In addition to that, the qooxdoo framework restricts the usage of these references in other classes. When a user explicitly uses these private variable references in other classes, all these references will not be updated and may fail to initialize—creating a runtime error. So, it is better to make sure that the private variables are used in the private scope only.

Base calls

This category reduces the method calls on the stack. Calls to the base class methods such as `this.base()` method calls are in-lined, that is, the superclass method content is inserted in place of the `this.base()` call. This is something similar to the method's `in-line` feature, available in some of the IDEs.

All these four categories, by default, will be enabled on the build version. To alter these, one should override the `optimize` property on the `compile-options` job, as shown in the following code snippet:

```
"compile-options" :
{
  "code" :
  {
    "optimize" : ["variables", "basecalls", "strings"]
  }
}
```

All these compile options mainly reduce the size of the `.js` file, which in turn reduces the initial JavaScript loading time on the browser and reduces the network bandwidth as it transfers less bytes. Finally, this reduces the GUI initialization time of the qooxdoo application.

To further reduce the final size of the generated JavaScript file, the developer can identify the unused classes and remove those classes.

Identifying unused classes

On building the source code with the `build` job, qooxdoo generates a single `.js` file by including all the qooxdoo classes defined. Even though qooxdoo creates the `.js` file after doing a lot of compressions, it is still better to identify the unused classes and remove those classes; the developer can reduce the final `.js` file size as much as possible. But it may be a big problem to identify the unused classes by going through each and every file in a step-by-step process. The qooxdoo framework simplifies this process. If you set the `classes-unused` property in the `log` setting of the `source` job, the qooxdoo framework directly lists out all the unused classes. You should set the packages to search for the unused classes. Typically, you can set the root package of the application to search all the classes.

The following code snippet is a part of the `config.json` file to set `classes-unused` in the `log` section of the `source` job:

```
"source" :
{
  "variants" :
  {
    "qx.disposerDebugLevel" : "9",
    "qx.aspects" : ["on"],
    "qx.debug" : ["on"]
  },

  "log" :
  {
    "classes-unused" : [ "teamtwitter.*" ]
  }
}
```

The preceding configuration identifies the unused classes inside the `teamtwitter` package. On running the source target on our Team Twitter application, we can find out all the unused classes such as `User`, `Composite`, `Menu`, `TextField`, and so on, which are not used anywhere in the application. Just by removing these files, we can reduce the generated `teamtwitter.js` file's size a lot, and thus reduce the initial application's loading time. When you run the `source` job with the earlier mentioned configurations, the output displays all the unused classes, as shown in the following screenshot. You should remove those unused classes identified by the job to reduce the application's loading time.

```
    [exec]    - Processing translations for 4 locales...
    [exec]    - Analyzing assets...
    [exec]      - Compiling resource list...
    [exec]    - Generating boot script...
    [exec] >>> Find unused classes...
    [exec]    - Checking namespace: teamtwitter.*
    [exec]      - Unused class: teamtwitter.model.User
    [exec]      - Unused class: teamtwitter.samples.Composite
    [exec]      - Unused class: teamtwitter.samples.Menu
    [exec]      - Unused class: teamtwitter.samples.TextField
    [exec]      - Unused class: teamtwitter.test.DemoTest
    [exec]      - Unused class: teamtwitter.ui.UserLoginPopup
    [exec]      - Unused class: teamtwitter.test.LoginUserTest
    [exec] >>> Done
deploy.client.source:
    [copy] Copying 35 files to D:\softwares\tomcat5.5\webapps\teamtwitter\source
BUILD SUCCESSFUL
Total time: 24 seconds
```

Lint check

qooxdoo, by default, provides a `lint` job within the framework to validate the application's source code against most common mistakes such as missing semicolons, missing braces for single line `if` blocks, undefined variables, global references, use of deprecated identifiers, and so on. By following the `lint` check instructions, we can improve the application's performance slightly.

Let us run the `lint` job with the default options and find what information it gives. The developer can run the `lint` job by using one of the following two ways— `.\generater.py lint` or run the `client.generate-lint` target from our `ant` file.

The resultant `lint-check` output is shown in the following screenshot:

qooxdoo includes its own JavaScript validator—**Ecmalint**. Using that, application developers can check their source. Still, developers have the choice to particularly ignore some warnings by using the following specific `doc` comment statements:

- `@lint ignoreUnused(x,y)`: It ignores the `lint` warnings for unused variables statements on `x` and `y`

- `@lint ignoreDeprecated(alert)`: It ignores displaying the alert deprecated statements

- ◆ `@lint ignoreUndefined(button1, foo)`: It ignores displaying the undefined statements for `button1` and `foo`

- ◆ `@lint ignorereferencedField(x)`: It ignores displaying the cross referenced filed statements on `x`

- ◆ `@lint ignoreGlobal(qx)`: It ignores displaying the global reference warnings on the variable `qx`

All the `doc` comments should be written inside the API documentation for the particular methods, classes, or variable declarations. Before `lint` prints a warning, it searches the AST and looks for the next enclosing API `doc` comment. Usually these comments should be placed in the method's `JsDoc` comments or in the `class` comment.

By removing all these `lint` warnings, we can overcome most of the errors at the early stages of application development.

Improvements

The following are the improvements:

- ◆ Unused variables can be reduced.

- ◆ Proper code formation by identifying the blocks with braces.

- ◆ Identifying the global references, where the scope for these variables will be at the application level, so that the developer could redefine the scope for those variables, if those variables are not required to be global. If you redefine it to the local variables (if possible), you will get the compile time optimization for the local variables.

- ◆ Points out the use of deprecated items such as deprecated variables or method calls.

We have learnt the techniques to configure specific jobs, identify certain things, and optimize the application code on compilation. By doing so, the application code is optimized and the final `.js` file size is reduced, which reduces the application's loading time. We have learnt how to identify unused classes, to remove those classes, and improve performance. We have learnt how to check the application with the `lint` job and fix the reported issues.

Partitioning and lazy loading

Package is the concept of grouping related information or classes. Simply, packages allow you to partition your application physically. It is a good idea to load the required information as needed, instead of loading everything in the beginning. The major advantage of loading each partition on demand is reduction in the initial application's startup time.

Note that this feature is not completely implemented in older releases of qooxdoo and it is fully implemented in qooxdoo 1.4+ versions. We will see what are the major issues that have been fixed and improvements in this feature.

A developer can partition the application into any number of partitions and the developer can load each partition as and when it is required in the application. In our Team Twitter application, we have the `teamtwitter` functionalities and we have also included the samples that contain all the experimental samples that we have featured in this book to explain various concepts. Here, the `teamtwitter` and samples are two physical parts. It is not a good idea to load both of them on initializing the application. Instead, we can create two partitions, one for the Team Twitter application-related classes and one for the samples-related classes and load the partition as required. On loading the application, only the Team Twitter partition is loaded, and on clicking the **samples** button, the samples partition is loaded. This is a typical example for the partition feature. You can create one partition for each of the modules in the application and load that partition when a user tries to use the features from that module.

Configuration

Let us configure our Team Twitter application by defining `parts` in `config.json` as follows:

```
"my-parts-config":
{
  "packages" :
  {
    "parts" :
    {
      "boot" :
      {
        "include" : [ "${QXTHEME}", "${APPLICATION}.Application" ]
      },
      "samples" :
      {
        "include" : [ "${APPLICATION}.Samples" ]
      }
    }
  }
}
```

On running either the `source` or `build` target, the total application is split into two partitions, namely, `boot` and `samples`. When a user opens the application in a browser, first the `boot` part will be loaded. The `boot` part contains all the qooxdoo framework classes completely and the initial application classes that are required to start the application. The `samples` part remain in the server itself and will be loaded lazily as and when required.

Coding to load parts on demand

Lazy loading can be done with the `qx.io.PartLoader` API available in the framework. This `PartLoader` is a singleton class and it knows about all the parts and packages in the application. This class contains the functions to load the parts and to retrieve part instances.

The following are the different methods available:

- `getPart(String partName)`: It returns the part instance of the given part name, where part name is the name defined in the `config.json` file.

- `getParts()`: It returns all the parts in a map instance.

- `hasPart(String partName)`: It checks if the part with the `partName` method defined is available.

- `Require(String/String[] partName(s), func callback, Object self)`: It loads one or more parts asynchronously. The `callback` function is called after all the parts and their dependencies are fully loaded. If the parts are already loaded, the `callback` is called immediately.

As this is a singleton class, a static `getInstance()` method is provided to get the single instance. A static require method is also provided to serve the same require (member function) functionality.

Verification

Generate the `build` version and check the number of final `.js` files created. You can observe that two `.js` files are generated, as we defined exactly two parts in our configuration. Let us observe when exactly the second `.js` file was loaded on the browser.

Observe the scripts loaded in the Firebug **Script** tab.

Recent improvements

In the newer versions of qooxdoo, this part loading feature has improved a lot on some of the areas. The different areas include:

Part collapsing or merging

This area is enhanced to avoid issues with class dependencies during the process. The generator now employs new constraints that take better care of dependencies between packages. At the same time, the part verifier has been augmented with additional checks to test for violations of these dependencies. It will now raise an exception when a violation is detected (rather than just issue warnings). However, this behavior can be toggled with the `packages/verifier-bombs-on-error` configuration setting.

Sometimes packages derived with the basic procedure turn out to be too small; this may cause too much fragmentation of classes over packages. Such situations are good examples of where part collapsing is useful and packages are merged into one another. Thus a part size is being maintained and this merging can be done in two ways, namely, based on the size and based on the load order.

Remove dependencies from the part loader

Some applications use the part loader at a very early state. So, the first `Bootstrap` class should be as minimal as possible. By rewriting the part loader using only functionality provided by `qx.Bootstrap`, we were able to shrink the size by a factor of 5! Now a package containing a part loader is usually smaller than 20 KB. As a result, the application startup time is reduced.

Load packages in parallel

The framework loads the parts or classes in two phases. In the first phase, the framework evaluates all the classes, as specified in the order, and this should be in the correct order. In the second phase, the framework loads the evaluated classes, once there are no issues. Otherwise, the framework doesn't load the classes failed in the evaluation phase. These evaluated packages (set of classes) can be loaded in parallel.

Error handling

An issue with the old implementation came up recently. An application had unexpected errors in IE, which seemed to be related to part loading but were very hard to track. It turned out that the server was busy and occasionally could not deliver a JavaScript file. To load the scripts, we dynamically insert script tags, but Opera and Internet Explorer do not fire an error event to signal server errors. As each package now calls a global `notify` function once it is loaded, we can simply start a timer when we start loading a file and stop the timer once the global function is called. If the timer is not stopped, we will assume that loading the file failed and we fire an error event. This way, we have proper error handling in all supported browsers.

Advantages

The following are the advantages:

◆ Reduces initial application loading time. Physical partitions can be loaded at any point of time, as the package requires.

◆ A `partLoader` checks if any of the classes in that package have already been loaded before loading the package. If so, the `partLoader` won't load any of the already loaded classes. It loads all the remaining classes and completes the part loading.

◆ The framework provides features for part collapsing and merging too.

◆ In the newer versions, the part loading is improved a lot and loads all the packages in part in parallel. A developer can tell the part loader to pre-load a part from the server without evaluating the code until it is actually required.

Time for action – partitioning

Let us include a few samples as a separate component and link that to the Team Twitter application as a part and load that part only when the samples module is opened.

1. We have provided the set of samples in the `samples.zip` file. Create the directory `C:/teamtwitter/source/class/teamtwitter/samples` and extract `samples.zip` under the `samples` directory.

2. One class, `teamtwitter.Samples`, has been written to display all the samples that have been developed during the course of the Team Twitter application development. That class is available in the file `978-1-849513-70-8_10_01.txt` under Chapter 10. You can copy that code file into `teamtwitter` as `C:/teamtwitter/source/class/teamtwitter/Samples.js`.

3. As mentioned in the configuration section, let us configure two parts for the Team Twitter application; one for the main Team Twitter application and another one for samples. The updated `config.json` is available as a file `978-1-849513-70-8_10_02.txt`.

```
"my-parts-config":
{
  "packages" :
  {
    "parts" :
    {
      "boot" :
      {
        "include" : [ "${QXTHEME}", "${APPLICATION}.Application" ]
      },
      "samples" :
      {
        "include" : [ "${APPLICATION}.Samples" ]
      }
    }
  }
},

"build" :
{
  "extend" : [ "my-parts-config" ]
},

"source" :
{
  "extend" : [ "my-parts-config" ],
  "variants" :
  {
    "qx.disposerDebugLevel" : "9",
    "qx.aspects" : ["on"],
    "qx.debug" : ["on"]
  },

  "log" :
  {
    "classes-unused" : [ "teamtwitter.*" ]
  }
}
```

4. Add a button in Team Twitter's `Application.js` file to display the samples. On loading the samples, inform that you require the `samples` part. Updated `Application.js` is available as a file `978-1-849513-70-8_10_03.txt`.

```
var samples = new qx.ui.form.Button(this.tr("Samples"));
samples.addListener("execute", function(){
  qx.io.PartLoader.require(["samples"], function(){
    // if the window is not created
    if (!this.__samples) {
      // create it
      this.__samples = new qx.ui.window.Window("Samples");
      this.__samples.setLayout(new qx.ui.layout.Dock());
      this.__samples.add(new teamtwitter.Samples());
      this.getRoot().add(this.__samples);
    }
    // open the window
    this.__samples.center();
    this.__samples.open();
  }, this);
}, this);
```

5. Compile, deploy, run the application, and verify the parts. You will observe that two `.js` files were generated, as we defined exactly two parts in our configuration. Let us observe when exactly the second `.js` file is loaded on the browser.

Access the Team Twitter application in the browser. After the GUI is initialized and before loading the samples part, check the Firebug's **Script** tab. Only one `.js` file, the `teamtwitter` part of the application, should get loaded and the second part shouldn't get loaded. If you run the source version, you can search for the `Samples` class, which cannot be found because that part is not yet loaded.

In the following screenshot, you can see only one `.js` file, namely, `teamtwitter.js` loaded. This is a `build` version snapshot.

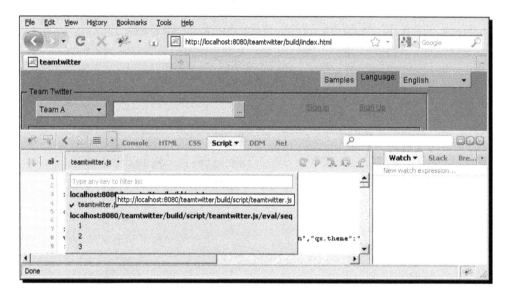

Now, click on the **Samples** button and observe the loaded scripts again to check the newly loaded part that is loaded on demand. In the following screenshot, you can see two `.js` files, `teamtwitter.js` and `teamtwitter-0.js`, loaded. The `teamtwitter.js` file is loaded on initialization and the `teamtwitter-0.js` file is loaded on demand, on click of the **Samples** button.

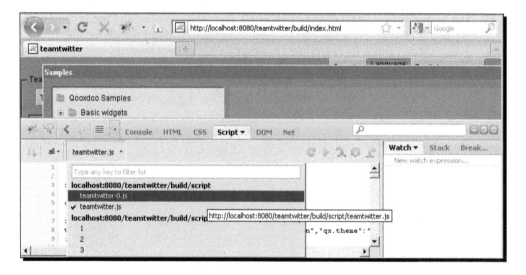

What just happened?

We just learnt how to partition the application and load each part as required, lazily. We understood how this part loading improves the application. We implemented this partitioning in our Team Twitter application, created a part for samples, and verified the part loading in operation.

Good practices for performance

In a few applications, you may have to handle huge data sets. You need to follow certain good practices from the beginning of the application development to avoid any failure in the application after deploying it.

While developing the application, you should design it to reduce the data set handled at any point of time using good design principles. Let us see a few of the good practices in this section.

Restrict the data in certain widgets

Certain widgets in qooxdoo do not scale to handle huge data. It is not a good idea to load more than a certain number of items (say 500 or 1000 items) in widgets such as `ComboBox`, `SelectBox`, `List`, and so on. It takes a lot of time to load these items into the widget and it also takes time to remove all the items from the widget. Either you avoid the data by adding filters at different levels, or if you cannot avoid the number of items, you should design custom widgets to display the limited data, either with search or some way to navigate and see all the data.

Use filters

When the data set is huge, the performance of the application goes down and it will also lead to information overload. The user of the application cannot go through the information that easily. So use the filter wherever possible.

In our application, the first level of the filter is a team. In a team, the number of team members will be countable. The tweets from the members of a team are considerably less when compared to the tweets from an organization or compared to tweets from the entire world.

Even within a team, the number of tweets may be more. So the second level of filters are tags and team members. A user of the application can filter by the tags that they are interested in, by the team members whose tweets the user wants to read, or a combination of tags and the team members.

With all those filters, you can still filter the tweets by searching for any text in a tweet search.

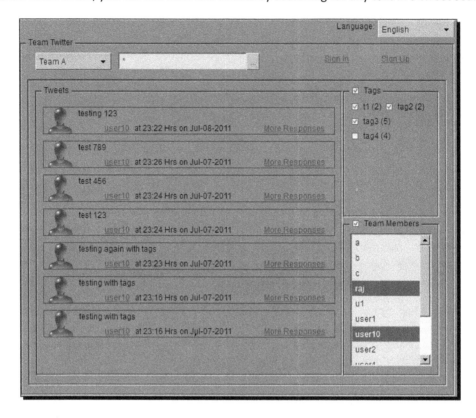

Pagination

Use pagination to navigate through the large data set. We can implement the pagination for the `Tweets display` widget. We haven't implemented that yet in the Team Twitter application. The logic is to have a page size and retrieve one page of tweets matching all the filter conditions and provide some links to navigate to the next and previous pages, if there are any.

You can also make use of `RemoteTableModel`.

.gz compression

To optimize at the transport level, one can compress the generated files and zip the script file. This reduces the network bandwidth usage and improves efficiency. But this again should be supported on the web server too, for example, jetty or Tomcat 7. Both of these by default supports `.gz` files.

We have learnt a few good practices to follow to get better performance in the application.

Pop quiz

1. How to identify unused classes in the qooxdoo application

    a. Fire a bug while running application

    b. Profiling

    c. `log` setting of the `source` job in `config.json` file

    d. All of the above

2. Is lazy loading of the partition possible

    a. True

    b. False

3. Packages inside the parts can be loaded in parallel

    a. True

    b. False

4. `lint` check gives information on

    a. Unused classes

    b. Unused variables

    c. Global references

    d. Use of deprecated variables

    e. Common coding mistakes

    f. All the above

5. Which parameters does the qooxdoo framework optimize during compilation

    a. Strings

    b. Variables

    c. Privates

    d. Base calls

    e. Method calls

6. Which API class helps in maintaining Object pooling

    a. `ObjectRegistry`

    b. `Object`

    c. `ObjectPool`

    d. `Pool`

7. Which API class helps in profiling

    a. `Profile`

    b. `ObjectRegistry`

    c. `ObjectPool`

    d. `Aspect`

8. Part collapsing is possible based on

    a. Part size

    b. Load order

    c. None of them

    d. Both of them

9. qooxdoo profiling gives statistical information on

    a. Method call type

    b. Method call count

    c. Method name

    d. Average and actual method execution time

10. One of the famous garbage collector algorithms

    a. Generational mark-and-sweep

    b. Non-generational mark-and-sweep

    c. Not applicable

Summary

In this chapter, we have learnt various ways to improve the performance of the qooxdoo application and the various tools provided with the qooxdoo framework that help to identify the performance hurdles in the application.

In particular, we have covered:

♦ The object life cycle and the efficient way of managing the browser memory. Disposing of the objects without failure.

♦ Object pooling is a very good concept where the user has a pool of objects, where object-creation time can be avoided by reusing a pooled object.

♦ Various ways to have statistical profile information.

- ◆ Compile-time settings to optimize the application and find the unused classes during the compilation process itself.

- ◆ Partitioning the application, where each chunk can be loaded lazily.

- ◆ Some best practices to implement in the application for best performance.

We have learnt and implemented most of the techniques on our Team Twitter application and have improved the initial loading time as well as the application's overall performance.

11
Miscellaneous

This chapter explains a few things, without which this book is incomplete.

Up to the last chapter, we have learnt about most of the things that we should know about developing the qooxdoo application. In this chapter, we will learn about few extra things without which our learning on the qooxdoo framework is not complete.

In this chapter, we shall discuss the following topics:

- Configuration
- Migration
- Back button support
- qooxdoo license

Configuration

In various chapters, we used `generate.py` to perform jobs to create a qooxdoo application, to compile the code, to translate, to optimize, and so on. For these jobs, a developer can configure many parameters. The qooxdoo framework allows the developer to configure these details in JSON files. We had already learnt about the JSON file format in the beginning of this book. In this section, we will mainly concentrate on how to define and configure the jobs.

A developer can configure many parameters in the JSON files and these various parameters include class selection, variants or environment, parts, internationalization, themes, compile-time cache support, API data, and so on. These parameters are configured in the `config.json` file, which will be available in the application's root folder. This application configuration file imports framework configuration files, by default, which contain a default implementation for some of the common activities such as build, compile, localize, and so on.

config.json

A sample `config.json` file that is generated on creation of the qooxdoo application is shown in the following blocks of code. The qooxdoo application is created using the `create-application.py` tool:

```
{
  "name" : "testAPP",

  // Includes the application.json from the qooxdoo framework
  //This imports set of jobs and environments from the framework
  "include" :
  [
    {
      "path" : "${QOOXDOO_PATH}/tool/data/config/application.json"
    }
  ],

  "export" :
  [
    "api",
    "api-data",
    "build",
    "clean",
    "distclean",
    "fix",
    "info",
    "inspector",
    "lint",
    "migration",
    "pretty",
    "profiling",
    "source",
    "source-all",
    "test",
    "test-source",
    "translation"
  ],
```

```
    "let" :
    {
      "APPLICATION" : "testapp",
      "QOOXDOO_PATH" : "../bkup/teamtwitter/qooxdoo-1.2-sdk",
      "QXTHEME" : "testapp.theme.Theme",
      "API_EXCLUDE" : ["qx.test.*", "${APPLICATION}.theme.*",
        "${APPLICATION}.test.*"],
      "LOCALES" : [ "en" ],
      "CACHE" : "${TMPDIR}/cache",
      "ROOT" : "."
    }

// You only need to edit the remainder of this file, if you want to
// customize specific jobs, or add your own job definitions.

    /*
    "jobs" :
    {
// Uncomment the following entry to add a contrib or library to your
// project; make sure to adapt the path to the Manifest.json; if you
// are using a contrib: library, it will be downloaded into the path
// specified by the 'cache/downloads' config key
      "libraries" :
      {
        "library" :
        [
          {
            "manifest" :
              "contrib://SkeletonApplication/trunk/Manifest.json"
          }
        ]
      },

// If you want to tweak a job setting, see the following sample where
// the "format" feature of the "build-script" job is overridden.
// To see a list of available jobs, invoke 'generate.py x'.
      "build-script" :
      {
        "compile-options" :
        {
          "code" :
          {
            "format" : false
          }
        }
      }
    }
    */
}
```

A developer can configure a new job or override any of the existing jobs. To override an existing job, one should know the possible job keys, its purpose, and usability. Each job has to be placed under job keys. All the possible keys were grouped into the following five categories:

- **Structure-changing keys**: These are the keys that influence or change the configuration itself; for example, re-using the existing jobs, inheriting, overriding, changing the job structure, job queue, and so on. The different keys include `extend`, `include`, `run`, `let`, `jobs`, and many more.

- **Action keys**: These keys trigger certain actions to carry out in the generator, which usually results in some output; for example, cleaning files, generating API, combining or copying images, packing resources, compiling source, and so on. The different keys include `api`, `clean-files`, `copy-images`, `compile`, and many more.

- **IO-setting keys**: These keys help in setting input and output options such as path settings, library, classes to create, packaging, and so on. The possible keys include `add-script`, `asset-let`, `compile-options`, `dependencies`, `use`, and more.

- **Runtime-setting keys**: These keys pertain to the working needs of the generator; for example, `cache` and `log`.

- **Miscellaneous keys**: All the remaining keys; for example, `desc`, `name`, and more.

Listing of keys in context

This section describes the complete possible contents of the top-level configuration map in the configuration file. Further information is linked to the respective keys.

Key	Description
name	A name or descriptive text for the configuration file.
include	Includes external configuration files.
let	Defines the default macros. This `let` map is included automatically in every job run. There is no explicit reference to it, so be aware of side effects.
export	List of jobs to be exported if this configuration file is included by another.
default-job	The name of a job to be run as the default setting, that is, when invoking the generator without job arguments.
jobs	Map of jobs. Each key is the name of a job. Each job's value is a map describing the job.

The job-describing map can have any number of the following keys:

Key	Description
add-script	A list of URIs that will be loaded first thing when the app starts.
api	Triggers the generation of a custom API viewer application.
asset-let	Defines macros that will be replaced in #asset hints in source files.
cache	Defines the path to cache directories, most importantly, to the compile cache.
clean-files	Triggers the clean-up of files and directories within a project and the framework; for example, deletion of generated files, cache contents, and so on.
collect-environment-info	Collects information about the qooxdoo environment, such as version, cache, and more and prints it to the console.
combine-images	Triggers the creation of a combined image file that contains various images.
compile	Triggers the generation of a source or build version of the application.
compile-options	Defines various options that influence compile runs of both the source and build version.
copy-files	Triggers the files/directories to be copied, usually between the source and build version.
copy-resources	Triggers the copying of resources, usually between the source and build version.
dependencies	Fine-tunes the processing of class dependencies.
desc	A string describing the job.
environment	Defines key-value pair environment settings for the application, covering settings, variants, and features.
exclude	Lists classes to be excluded from the job. Takes an array of class specifiers.
extend	Extends the current job with other jobs. Takes an array of job names. The information of these jobs is merged into the current job description, so the current job sort of "inherits" their settings.
fix-files	Fixes white space in source files.
include	Lists classes to be processed in the job. Takes an array of class specifiers.
let	Defines macros. Takes a map where each key defines a macro and the value defines its expansion.

Key	Description
library	Defines libraries to be taken into account for this job. Takes an array of maps, each map specifying one library to consider. The most important part therein is the "manifest" specification.
lint-check	Checks source code with a lint-like utility.
log	Tailors the log output of the job.
migrate-files	Migrates source code to the current qooxdoo version.
packages	Defines packages for the application.
pretty-print	Triggers code beautification of source class files. An empty map value triggers default formatting, but further keys can tailor the output.
provider	Collects classes, resources, and dependency information and puts them in a specific directory structure under the provider root.
require	Defines prerequisite classes needed at load time. Takes a map of where the keys are class names and where the values are lists of prerequisite classes.
run	Defines a list of jobs to run in place of the current job.
settings	Defines qooxdoo settings for the generated application.
shell	Triggers the execution of one or more external command(s).
simulate	Triggers the execution of a GUI test (simulated interaction) suite.
slice-images	Triggers cutting images into regions.
translate	Regenerates .po files from source classes.
use	Defines prerequisite classes needed at runtime. Takes a map where the keys are class names and where the values are lists of prerequisite classes.
variants	Defines variants for the generated application.

Job resolution

Let us further understand how the generator resolves jobs, when multiple jobs are defined or redefined in one or more configuration files. Each configuration file describes and defines a few jobs and imports one or more configuration files. Hence the application's config.json will have few local job definitions and zero to many imported job definitions. All the precedence and overwriting has to be resolved among all the jobs before running any job. To refer to a job from another job, a same level job can be referenced directly by its job name, whereas the other level or inner level jobs can be referenced as the parent job name, followed by /, and then the required job name.

The extend key

The extend key allows us to extend one or more jobs. This key takes an array of job names. These will be resolved by merging all the job information into the current job. A sample usage of this key is as follows:

```
extend : [ "job1", "job2"]
```

Where job1 and job2 are two different jobs defined either in the local configuration file or in other configuration files.

Now, how exactly does the job (let us call this the primary job) treat the extended jobs (let us call this the secondary jobs)? Here is what happens:

- The primary job provides a sort of a master definition for the resulting job. All its definitions take precedence.

- The secondary job is searched in the context of the current "jobs" map.

- Keys of the secondary job that are not available in the primary job are just added to the job definition.

- Keys of the secondary job that are already present in the primary job and have a scalar value (string, number, boolean) are discarded.

- Keys of the secondary job that are already present in the primary job and have a list or map value are merged. The extending rules are applied on the element level recursively, that is, scalar elements are blocked, new elements are added, and composed elements are merged.

- There is a way of preventing this kind of merge behaviour; if you prefix a job key with an equal sign (=), then no subsequent merging will be done on this key. That means all following jobs that are merged into the current job will not be able to alter the value of this key anymore.

- Obviously, each secondary job extends itself before being processed in this way, so it brings in its own full definition. As stated before, it is important to note that this extending is done in the secondary job's own context, which is not necessarily the context of the primary job.

- If there is more than one job in the extend list, the process is re-applied iteratively with all the remaining jobs in the list. This also means that the list of secondary jobs defines a precedence list—settings in jobs earlier in the list take precedence over those coming later, so order matters.

As an example, let us take some sample jobs that are defined under `base.json` of the qooxdoo framework:

```json
"libraries" :
{
  "desc" : "includer job, to hold the essential libraries
            for the compile jobs",

  "library" :
  [
    {
      "manifest" : "${QOOXDOO_PATH}/framework/Manifest.json"
    },

    {
      "manifest" : "${ROOT}/Manifest.json"
    }
  ]
},

"cache" :
{
  "cache" : "${CACHE_KEY}"
},

"includes" :
{
  "include" :
  [
    "${APPLICATION_MAIN_CLASS}",
    "${QXTHEME}"
  ]
},

"common" :
{
  "desc" : "common settings for base.json jobs",

  "extend" : ["libraries", "includes", "cache"],

  "settings" :
  {
    "qx.version" : "${QOOXDOO_VERSION}",
    "qx.theme" : "${QXTHEME}",
    "qx.application" : "${APPLICATION_MAIN_CLASS}"
  },
```

```
    "asset-let" :
    {
      "qx.icontheme" : "${QXICONTHEME}"
    }
  },
```

Here, the common job extends `library`, `includes`, and `cache`. As per the above-mentioned resolution rules on the `extend` key, the `common`'s scalar property, `desc`, is given precedence over the `desc` in the `library` job, and all the other properties will be merged. So finally, it is completely equivalent to the job defined as follows:

```
"common" :
{
  "desc" : "common settings for base.json jobs",

  "include" :
  [
    "${APPLICATION_MAIN_CLASS}",
    "${QXTHEME}"
  ]

  "cache" : "${CACHE_KEY}"

  "library" :
  [
    {
      "manifest" : "${QOOXDOO_PATH}/framework/Manifest.json"
    },

    {
      "manifest" : "${ROOT}/Manifest.json"
    }
  ]

  "settings" :
  {
    "qx.version" : "${QOOXDOO_VERSION}",
    "qx.theme" : "${QXTHEME}",
    "qx.application" : "${APPLICATION_MAIN_CLASS}"
  },

  "asset-let" :
  {
    "qx.icontheme" : "${QXICONTHEME}"
  }
}
```

The run key

The `run` job simply runs or invokes an array of jobs in a specified sequence. When a `run` key is encountered in a job, for each sub-job in the `run` list, a new job is generated with an auto-generated name, where the actual job name is a prefix for this job. As for the contents, the initial job's definition is used as a template for the new job. The `extend` key is set to the name of the current sub-job (it is assumed that the initial job has been expanded before), so the settings of the sub-job will eventually be included and the `run` key is removed. All other settings from the initial job remain unaffected. This means that all sub-jobs inherit the settings of the initial job (this is significant when sub-jobs evaluate the same key, and may be do so in a different manner). In the overall queue of jobs to be performed, the initial job is replaced by the list of new jobs just generated. This process is repeated until there are no more `run` jobs in the job queue, and none with any unresolved `extend` key.

A good example for this is to split the build job into sub-jobs and call those sub-jobs in the order that we run them, which can be specified in the run key as a sequential array of sub-jobs.

```
// -- build jobs -----------------------------------------------

"build-script" :
{
  "desc" : "create build script of current application",

  "extend" : ["common"],

  "variants" :
  {
    "qx.debug" : ["off"]
  },

  "compile-options" :
  {
    "paths" :
    {
      "file" : "${BUILD_PATH}/script/${APPLICATION}.js"
    },
    "uris" :
    {
      "script" : "script",
      //"resource" : "resource",
      "add-nocache-param" : false
    },
    "code" :
    {
      "format" : true,
      "locales" : "${LOCALES}",
      "optimize" : "${OPTIMIZE}"
```

```
      }
    },

    "compile" : { "type" : "build" }
  },

  "build-files" :
  {
    "desc" : "copy files of current application to build dir",

    "extend" : ["common"],

    "copy-files" :
    {
      "files" :
      [
        "index.html"
      ],

      "source" : "${ROOT}/source",
      "target" : "${BUILD_PATH}"
    }
  },

  "build-resources":
  {
    "desc" : "copy necessary resources for current application
              to build dir",

    "extend" : ["common"],

    "copy-resources" :
    {
      "target" : "${BUILD_PATH}",
      "resource-filter" : true
    }
  },

  "build" :
  {
    "desc" : "create build version of current application",

    "run" :
    [
      "build-resources",
      "build-script",
      "build-files"
    ]
  }
```

The include key

The `include` key allows re-using external configuration files. One can simply re-use jobs defined in some other applications and components. For example, if a user wants to use the jobs defined in some other applications or components such as API viewer, Test Runner, Test Simulator, and others, this `include` key takes a list of maps, where each map specifies an external configuration file and options how to include those jobs.

Practically, there are two steps involved in using external jobs:

◆ You have to include the external configuration file that contains the relevant job definitions. So, all the external jobs are added to the list of jobs of your local configuration. This can be done as follows:

```
"include" :
  [
    {
      "path" : "./base.json"
    }
  ],
```

◆ You can run the following command to get a list of all available jobs; the external jobs will be among this list:

```
generator.py
```

There are now two ways to utilize these jobs:

◆ You can invoke them directly from the command line, passing them as arguments to the generator

◆ You can define local jobs that extend the external jobs

Job shadowing and partial overriding

One can define a job with the same name as defined before in any of the imported configuration files. Such a job shadows the imported job. Here, in such a case, the local job takes precedence and the imported job gets automatically added to the local job's extend list. As we already know how the generator resolves the extended job, this shadowed job also does the same.

In a simple way, the `local` job is used to modify or add whichever specific keys are required and the remaining keys will be merged from the shadowed job from the imported configuration file.

For example, if we define the `build` job in the application's `config.json` (`local`), this `build` job shadows the imported `build` job from the qooxdoo framework. The `local` `build` job automatically extends the imported `build` job and merges the local changes defined in `config.json`. Let us just define the variants in the new `build` job and analyze how the generator resolves this:

```
"build" :
{
  "variants" :
  {
    "qx.debug" : ["on"],
    "qx.aspects" : ["on"]
  },
}
```

This is exactly equivalent to the following one:

```
"build" :
{
  "desc" : "create build version of current application",
  "variants" :
  {
    "qx.debug" : ["on"],
    "qx.aspects" : ["on"]
  },

  "run" :
  [
    "build-resources",
    "build-script",
    "build-files"
  ]
}
```

You can again use = to control the merging. Selectively, block the merging of features by using = in front of the key name. This is shown as follows:

```
. . .
{
  "=open-curly" : ...,
. . .
}
. . .
```

Override an imported job entirely by guarding the local job with =, shown as follows:

```
"jobs" : {
  "=build-script" : {...},
...
}
```

We have learnt the internal details of how to configure the jobs in the `config.json`, which is used by the qooxdoo generator. We have learnt to define the jobs or to override the existing jobs, learnt how the job is resolved, and learnt how the job is shadowed.

Migration

The qooxdoo framework is one of the fastest growing frameworks. The qooxdoo team publishes weekly news on their website and they release the new version of the framework every few months to add more features, improve the existing features, and more. There might be changes in the API while moving from one version to another. To support the existing customers, the qooxdoo team provides the migration tools in the framework which will help the customers to move into the new version of the qooxdoo framework.

Time for action – migration

If you want to migrate from any release equal to or later than qooxdoo 1.0, you can migrate directly to the target version, say qooxdoo 1.4.2.

Any release equal or prior to qooxdoo 0.8.3 is considered as a qooxdoo legacy release. If you are migrating from any release prior to qooxdoo 0.8.3 to a newer version, say qooxdoo 1.4.2, then firstly you should migrate to the version qooxdoo 0.8.3 and then migrate to the target version, that is, qooxdoo 1.4.2. You can download this version from `http://sourceforge.net/projects/qooxdoo/files/qooxdoo-current/1.4.2/`.

1. The qooxdoo migration tool updates the source files and cleans/deletes certain directories. To be on the safe side, let us make a backup of the whole application before migrating to the newer version.

2. Let us update the configuration files to refer to the new version of qooxdoo SDK. In the Team Twitter application, we are referring to qooxdoo 1.2 SDK. The qooxdoo team has released a few releases by now. Let us migrate to one of the new releases—qooxdoo 1.4.2 SDK. Download the new qooxdoo SDK and set QOOXDOO_PATH to the new qooxdoo SDK. To enable us to deploy the source version in the web server, we are keeping the SDK inside the Team Twitter application directory. That is why the QOOXDOO_PATH is just set to the qooxdoo SDK directory name; otherwise the QOOXDOO_PATH will have a relative path (for example, /qooxdoo-1.2-sdk). Remove the old SDK directory and copy the new SDK directory under the Team Twitter application. Update the configuration files mentioned as follows to refer to the new version of qooxdoo SDK.

Each application will have the reference to the qooxdoo framework in the `let` section of the `config.json` file. In the `config.json` file, change the QOOXDOO_PATH, as shown in the following code snippet:

```
"let" :
{
  "APPLICATION" : "teamtwitter",
  "QOOXDOO_PATH" : "qooxdoo-1.4.2-sdk",
  "QXTHEME" : "teamtwitter.theme.Theme",
  "API_EXCLUDE"   : ["qx.test.*", "teamtwitter.theme.*",
    "teamtwitter.test.*"],
  "LOCALES" : [ "en", "fr", "de" ],
  "CACHE" : "${TMPDIR}/cache",
  "ROOT" : ".",
  "APPLICATION_MAIN_CLASS" : "${APPLICATION}.Application",
  "include": ["qx.dev.Profile"]
}
```

In the `generate.py` file also, change the QOOXDOO_PATH, as shown in the following code snippet:

```
import sys, os, re, subprocess

CMD_PYTHON = 'python'
QOOXDOO_PATH = 'qooxdoo-1.4.2-sdk'
```

The migration process just updates the source code; it does not migrate the `config.json` file. You need to update the `config.json` file, if required. Check the release notes of all the versions from your current qooxdoo version to the target qooxdoo version. Release notes of all the qooxdoo versions are available at `http://qooxdoo.org/about/release_notes`.

In qooxdoo 1.4, as per the release notes (http://qooxdoo.org/about/
release_notes/1.4), the new `environment` implementation replaces the
old `variants` implementation. Let us update the `variants` section to the
`environment` section in the Team Twitter's `config.json`, which is mentioned
as follows. The qooxdoo framework also supports the `variants` section to have
backward compatibility:

```
"source" :
{
  "extend" : [ "my-parts-config" ],

  "environment" :
  {
    "qx.disposerDebugLevel" : "9",
    "qx.aspects" : true,
    "qx.debug" : true
  },

  "log" :
  {
    "classes-unused" : [ "teamtwitter.*" ]
  }
}
```

3. We have set up the new SDK and configured it. Now, let us run the following
    command to migrate the application code to the target version of the qooxdoo SDK:

    ```
    C:\teamtwitter>generate.py migration
    ```

```
===============================================================================
   INITIALIZING: TEAMTWITTER
===============================================================================
>>> Configuration: config.json
>>> Resolving config includes...
  - Warning: ! Shadowing job "source" with local one
  - Warning: ! Shadowing job "build" with local one
  - Warning: ! Shadowing job "translation" with local one
>>> Jobs: migration
>>> Resolving jobs...
>>> Incorporating job defaults...
>>> Resolving macros...
>>> Resolving libs/manifests...

===============================================================================
   EXECUTING: MIGRATION
===============================================================================
>>> Initializing cache...
  - Cleaning compile cache, as tool chain has changed
  - Deleting compile cache
>>> Checking configuration files...
>>> Migrating Javascript source code to most recent qooxdoo version...

NOTE:    To apply only the necessary changes to your project, we
         need to know the qooxdoo version it currently works with.

Please enter your current qooxdoo version [1.3] :
```

It will ask for the current qooxdoo version. Enter the version that you used to develop the application. Once you enter the current version, the migration path will be shown to you as follows:

```
MIGRATION SUMMARY:

Current qooxdoo version:    1.2
Upgrade path:               1.2.1 -> 1.2.2 -> 1.3 -> 1.3.1 -> 1.4

Affected Classes:
    teamtwitter.samples.RadioButtons
    teamtwitter.Application
    teamtwitter.ui.CTweet
    teamtwitter.samples.AsyncValidator
    teamtwitter.samples.Menu
    teamtwitter.ui.tweetWidget
    teamtwitter.samples.Composite
    teamtwitter.theme.Appearance
    teamtwitter.test.LoginUserTest
    teamtwitter.ui.CVideoTweet
    teamtwitter.ui.MainWidget
    teamtwitter.theme.Decoration
    teamtwitter.theme.Theme
    teamtwitter.ui.UsersListWidget
    teamtwitter.theme.Color
    teamtwitter.ui.TweetsDisplayWidget
    teamtwitter.test.TagsWidgetTest
    teamtwitter.samples.Atom
    teamtwitter.ui.UserSignUpForm
    teamtwitter.samples.TreeVirtual
    teamtwitter.ui.TagsWidget
    teamtwitter.samples.TextField
    teamtwitter.test.DemoTest
    teamtwitter.samples.PopupTooltip
    teamtwitter.ui.UserLoginForm
    teamtwitter.samples.FormWidgets
    teamtwitter.theme.Font
    teamtwitter.samples.Label
    teamtwitter.ui.TweetSearchWidget
    teamtwitter.samples.Table
    teamtwitter.Samples
    teamtwitter.ui.TweetInput
    teamtwitter.samples.Popup
    teamtwitter.samples.Image

NOTE:    It is advised to do a 'generate.py distclean' before migrating any files.
         If you choose 'yes', a subprocess will be invoked to run distclean,
         and after completion you will be prompted if you want to
         continue with the migration. If you choose 'no', the distclean
         step will be skipped (which might result in potentially unnecessary
         files being migrated).

Do you want to run 'distclean' now? [yes] :
```

It is advisable to run the `distclean` job before the migration. If you say `yes`, it will execute the `distclean` job, which will delete the compile cache, download cache, the `test` folder, the `simulator` folder, the `inspector` folder, `build`, the `api` folder, and the clean-up source. You can recreate this content after the migration by running the corresponding jobs.

```
================================================================================
 INITIALIZING: TEAMTWITTER
================================================================================
>>> Configuration: config.json
>>> Resolving config includes...
  - Warning: ! Shadowing job "source" with local one
  - Warning: ! Shadowing job "build" with local one
  - Warning: ! Shadowing job "translation" with local one
>>> Jobs: distclean
>>> Resolving jobs...
>>> Incorporating job defaults...
>>> Resolving macros...
>>> Resolving libs/manifests...

================================================================================
 EXECUTING: DISTCLEAN
================================================================================
>>> Initializing cache...
>>> Cleaning up files...
  - Deleting compile cache
  - Deleting download cache
  - Cleaning up source
  - Deleting test folder
  - Deleting simulator folder
  - Deleting inspector folder
  - Deleting build
  - Deleting api folder

WARNING: The migration process will update the files in place. Please make
         sure, you have a backup of your project. The complete output of the
         migration process will be logged to 'migration.log'.

Do you want to start the migration now? [no] :
```

After running the `distclean` job, it will ask for confirmation to migrate the application. If you say `yes`, it will migrate the application following the migration path. All the migration details at each migration step are printed in the console and also logged in the file `migration.log`.

In qooxdoo 1.4, the `qx.debug` variant is moved to the `environment` section. In the upgrade 1.4 migration step, the migration process updates the code to use the new API, which can be observed in the `migration.log` file, mentioned as follows:

```
- File: E:\test2\source\class\teamtwitter\Application.js

   - E:\test2\source\class\teamtwitter\Application.js:45
Replacing match 'qx.core.Variant.isSet("qx.debug", "on")' to '(qx.
core.Environment.get("qx.debug"))'

   - E:\test2\source\class\teamtwitter\Application.js has been
modified. Storing modifications ...
```

What just happened?

We have learnt to migrate a qooxdoo application from one SDK version to another SDK version. We have also migrated our application, Team Twitter, from qooxdoo 1.2 SDK to qooxdoo 1.4.2 SDK.

Back button support

In AJAX applications, for most of the actions, the URL does not change in the browser. Because of this, the browser back button might not work as it works in traditional web applications. qooxdoo provides a way to work with the browser back button.

If there is a requirement, we may need to make the browser back button functional. A good example is the API viewer component in the qooxdoo framework. The qooxdoo framework provides an API to manage the history and navigate through the various states through the browser's "forward" and "back" buttons.

Identify application states

Each point that we want to navigate through the browser's "back" button has to be identified as a `state` with the respective `title`. `state` and `title` strings. The `state` string must be an encoded string that will be set as the fragment identifier of the URL after the # character. When we click on the browser's "back" and "forward" buttons, this state is fetched by the qooxdoo history manager to act accordingly in the application.

It is up to us to decide what states we want to remember, based on the application's requirements . It could be coarse-grained or fine-grained, depending on requirements.

In the case of the API viewer component, each node click on the API tree is a `state`. The `state` string can be the node name itself, so that it is easy to select the node on the browser button actions.

Update history upon state change

In the qooxdoo application, whenever we reach a state that we want to remember in the history and navigate back to it later, we should register that state in the history manager by calling the following API:

```
qx.bom.History.getInstance().addToHistory(state, title);
```

The `state` is used in the qooxdoo application code and the `title` is set as the browser title for that `state`.

In the case of the API viewer component, whenever we click on the node in the API tree, it is a state. We should register it in the history manager. If we take a look at the API viewer class (C:\qooxdoo-1.4.2-sdk\component\apiviewer\source\class\apiviewer\ Controller.js), the method _updateHistory() updates the history manager. This method is called upon click of the node.

The following code snippet from the API viewer component registers the state in the history manager:

```
/**
* Push the class to the browser history
* @param className {String} name of the class
*/
_updateHistory : function(className)
{
  var newTitle = className + " - " + this._titlePrefix;
  qx.bom.History.getInstance().addToHistory(
    this.__encodeState(className), newTitle);
}
```

Add the event listener to the history manager

In the previous steps, we have identified states and registered the states in the history manager. Now, we need to act on the event. On the browser's "back" and "forward" actions, the history manager dispatches a request event. In the listener method, based on the state of the event, we have to do the application-specific update.

The following code snippet from the API viewer component adds a listener to the history manager:

```
__bindHistory : function()
{
  this._history.addListener("request", function(evt) {
    var state = e.getData();

    //Do application specific state update
    var item = this.__decodeState(state);
    if (item) {
      this.__selectItem(item);
    }

  }, this);
}
```

Retrieve initial state

In addition to the browser's "back" and "forward" buttons, the bookmarks in the browser should work. When a user loads the bookmark, the application should interpret the state that is bookmarked and load that state. We can get the state from the history manager using the following API:

```
var state = qx.bom.History.getInstance().getState();
```

In the API viewer component, if we have bookmarked the URL and loaded it again from the bookmark (`http://api.qooxdoo.org#qx.bom.History`), it should load that particular class based on the `state`.

The following code snippet from the API viewer component identifies and loads the `state`:

```
load : function(url)
{
---
---
  qx.event.Timer.once(function()
  {
    // Handle bookmarks
    var state = this._history.getState();
    if (state)
    {
      this.__selectItem(this.__decodeState(state));
    }
    else
    {
      // Load the first package if nothing is selected.
      var firstPackage = this.__getFirstPackage(treeData);
      var fullName = firstPackage.attributes.fullName;
      this.__selectItem(fullName);
    }
  }, this, 0);
---
---
}
```

We have learnt about the history support in the qooxdoo framework and learnt how to support the browser's "back" button, "forward" button, and bookmarks in the qooxdoo application. We have learnt how the history manager is used in the API viewer component of the qooxdoo framework.

qooxdoo license

qooxdoo may be used under the terms of either one of the following two licenses:

- **GNU Lesser General Public License (LGPL)**:
  `http://www.gnu.org/licenses/lgpl.html`

- **Eclipse Public License (EPL)**:
  `http://www.eclipse.org/org/documents/epl-v10.php`

As a recipient of qooxdoo, you may choose which license to receive the code under. Certain files or entire directories may not be covered by this dual license, but are subject to licenses compatible to both LGPL and EPL. License exceptions are explicitly declared in all relevant files or in a `LICENSE` file in the relevant directories.

Legacy version 0.6.4 and below are licensed solely under GNU Lesser General Public License (LGPL).

Pop quiz

1. The qooxdoo legacy version is until

   a. 0.7.0

   b. 0.8.3

   c. 1.2.2

2. qooxdoo migration updates the configuration (`config.json`) too

   a. True

   b. False

3. Generator configurations are written in which file format

   a. Ant

   b. JSON

   c. Properties

   d. Normal text files

   e. None

4. Which key triggers the execution of one or more external command(s)

    a. run

    b. shell

    c. simulate

    d. command

5. Which key allows you to configure a list of classes to be processed in the job

    a. include (top-level)

    b. include (inside job)

    c. classes

    d. library

6. Which key exports a list of jobs, if the configuration is imported in another

    a. combine

    b. export

    c. import

    d. dependencies

7. Which key triggers the generation of the custom API viewer for the application

    a. compile

    b. api

    c. generate

    d. translate

8. Which key allows you to define user environment settings

    a. environment

    b. let

    c. let (inside job)

    d. export

9. The command generate.py ? displays all the exported jobs, even from the imported configuration

    a. True

    b. False

10. Which key allows splitting application into pieces

   a. `packages`

   b. `parts`

   c. `combine`

   d. `run`

11. qooxdoo supports the browser's "back" and "forward" button

   a. Without any additional code

   b. Coding through the history manager

12. qooxdoo is available under the following licenses

   a. GNU Lesser General Public License (LGPL)

   b. Apache License 2.0 (Apache-2.0)

   c. Eclipse Pubic License (EPL)

   d. Open Software License 3.0 (OSL-3.0)

Summary

In this chapter, we have learnt about the miscellaneous items that complete this book.

In particular, we have covered:

- The configuration of the qooxdoo application
- How to migrate to a newer version of qooxdoo SDK and we migrated the Team Twitter application to qooxdoo 1.4.2 SDK
- How to support the browser's "back" and "forward" buttons
- The license of qooxdoo

In this book, we have learnt about the qooxdoo framework. We have also learnt most of the concepts by applying them in the Team Twitter application.

Pop Quiz Answers

Chapter 1: What is qooxdoo?

1	2	3	4	5	6
d	a	e	d	d	b

Chapter 2: Say Hello to the qooxdoo World!

1	2	3	4	5	6
b	b	a	a	c	c

Chapter 3: Core Programming Concepts

Pop quiz-I

1	2	3	4	5	6	7
d	e	b	c	b	d	b, c, and f

Pop quiz-II

1	2	3	4	5	6	7	8
a	e	a	a	c	b	a and d	a, b, and c

Chapter 4: Working with Layouts and Menus

1	2	3	4	5	6
a	a	c	b	a	a
7	8	9	10	11	
d	d	a	d	d	

Chapter 5: Working with Widgets

1	2	3	4	5	6	7
b	a	a and b	c	d	e	b
8	9	10	11	12	13	14
a	a and b	a	c	c	d	b

Chapter 6: Working with Forms and Data

1	2	3	4	5	6	7	8	9	10
d	a	c	a	g	d	a	e	b	c

Chapter 7: Testing and Debugging

1	2	3	4	5	6	7	8
a	b and c	b and c	b	a	d	b	e

Chapter 8: Internationalization

1	2	3	4	5
c	b	c	d	a

Chapter 9: Working with Themes

1	2	3	4	5	6	7
a, b, and d	a	a and d	d	d	e	a

Chapter 10: Performance

1	2	3	4	5	6	7	8	9	10
c	a	a	f	a, b, c, and d	c	a	d	a, b, c, and d	a

Chapter 11: Miscellaneous

1	2	3	4	5	6
b	b	b	b	a	b
7	8	9	10	11	12
b	a	a	b	b	a and c

References

The following sources have been referred to, for this book:

- ◆ The qooxdoo framework website: `http://qooxdoo.org/`
- ◆ The JavaScript Object Notation (JSON) website: `http://www.json.org/`
- ◆ The Selenium framework website: `http://seleniumhq.org/`
- ◆ The Firebug website: `http://getfirebug.com/`
- ◆ *"Object-Oriented Modeling and Design"* by *James Rumbaugh, Michael Blaha, William Premerlani, Frederick Eddy,* and *William Lorensen, Prentice-Hall*

Index

R

Thank you for buying
qooxdoo Beginner's Guide

About Packt Publishing

Packt, pronounced 'packed', published its first book "*Mastering phpMyAdmin for Effective MySQL Management*" in April 2004 and subsequently continued to specialize in publishing highly focused books on specific technologies and solutions.

Our books and publications share the experiences of your fellow IT professionals in adapting and customizing today's systems, applications, and frameworks. Our solution based books give you the knowledge and power to customize the software and technologies you're using to get the job done. Packt books are more specific and less general than the IT books you have seen in the past. Our unique business model allows us to bring you more focused information, giving you more of what you need to know, and less of what you don't.

Packt is a modern, yet unique publishing company, which focuses on producing quality, cutting-edge books for communities of developers, administrators, and newbies alike. For more information, please visit our website: www.packtpub.com.

About Packt Open Source

In 2010, Packt launched two new brands, Packt Open Source and Packt Enterprise, in order to continue its focus on specialization. This book is part of the Packt Open Source brand, home to books published on software built around Open Source licences, and offering information to anybody from advanced developers to budding web designers. The Open Source brand also runs Packt's Open Source Royalty Scheme, by which Packt gives a royalty to each Open Source project about whose software a book is sold.

Writing for Packt

We welcome all inquiries from people who are interested in authoring. Book proposals should be sent to author@packtpub.com. If your book idea is still at an early stage and you would like to discuss it first before writing a formal book proposal, contact us; one of our commissioning editors will get in touch with you.

We're not just looking for published authors; if you have strong technical skills but no writing experience, our experienced editors can help you develop a writing career, or simply get some additional reward for your expertise.

Learning jQuery, Third Edition

ISBN: 978-1-84951-654-9   Paperback: 428 pages

Create better interaction, design, and web development with simple JavaScript techniques

1. An introduction to jQuery that requires minimal programming experience

2. Detailed solutions to specific client-side problems

3. Revised and updated version of this popular jQuery book

Squid Proxy Server 3.1: Beginner's Guide

ISBN: 978-1-84951-390-6   Paperback: 332 pages

Improve the performance of your network using the caching and access control capabilities of Squid

1. Get the most out of your network connection by customizing Squid's access control lists and helpers

2. Set up and configure Squid to get your website working quicker and more efficiently

3. No previous knowledge of Squid or proxy servers is required

4. Part of Packt's Beginner's Guide series: lots of practical, easy-to-follow examples accompanied by screenshots

Please check **www.PacktPub.com** for information on our titles

www.ingramcontent.com/pod-product-compliance
Lightning Source LLC
Chambersburg PA
CBHW080145060326
40689CB00018B/3856